Informix®
Dynamic
Server.2000™

ISBN 0-13-013709-X

9 780130 137098

90000

Inform**ix**® Press

For a complete list of Informix Press titles, please visit
www.phptr.com or www.informix.com/ipress

Informix®
Dynamic
Server.2000™
Server-Side Programming in C

Jacques Roy

Prentice Hall PTR
Upper Saddle River, New Jersey 07458
www.phptr.com

Library of Congress Cataloging-in-Publication Data

Roy, Jacques, 1958-
    Informix Dynamic Server.2000 : server-side programming in C / Jacques Roy.
      p.   cm. — (Prentice Hall PTR Informix series)
    Includes bibliographical references (p.   ).
    ISBN 0-13-013709-X (paper)
    1. Client/server computing.   2. INFORMIX Dynamic server.   3. Internet programming.
   I. Title.   II. Series.

QA76.9.C55 R69 1999
005.75'65 21—dc21

99-044857

Editorial/Production Supervision: *Precision Graphics*
Acquisitions Editor: *Miles Williams*
Editorial Assistant: *Noreen Regina*
Marketing Manager: *Kate Hargett*
Cover Design: *Anthony Gemmellaro*
Cover Design Direction: *Jerry Votta*
Manufacturing Manager: *Alexis R. Heydt*
Project Coordinator: *Anne Trowbridge*

Prentice Hall books are widely used by corporations and government agencies for training, marketing, and resale.

The publisher offers discounts on this book when ordered in bulk quantities. For more information, contact Corporate Sales Department, phone: 800-382-3419; fax: 201-236-7141; e-mail: corpsales@prenhall.com or write:

Prentice Hall PTR
Corporate Sales Department
One Lake Street
Upper Saddle River, NJ 07458

Printed in the United States of America
10 9 8 7 6 5 4 3 2 1

ISBN 0-13-013709-X

Prentice-Hall International (UK) Limited, London
Prentice-Hall of Australia Pty. Limited, Sydney
Prentice-Hall Canada Inc., Toronto
Prentice-Hall Hispanoamericana, S.A., Mexico
Prentice-Hall of India Private Limited, New Delhi
Prentice-Hall of Japan, Inc., Tokyo
Prentice-Hall (Singapore) Pte. Ltd., Singapore
Editora Prentice-Hall do Brasil, Ltda., Rio de Janeiro

To Tina, Derek, and Andrew

Contents

Preface

The Informix object relational technology consists of the integration of the Informix dynamic system architecture (DSA) relational database management system (RDBMS) with the extensibility features acquired from the Illustra database. It first came out around January 1997 and has since been through heavy testing and functionality improvements.

Since Informix Dynamic Server.2000 (IDS.2000) is a superset of a relational database system, legacy systems using a relational database system can run without modification, preserving IT investment. This is a double-edged sword: On the one hand existing systems can continue to support the corporation while improvements can be implemented gradually to take advantage of the new functionality to increase applications performance. However, since IDS.2000 is a full-featured relational database system, it is easy to continue developing within the well-known context of relational database systems and their limitations.

IDS.2000 is an excellent relational database. Of course, if this technology is used to develop relational database solutions, we can only expect our systems to perform as well as any relational database solution—no more, no less. So the real challenge of this technology is for us to imagine better solutions to our business problems through more creative use of its object-relational features.

The main goal of this book is to show how to use the DataBlade API to exploit the object-relational features of IDS.2000. This way, you can augment the database system to better fit your business environment instead of compromising your design to fit the database. Another goal is to provide practical examples that stimulate a new way of thinking about better solutions to your business problems. The pay-off will be simpler applications, faster development, and increased performance. Furthermore, if the application is simpler, it should also reduce the effort required for maintenance.

Book Organization

This book approaches the subject on different fronts. It includes tutorial, "how to," and reference material. I've tried to organize it logically so that it first provides the information needed to understand the product as a whole and then delves into more technical details, beginning with the simpler features and building up to the most complex ones.

> ***Chap. 1. IDS.2000 = Business Advantage:*** *Chapter 1 puts this technology in perspective and gives an overview of its main features, along with examples that show practical use of these features. It also discusses the advantages of using this technology. This overview should help you figure out how to take advantage of object-relational technology in your environment.*
>
> ***Chap. 2. User-Defined Routines:*** *User-defined routines implement your business rules and the support functions for your business types (user-defined types). This chapter describes how they are implemented and the context of their execution. This information is essential to understanding the rest of the book.*
>
> ***Chap. 3. SQL Statements:*** *This reference material describes the syntax of the SQL statements needed to take advantage of the extensibility features. You may skip this chapter at first and come back to it when studying specific features.*
>
> ***Chap. 4. Handling Data Types:*** *A big part of this technology is to add business rule processing to manipulate the database data. This means that a large part of the utilization involves calling a function at the SQL level. The function must receive*

and return any SQL types. This reference material describes how to receive and return any SQL types.

Chap. 5. Computational Functions: *There are some issues that apply to any user-defined routines. These issues are presented within the context of computational functions that are simple user-defined routines intended to do simple processing by taking an argument and returning a computed result. This chapter is essential to understanding the rest of the book.*

Chap. 6. User Defined Types: *This chapter discusses mainly complex types and the execution of SQL statements within user-defined routines. It complements the information provided in Chaps. 4 and 5.*

Chap. 7. Opaque Types: *Opaque types are really user-defined types. They are covered in their own chapter because they are the heart of the type extensibility of IDS.2000. They require a set of support functions so that the database server can store, retrieve, and handle them.*

Chap. 8. Iterator Functions: *It is possible to write a function that returns a set of values instead of a single result. This chapter explains how to write such a function.*

Chap. 9. The Fastpath Interface: *A user-defined routine cannot always call another user-defined routine directly. Sometimes it must be done using a special API provided by the DataBlade API. This chapter discusses why and when this interface should be used.*

Chap. 10. Smart Blobs and Multirepresentation: *IDS.2000 provides new types of large objects for storing business types that cannot fit a table row. This chapter shows how to manipulate them and how to use them within opaque types.*

Chap. 11. Aggregate Functions: *An aggregate function takes values from a set of rows and returns a result. The AVG() SQL function is an aggregate function. This chapter shows how to extend the existing SQL aggregate functions to handle new data types and how to create totally new aggregate functions.*

Chap. 12. Tracing and Debugging: *The database server is a totally different development environment. This chapter gives some pointers on problems you may encounter and shows how to trace and debug your functions to solve the problems rapidly.*

Appendix. Functions Reference: *This Appendix describes all the Informix functions available to you when writing user-defined routines.*

How to Approach Extensibility

IDS.2000 provides some very powerful features. You may find very quickly that features such as opaque types and user-defined aggregates are perfect for your business solution. In any case ask yourself what little extra functionality in the database would greatly simplify your application and significantly improve performance. In other words, what is the least effort needed for the biggest return? Thinking this way, you can get a fast return on your investment and gain some experience with the product before diving into larger, more complex projects. If you can quickly prove the value of this new technology, you will have more time to experiment and become familiar with how this technology works. Then you will really be ready for more complex solutions.

What's in a Name? A Brief History

The Informix object-relational technology started from the Illustra database product. The first implementation based on the Informix dynamic server architecture was called Informix Universal Server (IUS). The name lasted until a decision was made to reflect the common base architecture of the Informix products. IUS was then renamed Informix Dynamic Server with Universal Data Option or Informix-UDO for short.

Informix had been working on merging the IDS 7.x code line with the UDO 9.x code line. It took a few years because both products were still evolving. In July 1999, Informix announced a new product, code name Centaur, that completed this task, rendering the IDS 7.x code line irrelevant. The decision was made to rename the product once again to reflect the fact that all IDS 7.x customers can safely use this new product, keep their current systems intact with all the benefits they currently enjoy, and also take advantage of the new functionality. The new product is now Informix Dynamic Server.2000, or IDS.2000 for short. It is the core database server for Informix Internet Foundation.2000 also announced in July 1999.

Acknowledgments

There are several people whose professionalism eased the process of making this book a reality. I'd like first to thank Brian Miezejewski for his numerous comments and his sharp technical eye. His extensive experience in a wide range of topics helped in fine-tuning the manuscript. As usual, it was a delight to work with Brian.

The production team led by Anne Trowbridge of Prentice Hall and Kirsten Dennison of Precision Graphics made a book out of my manuscript. In going over every single change that was made to the manuscript, I was able to appreciate the improvements, especially the rework of the more convoluted sentences. Thank you for all the work that produced this final result.

On the Informix press front, Judy Bowman was helpful in resolving several issues. I also appreciate our several conversations and Judy's advice on many aspects of this project.

I'd like to thank my parents, especially my father, who taught me so much by his example. Also, thanks to Marc Lambert and Lan Tran, who got me started the right way in the computer field.

Finally, congratulations, Miles, for your first one, end-to-end.

Jacques Roy
August 1999

IDS.2000 = Business Advantage

Informix Dynamic Server.2000 (IDS.2000) provides so many new capabilities that it might well be regarded as a radically new database environment. A closer look shows, however, that IDS.2000 is a logical next step in the software industry's evolution. Because it is a superset of the relational model, IDS.2000 allows for easy migration of relational schemas. The schemas can then be improved by gradual implementation of features using the new functionality.

Technology does not survive only for technology's sake. There have to be practical reasons for it. In our case, technological innovation has to provide business advantages over current database technologies. Because IDS.2000 can adapt to your business environment, it has the potential to provide more straight-forward business solutions. This translates into better performance and faster time to market.

The real challenge of this technology is for users to break down established solution patterns so new ones can be created.

A new approach to solving problems can provide significantly better solutions. Consider what the star schema did for data warehouses. Just so, dramatically new approaches exploiting its new object-relational features will provide the greatest returns with IDS.2000.

This chapter provides the foundation for thinking in new ways to make the most of this technology and reap business advantages.

A Logical Evolution

The logical evolution of object-relational database systems (ORDBMS) covers two aspects: the relational database management system (RDBMS) and the ORDBMS extensions.

Relational Evolution

The object-relational model is a superset of the relational model. In the case of IDS.2000, it is an extension of the dynamic scalable architecture (DSA). IDS.2000 takes advantage of years of research and development to provide a highly reliable and scalable database management system. It is possible to migrate easily from the relational product to the object-relational one, only gradually taking advantage of the additional features while continuing to use the features you had come to rely on.

The relational model provides two major features: a logical database model and a non-procedural language (SQL). The logical model provides independence from the physical organization of the data. Since the application does not contain any physical path to the data, the data can be organized to optimize its access without application dependencies. In addition to relieving application developers of responsibility for optimizing data access, the logical database model improves application stability because no changes are required when physical changes are made to data location.

This feature would not be complete, however, without a non-procedural language. SQL provides a means to express what must be done instead of how to do it. The database engine is then free to decide the best way to execute the query. The application takes advantage of highly tuned algorithms within the database engine that provide optimized access to the data. Over time, applications can use improved versions of the database engine without requiring modifications.

IDS.2000 takes these features one step further. Instead of providing a logical view of the data, it now allows for a business view of it. You can define business types and the business rules that apply to these types within the server. The application now works at the business-type level. If business rules change, the definitions of the business types can be changed without impacting the application. Of course, this also provides significant performance advantages, as we'll see later.

Customization Evolution

The most important benefit of IDS.2000 is that it can adapt to your business environment. In many cases, having the database understand simple business rules can dramatically reduce the size of the application code and also improve performance. Many, if not all, of the IDS.2000 features aim at providing a better fit in the business environment. Its flexibility in this regard is so surprising that it may seem to come from nowhere.

Software customization is nothing new. Operating system vendors allow third-party vendors to create device drivers that are integrated with the operating system to provide added value to the users. One of the most prominent examples of added value through device drivers is their support for new hardware and files systems with expanded capabilities.

In the mainframe environment, software packages often include what are called user exits. User exits are functions that are called by the software at specific locations within the processing. For example, user exits may be provided before and after a record is written to or read from a disk. These exits provide capabilities such as encoding or compressing the record. The customization functions are then linked with the software, which would otherwise have made the empty calls defined by the default user exit implementations. The user exit processing flow is illustrated in Fig. 1–1.

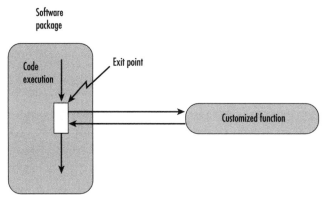

Fig. 1–1 *User exit execution flow.*

The user exit mechanism is relatively rigid. Exits are located at specific points in the software package. They take a predefined number of arguments and are expected to return a specific type of result. There are similarities between user exits and the flexible mechanism provided in IDS.2000, so we can say that IDS.2000 provides user definable exits: The location, number of arguments and their types, and return type of the exit can be defined by the user.

Software vendors have always tried to provide enough flexibility to accommodate specific user environments. With the flexibility included in IDS.2000, however, it becomes easier to implement design solutions with minimum compromises. The database engine becomes an integral part of the solution instead of a rigid storage mechanism.

IDS.2000 Features

IDS.2000 provides a large set of features. The following is a list of the features provided to date:

Distinct type	Opaque type	Row type
Set	Multiset	List
User-defined routine	Table/row type inheritance	Polymorphism
User-defined aggregate	Functional index	R-tree index
Smart blob	Primary/secondary access methods	

These features provide a lot of functionality that can improve business processing. They can take advantage of existing capabilities provided in the Informix Dynamic Server architecture, such as parallel execution of SQL queries. What follows is an explanation of these features and how to take advantage of them.

Distinct Type: *Because this type takes its internal representation from an existing type, the database server already knows how to handle it. Distinct types can be used for several purposes. They can provide strong typing for different types of revenues. Rules can be defined for manipulation of mixed types and conversion from one type to another. They can define units of measure and comparison and conversion rules.*

For example, you can create a distinct type from the date type. Because it is based on an existing type, the conversion functions between internal and external representations are already available. You can then create new operator implementations so that the date arithmetic follows your business rules. The SQL statements still use the same syntax that a relational database requires. Internally, IDS.2000 finds the right implementation for the type and executes it.

You can also use distinct types to differentiate different types of revenues or expenses. You may want to make sure, for example, that you cannot add capital expenses with operational expenses. By having distinct types for each, you can implement the business rules that apply to mixing types of revenues. If an improper operation is requested in an SQL statement, IDS.2000 will return an error message. A relational database does not provide strong typing. The SQL statement would execute to completion and return an answer because it is syntactically correct, but the answer could be wrong according to a particular business rule.

The strong typing capability of IDS.2000 can help catch business errors, a benefit similar to what function prototyping did for the C language. This can prevent major mistakes in business decisions, especially in environments that use a lot of ad hoc queries.

Opaque Type: An opaque type defines a new internal representation that, hopefully, better fits the business requirements. An opaque type requires more work to implement because it must include a set of functions that will allow the database server to manipulate it.

Two examples come to mind. You could create an opaque type that contains a revenue amount along with the conversion rate that applied at the time to convert to U.S. dollars. This way you can compare revenues from different time periods in their original currencies to see whether there was improvement instead of being misled by currency conversion variations. You can also get the exact value in U.S. dollars when consolidating your financial results.

You may also want to create a type representing a calendar that identifies holidays and special events. The application does not need to know how you keep the data. It just needs to work with an external representation.

Row Type: This type is similar to the column definition in a table. You can use a row type as a column type. It is also used in the table inheritance to provide row typing.

Set, Multiset, List: These three types represent collections of objects. A set is an unordered collection without duplicates. A multiset is an unordered collection allowing duplicates. A list is an ordered collection of objects allowing duplicates.

User-Defined Routine (UDR): These routines are used to provide support to your user-defined types (UDTs). They provide the implementation of the business rules that apply to your environment for both the existing types and the UDTs. The UDRs can implement all the arithmetic operations (+, −, *, /, etc.), *comparison operations (>, >=, =, <=, <), and any business processing that is required. The UDRs can execute SQL statements and can also call other UDRs, even if they come from other DataBlade modules. In addition to processing arguments and returning a scalar value, a UDR can return a set of values. Such a UDR is called an iterator function. Chapter 7 discusses iterator functions in detail.*

Table/Row Type Inheritance: Inheritance is provided through rows and tables. The table inheritance requires the use of named row types that are themselves built into a hierarchy. IDS.2000 supports only single inheritance.

The use of this feature is better explained through an example. Imagine that you are running a bank that has hundreds of branches. Each branch gives out loans to different industries. All loans have common characteristics but each industry adds its own loan characteristics, and subdivisions within an industry may require specific processing.

Figure 1–2 shows a potential table hierarchy. The top level, loans, contains the characteristics common to all loans. Each specialization applies to a specific industry. The retail industry is further subdivided into three separate groups to account for their different characteristics.

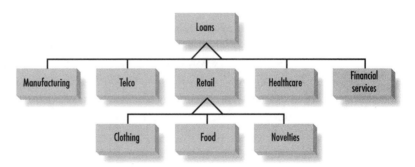

Fig. 1–2 *Table hierarchy.*

Each table is created separately. This has the additional advantage of allowing more ways to partition the data. A table definition includes a statement identifying where the table is in the hierarchy. An index created at the top of the hierarchy will span all the tables. Other indexes can be created at the appropriate levels. For example, an index created on the retail table will span clothing, food, and novelties.

It is possible to execute statements that give us information based on the entire hierarchy. The following statement returns the total number of loans for all industries:

```
SELECT count(*) FROM loans;
```

It is also possible to work directly with a table in the hierarchy:

```
SELECT SUM(loan_amount) FROM ONLY(Retail);
```

This statement returns the total amount of the loans given to retail customers. It does not use any loans in the clothing, food, and novelties divisions.

Polymorphism: *Polymorphism is the quality of a function to behave differently according to the type of its arguments. Arithmetic operations are obvious examples. They can process types such as integers, floats, and double precision numbers. In the IDS.2000 environment, you can create several functions with the same name, as long as they have different numbers of arguments or different argument types.*

Let's continue our loans table example. Bank executives may want to monitor their branches to make sure they stay within certain risk guidelines. The first step is to calculate a risk factor for each loan. As you can imagine, the risk factor is calculated differently for each industry. When loaning to a manufacturing company, you need to take into consideration the assets of that company. The risk is reduced by the value of the company assets. Part of the calculation of the asset value can impact the risk factor. This may work well for a manufacturing company; however, the assets of a novelty store may not enter the loan calculation. For example, if a novelty store selling pet rocks goes out of business, the bank will most likely get stuck with pet rocks.

You can create several `riskFactor()` functions, one for each table row type. These functions take a row of a specific row type and calculate the risk factor for that loan. The functions are relatively simple since they are dealing with only one loan of a specific type. With these functions in place, it is now possible to ask the database server to calculate for each bank branch an average risk factor that takes into consideration the different industries. This is done with a simple SQL statement:

```
SELECT branch_id, AVG(riskFactor(A)) FROM loans
AS A
GROUP BY 1
ORDER BY 2 DESC;
```

The result is a list of the average risk factors calculated for each branch and arranged in descending order. IDS.2000 makes sure to call the appropriate function based on the row types the function takes. The function number of arguments and their types are often referred to as the function signature. Using the same function name with different signatures is referred to as function overloading.

User-Defined Aggregate: IDS.2000 has added a few new aggregation functions. They include `RANGE()`, `STDEV()`, and `VARIANCE()`. All the predefined aggregates perform their calculations using specific functions. You can use these aggregation functions for your new types by overloading specific operators so they handle your types. For example, you can use `AVG()` on a newly defined type by providing "+", `PLUS()`, and "/", `DIVIDE()`, for that type.

You can take it one step further and create your own aggregation function. The average risk factor shown above does not provide the answer we are looking for. If we want to know the average risk taken by each branch, the calculation must take into account the loan amounts. We can, however, create an `AVGRISK()` aggregation function that will take all the factors into consideration. The SQL statement becomes:

```
SELECT branch_id, AVGRISK(A) FROM loans AS A
GROUP BY 1
ORDER BY 2 DESC;
```

Now, assuming that an average risk greater than one is too much, we can issue:

```
SELECT branch_id, AVGRISK(A) FROM loans AS A
GROUP BY 1
HAVING AVGRISK(A) > 1
ORDER BY 2 DESC;
```

We end up with an ordered list of branches we should investigate more closely. A user-defined aggregate is implemented with four support functions. These functions follow the same polymorphic dispatch as user-defined routines. This means that in the example above, if we receive a manufacturing row, the appropriate function is called. When a retail row is received, the database server again ensures that the appropriate function is called.

This example shows several benefits to using IDS.2000. The amount of code needed to implement the average risk calculation is smaller and simpler than its equivalent in a custom application. The performance is increased due to the database internal processing and because data did not need to be shipped to a custom application. Finally, a custom off-the-shelf product can be used instead of a custom application. This reduces future maintenance costs since only the basic functionality is implemented and the support functions of user interfaces, formatting, and printing are not needed.

Functional Index: *IDS.2000 allows you to create indexes on the result of user-defined routines. This adds several opportunities to use indexes to speed up performance. Some departments of motor vehicles encode multiple values within a license number: the type of vehicle, the county of registration, and the license number. It is possible to extract the type of vehicle and index it.*

Consider the following function that takes a datetime *as input. This function would extract the day of the week from the date and find out if it is a holiday or not. It would then return a value representing the day, day type, and hour of the day. The function provides up to 336 different values. It is then possible to execute queries that apply to specific days and specific times. The additional performance allows us to submit several requests to refine analysis of the data.*

R-Tree Index: *R-trees are heavily used in geographical information systems to index longitude and latitude. R-Trees include the standard comparison operations (<, =, >) and additional operations including overlap, contains, and within. Since they are so strongly associated with geographical locations, many dismiss them as useless in their business environment.*

You have to look at how r-trees work, not how they are used in a specific implementation. R-trees provide the capability to index two values. These values don't need to be longitude and latitude. They could represent age and income. Using two independent values within an index provides better data selectivity. This means that the index can return a number of values small enough to make it a better choice than a table scan. An index on one or the other values would not be selective enough, making the index a liability instead of an asset.

Smart Blobs: *Smart blobs come in two flavors:* BLOB *and* CLOB. *The two types differentiate between large objects that contain binary data and the ones containing only text data. The advantage of smart blobs over the traditional blobs is that you can access a specific section of the large object without first having to read it all into your application. As a result, it is possible to structure a large object so that operations will read specific sections of the large object to answer the query. This reduces the number of I/O operations required to return the answer and provides better performance.*

Access Method: *An access method is a set of server functions that implement table or index access to additional storage mechanism like a file system file. It can also be used to provide a table interface to a complex data structure stored in a database so that off-the-shelf products would think it is a standard relational table. IDS.2000 provides the capability to write your own access methods for tables and indexes. This should be considered an advanced feature, and the benefits of its use should be carefully weighed.*

Table access methods are referred to as primary access methods or virtual table interface (VTI). The Informix TimeSeries DataBlade module uses this mechanism to provide a traditional table view of a timeseries. This way, a common off-the-shelf product can access the timeseries with its performance advantages without having to include nonstandard database access codes.

Index access methods are called secondary access methods or virtual index interface (VII). They are used to provide new indexing schemes within the database server. Vendors—including Excalibur, Fulcrum, and Verity—provide indexing for text search capabilities. If your corporation has invented specialized search algorithms to improve your business processing, these algorithms can be implemented by using this mechanism.

More Features

Implementing all the features described above requires modifications to core components of the database system. First, the parser needs to be modified so it understands the new SQL3 syntax. It does not deal only with fixed keywords anymore. It needs to identify user-defined routines that can be located anywhere in an SQL statement. The parser uses new system catalog tables describing the functions.

The optimizer uses an exhaustive search algorithm to look at all possible ways of processing the query. During query optimization, the optimizer may rewrite the query, which may generate query plans that were not obvious when looking at the original text of the query. The cost of each plan is established by getting the cost of each operation and by getting an estimate of the amount of data that will be processed. This includes taking into account the cost included in the definition of each UDR. The optimizer must also consider entire table hierarchies when deciding whether to use an index or do a table scan.

The UDRs use memory that must be managed. If the database server detects contention for memory, it must decide which function should be unloaded to make space for others.

Integration of the object-relational features impacts several other components, including the b+tree index, access methods, and storage management. The key to all these modifications is to provide support for added functionality present and future.

What is a DataBlade Module?

A DataBlade module is a packaging of functionality. It can include any of the features mentioned above. The DataBlade module can come from Informix—the TimeSeries DataBlade module, for example. It can also come from a third-party vendor, generally a company that specializes in a specific problem domain. The availability of DataBlade modules from separate domain experts allows for the integration of best-of-breed solutions. Finally, a DataBlade module can come from departments within a corporation. The DataBlade packaging of functionality encourages consistent application of business rules throughout the corporation since it can be easily installed in other databases.

A DataBlade module could include the definitions of related business types and the business rules that apply to them. The business rules take the form of UDRs that perform operations on the business types. There is no minimum set of functionality that must be included in a DataBlade module. It is up to the creator to define a set of complete features.

A DataBlade module may also include a client component. It could be an application that provides a user interface or a programming API that knows how to manipulate the business types.

Performance

At the beginning of this chapter, I mentioned that IDS.2000 yields a performance advantage. Some performance benefits have been pointed out in the examples already provided. Before we can make any more specific statements on the performance benefits of this technology, however, we must define the elements that impact performance. The following sections look at the performance impact of each element, including hardware, operating system, database servers, and application code.

Hardware Components

A computer is made of many parts that have different characteristics. Their impact varies depending on what the application is doing. Here is a brief overview of the major hardware components:

- **CPU:** The central processing unit is what executes program instructions. UNIX vendors have supported symmetrical multiprocessing (SMP) since the late 1980s. The scalability of these systems has increased to support a large number of processors. With SMP, a machine contains several CPUs that are all equal in functionality: Any CPU can handle any task in the system, including interrupts and I/O.

  High-performance CPUs include on-chip memory and often use a secondary cache. For example, each UltraSPARC processor in the Sun ES10000 has 16 KB of instruction cache and 16 KB of data cache. It also has a 4 MB secondary cache. Why have a cache, and why such a large one? Let's again consider the Sun ES10000. The processor speed is listed at 336 MHz, and it uses a 128-bit (16 bytes) interface. For each CPU cycle, the processor can get 16 bytes:

$$336 \times 1{,}000{,}000 \text{ cycles/sec} \times 16 \text{ bytes/cycle} = \begin{array}{l} 5{,}376{,}000{,}000 \\ \text{bytes/sec} \\ (\sim 5.2 \text{ GB/sec}) \end{array}$$

  So, at peak performance, one UltraSPARC processor can go through 5.2 GB per second. Memory caches provide faster access to instructions and data in the hope of keeping the CPU busy.
- **Memory:** Memory subsystems use the concept of interleaving to increase data transfer performance. In the Sun ES 100000, a memory module achieves transfer rates of 1.3 GB per second.
- **System bus:** The system bus is the critical component of the I/O subsystem that allows communication between the I/O controllers and the system. The standard Sun SBus provides a data throughput rate of 100 MB per second.
- **Controllers:** Several types of controllers are available. They are used to access disk drives, networks, tape drives, and so forth. The standard SCSI controller can accommodate the

Table 1–1 Some disk drive characteristics.

Attribute	Value
Optional cache	4096 KB
Track-to-track seek	0.8/1.1 msec
Average seek, read/write	5.4/6.2 msec
Max seek, read/write	12.2/13.2 msec
Average latency	2.99 msec
Spindle speed	10025 RPM

performance of the SCSI bus at 20 MB/sec. Sun has come out with controllers for disk arrays based on fiber optic technology that are rated at 100 MB/sec. This matches the speed of the system bus.

- **Disks:** The standard disk drive used in high-performance systems is the SCSI drive. You can calculate the transfer rate of a disk by looking at its capacity, rotation speed, latency, seek time, track-to-track seek, and so on (see Table 1–1). The real throughput depends on all these factors and the size of the transfer requested. If you ask for disk transfers of a few disk blocks scattered all over the disk, seek time and latency will represent a large percentage of the operation. However, if you are transferring a large number of contiguous disk blocks, most of the time will be spent transferring data.

  The average seek time, average latency, and the track-to-track seek times are measured in milliseconds. A top-of-the-line drive may have an average seek time of 5.4 msec. During that time, the UltraSPARC processor can execute about 7,000,000 instructions. In an effort to reduce the impact of this overhead, most disk manufacturers include memory cache in their disk drives.

  The previous paragraph explains why it is always recommended to allocate contiguous space and avoid disk fragmentation. So what transfer rate should we expect from a disk drive? Some disk drives have peak transfer rates up to 80 MB/sec. Of course this is a best-case scenario. The performance will vary greatly depending on the type of I/O being done and the impact of latency and seek time. In a worst-case scenario, we could require the average seek time and average latency for each page, which would reduce the performance to around 240 KB/sec (2 KB every 8.4 msec). This is a huge range. The real performance will have to be evaluated by benchmarking the application.

- **Network:** The most popular network is the ethernet. The usual transfer rate is 10 Mbit/sec. Considering the standard overhead of control bits and data used for error detection, we can expect a transfer rate of at most 1 MB/sec. New network technology is rapidly appearing that provides transfer rates of 100 Mbits/sec (10 MB/sec).

    The ethernet protocol defines a format for sending information. Each packet of information has a maximum size of 1526 bytes. This includes 26 bytes of control information. The size of the data transfer will have a major impact on the effective transfer rate. For example, the transfer of 20 bytes of data will still incur 26 bytes of control data for more than 50 percent overhead.

- **Modems:** Modems are available at various speeds. The most popular are 14.4 Kbits/sec, 28.8 Kbits/sec, and 56 Kbits/sec. Because we've been dealing mostly with MB/sec up to now, let's convert the previous ratings. They translate to around 0.0014 MB/sec, 0.0028 MB/sec, and 0.0056 MB/sec respectively. With the advent of cable modems, these devices are moving more and more into the network devices realm.

Keeping the processors busy doing useful work is the key to hardware performance. You can improve I/O performance by distributing the queries over several disk drives and optimizing the I/O sizes by limiting fragmentation as much as possible.

Any data movement, even memory to memory, can have a negative impact on performance. This is even more obvious when the network is involved. System architects need to decide where it makes most sense to do the processing.

Operating System

The main goal of an operating system (OS) is to optimize the use of the hardware resources. The overhead incurred by the operating system is more than offset by improved resource utilization. Here is a description of the main components of an operating system:

- **Process control and scheduling:** The operating system schedules processes for execution. After a specified time has elapsed, a system interrupt occurs; or, when the currently running process executes a system call, the operating system reevaluates which process should be executing. If the process is still ready to run, the scheduler decides if it should continue its execution or if another process should take its place.

  In large systems, the process scheduler must also consider where a process ran last. This way, it is possible that the process memory pages are already available in the processor cache. Then, the processor does not have to wait for the pages to be loaded in the cache, and it can be productive right away.

- **Memory management:** Modern operating systems implement a concept called virtual memory. Each process is given a contiguous memory space of a predetermined size (4 GB for 32-bit systems). The operating system takes care of allocating the physical memory to each process. If a process references a memory address that is not part of the physical memory, a page fault occurs. The operating system takes over and retrieves the requested page, puts it in memory, and returns control to the process.

  A process requires a minimum amount of memory to run. If the sum of the memory required for all processes exceeds the amount of physical memory, the operating system will take steps to free up some pages. It may go as far as removing entire processes from memory to allow other processes to run. The situation can degrade to a point where the operating system itself uses a large percentage of CPU resources in trying to manage the memory.

  Processes can share memory regions by taking advantage of an operating feature called shared memory. Using operating system calls, a process can create a shared-memory segment of a given size. Another process can request access to a previously created shared-memory segment. This way, processes can collaborate on some tasks through that shared memory. Of course they have to handle any concurrent access issues.

- **File System Management:** File system management optimizes access to files by buffering file descriptors and file content. The I/O to files is often done in multiples of 8-KB blocks. This constitutes a tradeoff between optimizing the I/O and optimizing space utilization.

The two main structures in a file system are the directory and the I-node. A directory is a list of filenames with a pointer to an I-node. A file is found by scanning the directory to find the appropriate entry. Because of the hierarchical nature of a file system, this process is repeated for each level of directory until the requested file is found.

An I-node contains administrative information about the file and a set of pointers that either identify data blocks or index blocks. An index block contains a list of pointers. Depending on the pointer level of indirection, a pointer identifies either another index block or a data block. A UNIX I-node contains 12 direct pointers and 3 indirect pointers representing increasing levels of indirection. This is illustrated in Fig. 1–3.

The structure and buffering included in a file system is not appropriate for database management systems (DBMSs). The pointers' indirection increases the I/O, and the file system buffering forces additional data movement, first by reading the disk into the file system buffer and then by transferring the data to the DBMS. Since the DBMS also buffers the data, the file system buffering is unnecessary. Furthermore, it uses memory that could be better allocated to other purposes.

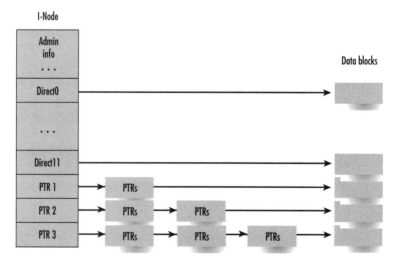

Fig. 1–3. *I-node representation.*

- **Network access:** UNIX systems provide access to the network through library functions. The two standard libraries are sockets and TLI (transport layer interface). A user program will establish a network connection by issuing a call to the network library, which will, in turn, issue system calls. Once the connection is established, either library calls or system calls can be used to transfer data over the network.

  The TCP (transmission control protocol) prepares data for transmission and adds 24 bytes of control information before passing it to the IP layer. The IP (internet protocol) also adds 24 bytes of control information and passes it to the physical layer. The physical layer needs to break down the data it receives into packets that include 32 bytes of control information.

  If a TCP packet fits into a physical frame, it incurs an 80-byte communication overhead. Otherwise, the TCP or, more precisely, the IP packet is divided into a number of physical packets. The maximum size of a physical packet varies with the network interface used. The ethernet format defines a maximum size of 1526 bytes, including the control information. The FDDI (fiber distribution data interface) format defines a maximum size of 4500 bytes.

  In addition to the speed and overhead of network communication, we have to consider the amount of traffic. The chances of collision and retransmission increase with the amount of traffic. Considering the number of people that can be using the network simultaneously, the use of this resource should be carefully planned.

- **System calls:** Processes request services from the operating system through system calls. This effectively gives additional privileges to a user so that she can access system resources. Because all of these resources are shared among a number of users, additional checks must be made to ensure the proper execution of the system call; otherwise the entire user community could be disrupted.

  Issuing a system call is a relatively expensive operation. The hardware switches into kernel mode; the operating system saves the process context, validates parameters, executes the operation, copies the return values to the proper location, and, finally, returns to user mode before giving control back to the user process.

  Some system calls are more expensive than others; opening a file is much more expensive than reading a shared memory segment, for example. Reducing the number of system calls made in an application will improve performance.

We see that the operating system tries to optimize the use of the system by keeping the CPUs busy with process scheduling. It manages the memory and reduces I/O requests by using large operations and by buffering files contents. This is consistent with what we saw at the hardware level.

IDS.2000

IDS.2000 extends the Informix dynamic server architecture (DSA). DSA has a multithreaded architecture. It implements its threading model using a concept of virtual processors (VPs). The server architecture is depicted in Fig. 1–4.

IDS.2000 includes several types of virtual processors including CPU, PIO, LIO, SHM, TLI, SOC, and EVP. Under the UNIX operating system, a virtual processor is implemented as an operating system process. In the Microsoft NT environment, it is imple-

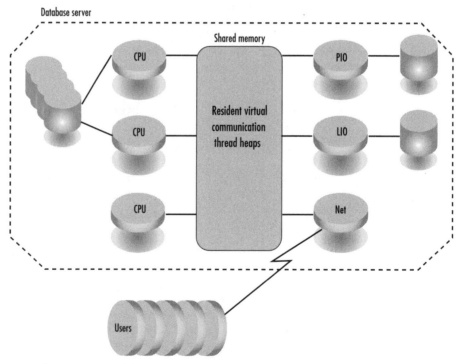

Fig. 1–4 *Simplified server architecture.*

mented as a thread. Each virtual processor manages a threaded environment containing several separate threads of execution.

Users communicate with the database server through either a network connection or a shared-memory connection. When a network connection is used, a user talks to the server through a networking virtual processor. The communication protocols supported are platform dependent. They include socket, TLI for TCP/IP and/or IPX/SPX, or stream pipe. More than one network virtual processor can be configured, and several protocols can be supported simultaneously.

A shared-memory connection is implemented using a small shared-memory area in the communication section of the database server. The communication functions linked into the application follow a predefined protocol to exchange information through that shared memory.

When a user establishes a connection to the server, the networking virtual processor authenticates the user, establishes the connection to the server, and starts a session thread. This thread is referred to as the sqlexec thread, and it does the primary processing for the client.

User threads execute within CPU virtual processors. Their contexts are kept in shared memory, which permits a thread to migrate to different CPU virtual processors. Some functions executed by a user thread may have to be executed in special virtual processors, referred to as extended virtual processors or EVPs. We'll come back to this when we cover user-defined routines in Chap. 2.

Virtual processors communicate with each other through shared-memory segments. IDS.2000 defines four shared-memory segments: resident, virtual, communication, and thread heap. The resident portion of shared memory stores shared-memory headers, internal tables, and the buffer pool. It is intended to always be in memory, never swapped out to disk. The virtual portion contains a variety of memory pools, including session and thread data among other things. The communication segment is used when shared-memory communication is used between the user and the server. The virtual portion contains, among other things, thread heaps for DataBlade modules and user-defined routines that run in extended virtual processors.

IDS.2000 manages its own disk space. It differentiates between different types of storage for standard pages, traditional large objects, and the new smart large objects. To improve performance, IDS.2000 also implements asynchronous I/O, read-ahead facilities, and data partitioning for row elimination and parallel processing.

For an in-depth discussion of IDS.2000 architecture, I recommend the following chapters of the *Informix Dynamic Server.2000: Administrator's Guide:*

- Chap. 10. "What is the Universal Server Architecture?"
- Chap. 12. "Shared Memory"
- Chap. 14. "Where is Data Stored?"
- Chap. 16. "What is Fragmentation?"
- Chap. 18. "What is PDQ?"

Query Execution

A user session is represented by a sqlexec thread. A sqlexec thread is a primary client thread. It executes the user's SQL statements. IDS.2000 starts additional threads to process the user requests. The execution of an SQL statement may involve a number of specialized threads for scans, joins, grouping, and aggregation.

Figure 1–5 provides a logical representation of a query execution. At the lower level, a number of scan threads read the table partitions. IDS.2000 then distributes the results of the scan threads to higher-level threads. In our example, the sort threads receive the result of the scans' execution. The sort threads are unaware of where the data comes from because they work through exchanges, which are not illustrated here. This allows for a more generic interface among threads. As soon as the scan threads start providing data to the sort threads, the sort threads can start executing, providing even more parallelism. This process continues up the tree until the result is returned to the user.

We can see that IDS.2000 possesses a lot of the characteristics of an operating system. It schedules threads for execution, manages memory, and buffers I/O. IDS.2000 has the additional advantage of dividing the user query into multiple threads that execute in parallel.

Performance Advantages

Now that we have covered some background information on performance, it will be easier to understand the performance bene-

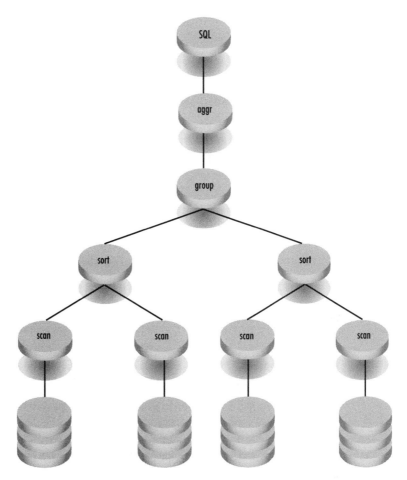

Fig. 1–5 *Query execution example.*

fits of UDRs. The performance advantages are best explained through examples.

Let's consider a company that wants to find out the total amount of sales it had for each quarter of the year. The SQL statement may look like this:

```
SELECT  'quarter 1', SUM(amount)
FROM orders
WHERE order_date BETWEEN '01/01/1998' AND
  '03/31/1998';
```

This statement returns the amount of sales for a specific quarter. Four statements must be submitted to find the total amount of sales for the year for each quarter. The impact of using four statements is that the system may be doing four table scans or using an index in the four separate statements, where a single table scan could be much more efficient. There is also the additional problem that including specific dates is error-prone. A user may make an error in the date range defining a quarter. For example, if a user identified the end of the quarter as '03/30/1999,' he would miss one day.

Database vendors don't provide functions that will identify quarters. This is because companies use different business years. With IDS.2000, it is easy to add a quarter function that will identify the right quarter for your business. The quarter function would take a date as input and return a character string in the form 'yyyyQn' where 'yyyy' identifies the year and 'n' identifies the quarter. Obtaining the total sales per quarter for the year 1999 becomes:

```
SELECT quarter(order_date), SUM(amount)
FROM orders
WHERE quarter(order_date) LIKE '1999Q?'
GROUP BY 1 ORDER BY 1;
```

The quarter function is very simple. It only knows how to take a date and convert it to a quarter string. This simple function enables the server to better process your data. Take the query plan illustrated in Fig. 1–5. Because the quarter function is used in the WHERE clause, the server is able to eliminate the rows that do not fit the query as soon as they are obtained in the scan threads. This reduces the amount of processing required by higher-level threads. The quarter function is also used in both the GROUP BY and the ORDER BY clauses. The quarter function gives the database server the information required to process the implied business type "quarter" all through its execution tree.

Date manipulations can become a lot more complex. In many industries it can be useful to analyze the activities based on the day of the week. Informix already provides functions to extract the day of the week from a date. This may not be sufficient, however. What about taking weekday holidays into consideration? Furthermore, there may be interesting distinctions between holidays that would affect the grouping: Is it a national holiday, is it observed, or is it a religious holiday for a specific group?

Other date manipulations include date arithmetic for financial calculations, date and time arithmetic that takes into consideration time zones and daylight savings time, and calculating the number of business days between dates.

The implementation of the proper data manipulation in the server allows the application developer to take advantage of the database server capabilities and reduce the amount of customized code required to get the answer. Some applications contain complex fields that include several pieces of information. For example, some departments of motor vehicles have a license field that contains the license number, the county of registration, and the type of vehicle. If we want to report on the number of registrations done in May for each type of vehicle, it requires a customized application.

The application will have to extract all the rows that apply to the month of May. The rows cannot be sorted properly, so the application must write the records to a temporary file and call a system sort utility. Then, the application reads the temporary file and counts the records. Since the records are now in the right order, it is a simple process.

With IDS.2000 you can add a function that will take a license number as input and return the county of registration. An SQL statement similar to the following will provide the desired answer:

```
SELECT county(license), COUNT(*) FROM registration
WHERE MONTH(reg_date) = 5
GROUP BY 1 ORDER BY 1;
```

The function "county" only has to return a subfield of the license column. With this result, the database server knows how to sort and group the rows to provide the answer. Here is the processing that we avoided:

- Transfer all the rows to the application, most likely through a network connection.
- Write a temporary file with the resulting rows.
- Execute an additional process to sort the temporary file.
- Read the temporary file and process its content.

The application has to manage all the steps and account for potential errors, one of them being running out of disk space for the temporary file. Implementing a server-side function is much simpler and provides significant performance benefits.

Performance Advantages Summary

Using user-defined routines improves application performance in several ways:

- **Reduces data movement:** If the server can process the data and return only the answer, all the data movement between the server and the application is eliminated. This is the main factor affecting the performance benefits of stored procedure. However, there are many situations where a stored procedure is too limited.
- **Eliminates data sooner:** We saw that user-defined routines can help the server eliminate rows at the scan level. This reduces the number of rows that other levels need to process and therefore improves performance.
- **Allows multithreaded processing:** A simple user-defined routine becomes part of the multithreaded processing of SQL queries. The application programmer takes advantage of it without having to deal with the complexity of writing multithreaded processes.
- **Provides straightforward approach:** As we saw in the license field example, several expensive steps can be avoided by having the server execute simple business processing. Extending the server to include simple business processing can result in major savings.
- **Permits new algorithms:** New approaches to problems can be implemented in the server. This includes new data representation and additional processing. The business domain experts can now augment the database server and, in some cases, change the processing characteristics from an exponential processing to linear processing. The performance benefit then increases with the size of the data that must be processed.
- **Eliminates need for marshalling:** Business data can be stored and retrieved from the database in their native

implementation instead of having to convert them to fit specific database requirements.

The software developers don't have a rigid persistence storage mechanism anymore. The domain experts do not have to wait for database vendors to add some piece of functionality that may only marginally improve their processing. They can augment the database themselves, applying their years of experience to a specific problem to make the database better suited to their environment.

Other Advantages

There are other advantages beyond better performance and simpler code. The implementation of business types changes the terminology used to address the problem. It is then easier to communicate with the domain experts because the system uses the domain terminology instead of computer terms. The improved communication with the domain experts will improve the quality of the solutions implemented.

The implementation of business types and their respective business rules are not application specific. They are specific to the business environment. This means that business objects can be used in multiple applications, providing a consistent framework throughout the corporation. The applications are more stable because they work with business objects. If the business rules change, the changes are made within the database server and not in the application code.

Having the business rules built into the database server can eliminate the need for customized applications. Common off-the-shelf products can then provide the user interface. Since customized applications also require the development of user interfaces and report formatting and printing, among other things, their elimination significantly impacts time to market.

IDS.2000 provides many object-oriented benefits, including encapsulation and inheritance. It provides a good fit between the object-oriented analysis and design and the implementation in the database.

How Far Can We Take IDS.2000?

The biggest challenge of this technology is to change the way we think about solving problems. Because IDS.2000 is a superset of a relational database, it is all too easy to continue to apply the same limitations. We have to develop solutions without considering the database and then define what the database should do to fit within the design.

With IDS.2000, we can implement our own processing and create new data representations. It is possible to allocate memory of various durations; we can also create table-type interfaces to other objects. We can even add new indexing schemes that apply to standard tables. Informix continues to improve the product and increase its extensibility.

Some third-party vendors already sell messaging DataBlade modules. IDS.2000 can also be used to join external data with existing tables. So what's next? With input from its customers, Informix will continue to improve its products to provide a business advantage.

Chapter 2

User-Defined Routines

IDS.2000 is a multithreaded database server. Multiple processes cooperate to execute many user and system threads in an effort to optimize the use of the machine. A user-defined routine executes within one of these threads. A user-defined routine is also referred to as a server-side function or a function. All these terms are equivalent and may be used interchangeably.

It is important to understand the environment where your functions execute. An application programmer must understand the operating system in which his application runs. Similarly, a developer of user-defined routines must understand the IDS.2000 environment. Furthermore, this environment is impacted by the underlying operating system; in our case it is either UNIX or Windows NT.

This chapter provides the necessary background for under-standing the running environment of user-defined routines. It covers processes, threads, thread implementations, and dynamic libraries. This sets the stage for subsequent discussion of the restrictions imposed on server-side functions as well as some ways to relax these restrictions. It then covers some important information about the environment. This information should be reviewed carefully before starting any database extensibility projects.

Processes

The operating system's main task is to optimize the use of system resources, including CPU(s), memory, controllers, disks, and network. These resources are shared among several users, and the operating system must ensure their proper use. Every request made to the operating system must be checked for errors so that they do not interrupt the other user processes executing on the machine.

Figure 2–1 illustrates the major components that make up a process. A process represents a program in execution and is described by its state of execution (running, runnable, sleeping, blocked, etc.), registers, program counter, memory (address space), and other information. The operating system uses a mechanism called virtual memory to give each process a view of memory as a contiguous space of physical memory. In 32-bit operating systems,

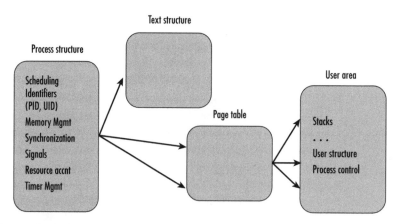

Figure 2–1 *Process structures.*

this address space is usually 4 GB. The operating system uses the concept of demand paging to allocate the system's physical memory to the processes. When a process tries to access a page that is not mapped to physical memory, a page fault is generated. The operating system catches the page fault and retrieves the page into memory. Then the process can resume its execution.

A process requires a minimum number of pages to execute. This number varies according to the processing performed, and is called a working-set size. Since the working-set size is much smaller than the amount of physical memory, many processes can be accommodated simultaneously. The operating system uses disk storage to make up the difference between the working-set size and the address space.

The creation of a process is quite expensive. It involves the following general steps:

- allocation of disk storage for the process,
- allocation and initialization of an entry into the process table,
- allocation of page tables for the process,
- allocation and initialization of a user structure, and
- initialization of the address space.

Operating systems also provide mechanisms where processes can communicate with each other. One of these is the signal mechanism. Signals can be used to indicate that the program should terminate or that a specific event has occurred. The process structure includes signal masks to set the proper behavior when a signal is received. Signals can be ignored, caught, or left to their default processing. Signal processing becomes an important issue in a multithreaded environment.

Other methods of interprocess communication include shared memory, messages, semaphores, pipes, and network communication. These methods allow processes to exchange information without violating the security requirements of discrete processes.

Operating systems simulate the simultaneous execution of processes by scheduling processes on the available processors. Each process runs for a small amount of time, called a time slice. When a process executes for the duration of its time slice or requests system services, the operating system evaluates the system situation. It then decides either to return control to the process or replace the process with another one that is ready to run. The operation of changing from the context of one process to another is called context switching. When a context switch occurs, the operating system needs to ensure that it will be able to complete the switch without interruption. It saves the process' state and moves the process descriptor to the appropriate queue. It then restores the state of another process including some special registers that identify the memory mapping for that process. Upon completion, the OS restores the machine's state before giving the control back to the original process.

The operating system adds noticeable overhead when creating new processes or when performing context switching. It must change the operation mode from user mode to kernel mode and then perform the operations briefly described above. Process scheduling always requires the intervention of the operating system. This is a necessary operation, but it should still be seen as overhead. Reducing this overhead provides more CPU cycles for productive work.

Threads

A process executes the program instructions sequentially, subject to the changes made by flow control instructions (branching). This flow of execution is called a thread. A process has one thread of execution by default.

A thread executes within the context of a process. Its structure is held in user space and can be accessed directly with thread library calls. The thread structures include a stack, program counter, state information, priority information, accounting information, and the like (see Fig. 2–2).

Threads share the process's resources, including memory, the process environment, user identification, and the file descriptors. The threads are presumed well behaved and cooperative; that is, they are expected to follow some conventions established within the program so that resources can be shared. They are expected to modify only memory elements that are allocated to them so as not to interfere with other threads.

Process

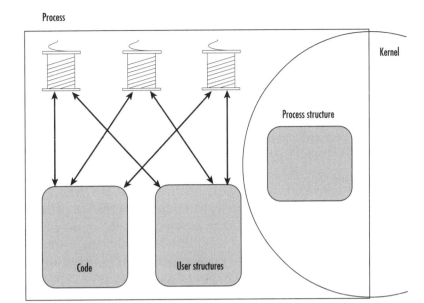

Figure 2–2 *Threads within a process.*

Threads implicitly trust each other because they come from the same process. There is no additional security necessary. As a result, threads are mainly concerned with a stack and a program counter, which allows much lower resource consumption than is required for a process. However, because several threads execute within the same address space, a single thread could terminate the process either voluntarily or by accident. If a thread writes outside its expected memory areas or simply overflows its stack, it can write into other thread spaces and cause them to fail. This may sound terrible, but it is not much different from an error in a function call that may cause the application to terminate.

It is simpler to use threads when coordinating multiple concurrent tasks than to use multiple processes. Because threads use the same address space, they share all the resources. Access to resources must be synchronized via mutexes based in user space.

Multithreading improves performance for several reasons. The advantage derives partly from the lower resource consumption. Furthermore, there is less context switching between user space and kernel space. The scheduling is done in user space, as is the resource synchronization. The savings are significant. In Solaris, creating a process is about 30 times slower than creating a thread; implementing synchronization variables are about 10 times slower, and context switching is about 5 times slower.[1]

These benefits come at a price. You must pay more attention when writing functions so they are reentrant. Since multithreading is relatively new in UNIX systems, some functions are not thread safe. Some functions, such as `asctime(3c)`, `readdir(3c)`, `strotk(3c)`, `gethostbyname(3n)`, and `tmpnam(3s)`, make use of static variables that would get clobbered if used concurrently in multiple threads. Most UNIX vendors provide equivalent functions that are thread safe. For example, the thread-safe equivalent of `tmpdir(3s)` is `tmpdir_r(3s)`. Not all functions have a thread-safe equivalent. You can still use these functions in a multithreaded environment as long as you ensure that their usage is serialized through the use of some synchronization mechanisms.

Since threads execute concurrently, you have to make sure you don't modify data structures in several threads simultaneously. You must use locking mechanisms to ensure that only one thread uses a specific data structure at a given moment. You can also separate what the work threads are doing to limit interaction between them. This reduces the need for synchronization overhead and therefore improves performance.

Thread Implementations

Thread packages come in two general implementations: user-level and kernel-level. User-level threads execute entirely in user space. They depend on the cooperation of the different threads to distribute the CPU resources. Scheduling of user-level threads is referred to as non-preemptible. The scheduling algorithm is called when either a thread API function or a system function handled by the thread package is called. A misbehaved thread could hog the CPU, starving the other application threads.

---

[1]Bil Lewis and Daniel J. Berg, *Threads Primer: A Guide to Solaris Multithread Programming* (Upper Saddle River, NJ: Prentice Hall, 1995), 21.

A user-level implementation of a thread package requires managing thread queues and events. The basic operations required are thread creation, scheduling, and removal. Thread creation requires allocation of a control block that will contain an execution stack, register information, and administrative information. The stack is initialized so that, once restored, the execution will continue as if the requested function was called. The control block is then put onto the execution queue, awaiting scheduling.

The thread scheduler saves the state of the current thread in the thread control block (TCB) and then replaces the stack pointer with the value of another thread stack. Once execution resumes, the thread indicated by the stack pointer executes while the first thread waits its turn in a queue. This is illustrated in Fig. 2–3.

This scheduling mechanism simulates concurrent execution by switching control from one thread to another. Because this process occurs often enough, it gives the impression that several

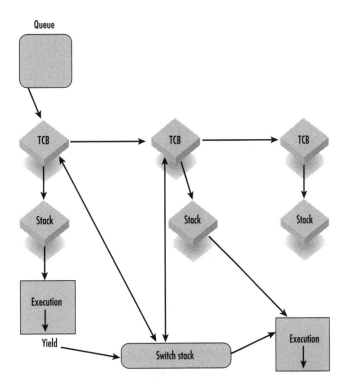

Figure 2–3 *Thread context switching.*

threads are executing simultaneously when in fact only one thread executes at a specific point. Since there is only one kernel-level execution thread, a process using this multithreaded mechanism can only take advantage of one CPU in a SMP environment. This still provides performance benefits because some threads can execute while others wait for specific events.

Each thread must voluntarily give up the CPU to allow other threads to run. If a thread executes a blocking system call or function call, no other thread can execute. For example, if a thread executes a sleep command (`sleep(3c)`), then the entire process will sleep for the requested duration. The same thing happens if a thread waits for I/O operations.

Kernel-level thread implementations depend on operating system features. They require more resources but, when executing multiple threads, they provide the additional capabilities of pre-emptible scheduling and simultaneous access to multiple CPU resources, if available.

Both thread creation and scheduling is more expensive than the user-level implementation since the operating system kernel is involved in these operations. However, it is still much better than having to create separate processes, which add virtual memory and security concerns.

Some operating-system providers implement a hybrid solution of these two methods. They provide a user-level thread implementation that schedules the threads on kernel-level threads, often called light-weight processes (LWPs). There is no set relationship between the number of threads and the number of LWPs.

Here is a short description of the most common thread packages available.

- **DCE threads:** The Open Software Foundation (OSF), since renamed The Open Group, was the first to make a thread package available on multiple UNIX platforms. This thread package is a small part of the distributed computing environment (DCE). This package is based on the POSIX 1003.4a Draft 4 specifications with some additions made to the POSIX draft standard to complete the DCE thread implementation.

  The drawback of this package is that it usually does not come with the operating system. It must be bought separately from organizations like Transarc. Furthermore, the

DCE thread package is a component of a much larger package and is not sold separately.

- **POSIX threads:** POSIX stands for portable operating system interface. Its purpose is to define a standard operating system interface and environment based on the UNIX operating system documentation to support application portability at the source level. The development of the many parts of the POSIX standard is done by committees from the Institute of Electrical and Electronics Engineers (IEEE) Computer Society.

  The IEEE published several drafts of the POSIX 1003.4a thread standard. Vendors either did not implement POSIX threads or relied on the most current draft. For this reason, some implementations are based on draft 4, draft 6, or draft 7. The POSIX standard that was recently adopted is called POSIX 1003.1c–1995 and is based on draft 10.

- **Microsoft Windows NT threads:** The Microsoft Windows NT operating system schedules processing at the thread level. The thread implementation comes for the Win32 module that is also available under Windows 95. The same scheduling applies to threads within a process and threads between processes. It is based on thread priority and round-robin scheduling. Threads are inherent to Windows NT and therefore provide their own de facto standard.

IDS.2000 Multithreading

IDS.2000 supports a large number of client connections and query executions through a few multithreaded processes. These processes are called virtual processors (VPs). They are implemented as processes on UNIX systems communicating over shared memory and as operating-system threads under Windows NT.

This architecture provides a fan-in effect where several user connections are handled by a few server processes. This reduces the operating-system overhead, leaving more CPU cycles to more useful processing.

Virtual processors are divided into classes based on the type of processing that they do. Each class is dedicated to processing certain types of threads. The processing categories include administrative tasks, disk I/O, network, user thread processing, and the like.

User requests are divided into specialized threads that can run in parallel. The operations include index building, sorting, scanning, joining, aggregation, and grouping. Parallel operations provide the ability to exploit all the CPU resources available on the system to process a single query.

Informix implemented its own thread library. When the dynamic server architecture (DSA) was implemented, few if any UNIX vendors provided threading support. Having its own thread library yielded Informix advantages: It provides a consistent thread library API. Only a small part of the thread library is platform dependent. The porting effort is kept to a minimum. The library is designed and optimized for the specific needs of a database server.

The thread library is non-preemptible. This means that threads must give up control voluntarily. The database server threads give up control of the CPU at specific points during their processing in order to optimize resource utilization. This optimization is important because the database threads include the query processing mentioned above.

The Informix threading model is similar to the user-level threading model described above. This affects what server-side functions can do and how they behave. We will discuss this later. First, let's look at how server-side functions are integrated into the Informix dynamic server architecture.

Dynamic Libraries

When a query requests a user-defined routine (UDR) for the first time, the database server loads the object code of the function into its address space. Once loaded, the UDR is available to any user until it is unloaded. Operating systems provide the capability of loading object code dynamically into running processes. This feature is usually called shared libraries or dynamic link library (DLL). In the following discussions, we will refer to them as dynamic libraries.

Dynamic libraries are heavily used in most operating systems. They allow sharing of functions among unrelated programs. This reduces the amount of memory required by the system, since only one copy of a function is required for multiple executables instead of having a copy in each one. The standard C library is a good example. The C library functions are utility functions. Having just one read-only copy in memory is sufficient for all programs. It is easy to see that the benefit increases with the number of programs using the dynamic libraries. On the other hand, it usually takes a little bit longer to initialize a program using dynamic libraries. This could be a consideration for short-lived programs, but in our case it is not important.

A dynamic library consists of a set of relocatable object files that are combined together. When a library gets loaded, some code automatically executes to convert the module addresses to actual locations in the executable.

An executable object file can be created as either static or dynamic. In static mode, all object code is included in the executable. In dynamic mode, the linker includes a list of libraries that will be used to resolve undefined symbols at runtime. In the UNIX environment the library names are included in the executable and the libraries' locations are determined by searching through a list of directories included in the `LD_LIBRARY_PATH` environment variable. A similar search is applied in the Windows NT environment by looking at the directories included in the `PATH` environment variable.

The linker also provides the capability to use dynamic libraries on demand. Because the symbols were not included directly in the executable, they are not visible outside the dynamic library. This is an important difference to understand. When a set of object files are linked together to make an executable, they include references to functions that are located in shared libraries. When the executable file is loaded into memory for execution, a special module is executed to resolve these references by opening the appropriate shared library, resolving its address, and modifying the executable accordingly. When a library is opened at runtime by the application program, there are no symbols to resolve in the executable. So how can we execute a function?

The executable program first opens the library. It then gets the address of the desired functions by passing the library and a symbol name to a function. The function can then be executed to provide the requested functionality.

Let's assume we want to execute the quarter function that is in the dynamic library `mylib.so`. A code excerpt shows this functionality in the UNIX environment:

```
void *handle;
char *pret, *(*pfn)(int);
. . .
handle = dlopen("mylib.so", RTLD_LAZY);
pfn = (char *(*)(int))dlsym(handle, "quarter");
pret = (*pfn)(date);
. . .
```

The `dlopen()` function is used to open the library and the `dlsym()` function retrieves the address of the function. The address is cast onto the appropriate function pointer type and then executed. The library could be closed later with the `dlclose()` function. The Windows NT environment provides similar capabilities with functions like `LoadLibrary()`, `GetProcAddress()`, and `FreeLibrary()`.

Symbol Visibility

UDRs are located in dynamic libraries, so IDS.2000 goes through a process similar to the one described above. A UDR can directly call functions that are located in the same dynamic library. This is also true for functions compiled from a different source file.

Keep in mind that these symbols are not visible outside the dynamic library. You cannot directly call a UDR that resides in a different dynamic library. IDS.2000 provides functions that allow you to execute other functions, as discussed in Chap. 8.

UDR Restrictions

At this point, it is obvious that a UDR is part of the server. The database server is the routine's operating environment. When you write a program, you have to consider the functionality and restrictions that the operating system imposes on your program. When writing a UDR, you have similar considerations about the functionality and restrictions within the database server environment.

As we saw earlier, IDS.2000 is a multithreaded database server. It communicates with users through shared memory or network connections; it accesses disk storage and manages execution threads over several processes; and it needs to recover from errors, which also involves catching signals that indicate errors or asynchronous events. You have to ensure that any UDR added to the server behaves properly so as not to interfere with the proper execution of the database server.

There are limits on the system calls and functions calls a UDR can execute. The calls can be divided into three general categories—forbidden calls, blocking calls, and global state calls. Table 2–1 lists some of the calls that are either forbidden or dangerous to use. There are other calls that should be used carefully if at all. It is not possible to identify them all because some of them are platform specific. The rest of this section explains some of the rules to follow in order to identify these functions or system calls.

Some functions, like `exec()` and `exit()` simply terminate the current executable. Any function that interferes with the proper environment of the server must be avoided. This includes changing the current owner or group identification of the process.

Any call that opens a file descriptor potentially interferes with the server. This impacts the maximum number of descriptors the server can open. This should be a minor issue for the server itself, but it causes a major problem for the UDR. A UDR may migrate to another virtual processor during its execution. If the UDR opens a file and is then rescheduled on a different virtual processor, the file descriptor is no longer valid since it was opened within a separate process. This can cause a situation where the

Table 2-1 Dangerous or forbidden calls.

alarm()	brk()	chdir()	dlopen()
dup()	exec()	exit()	fork()
getmsg()	ioctl()	malloc()	mmap()
open()	poll()	popen()	putmsg()
read()	sbrk()	select()	semop()
setgid()	setuid()	shmat()	signal()
sleep()	socket()	system()	write()

UDR works fine in the development environment with one CPU VP but fails in the production environment that includes several CPU VPs. This reasoning applies to any call that allocates a resource within a process and returns a handle to it, resources such as shared memory, sockets, message queues, and more.

Informix has identified a set of POSIX calls that are safe to use in user-defined routines. These calls are documented in the *DataBlade Developers' Kit User's Guide*,[2] and are listed in the Table 2–2.

Table 2-2 Safe POSIX calls.

date	`getdate`
sort/search	`bsearch, qsort, lfind, lsearch`
encryption	`crypt, setkey, encrypt`
memory management	`memccpy, memchr, memcmp, memcpy, memmove, memset`
environment	`getenv`
bit manipulation	`ffs`
byte manipulation	`swab`
structure member manipulation	`offsetof`
trigonometric functions	`acos, acosh, asin, asinh, atan, atan2, atanh, cos, cosh, sin, sinh, tan, tanh`
bessel functions	`j0, j1, jn, y0, y1, yn`
root extraction	`cbrt, sqrt`
rounding	`ceil, floor, rint`
IEEE functions	`copysign, isnan, fabs, fmod, nextafter, remainder`
error functions	`erf, erfc`
exponentials and logarithms	`exp, expm1, log, log10, log1p, pow`
gamma functions	`lgamma, lgamma_r`
euclidean distance	`hypot`

---

[2]*DataBlade Developers' Kit User's Guide* (Menlo Park, CA: Informix Software, 1998).

Table 2–2 should be taken as a guideline, not a complete list. Read the "man" pages for your UNIX platform carefully. Look for any mention of memory allocation and thread safety.

Ill-Behaved Functions

IDS.2000 can support functions that are not following the proper restrictions. In some cases this support may be needed to provide the desired functionality. Such functions are labeled ill behaved. In addition to the calls mentioned in Table 2–1, additional cases make a function ill behaved.

As we saw earlier, the IDS.2000 server implements its own threading model. These threads are nonpreemptible. This means that they must give up the control of the CPU voluntarily. If a function executes for a long time, the database server cannot attend to other tasks from this virtual processor. If your system is configured with only one CPU VP, nothing else gets done. Considering that a CPU VP can also be configured to handle network communication, this could be damaging. Long-running functions can cause the server to hang or crash. A function is considered long running if it executes for more than 1/10 second without calling `mi_yield()` to allow the database server to regain control.

In other situations a function may require the use of global status variables, or it may simply call other functions that are not thread safe. For example, in the UNIX environment, functions such as `asctime(3c)`, `readdir(3c)`, `strtok(3c)`, and `gethostbyname(3n)` make use of static local variables. If two threads execute a UDR using such a function, they will interfere with each other and cause erroneous results.

Ill-behaved functions can be defined to run on a special type of virtual processors called extended virtual processors (EVPs). These EVPs are defined within the server configuration file (`onconfig`) and are given names. Consider the following statement from a database server configuration file:

```
VPCLASS    MyClass,num=1,noyield
```

This statement creates a virtual processor type named MyClass (case insensitive). Only one process of this type will be started. The noyield option indicates that the virtual processor will run UDRs serially. Only one UDR can run on a noyield processor at a time. Furthermore, it must run to completion before another function begins. When this option is in use, only one virtual processor of this class should be started.

Using EVPs allows you to implement ill-behaved functions. Furthermore, by allocating only one process for a specific EVP, you ensure that your UDR will not migrate to a different process during execution.

For configuration purposes, EVPs are treated as CPU VPs. For this reason, you must set the SINGLE_CPU_VP configuration parameter in your onconfig file to zero, otherwise EVPs will not be accepted:

```
SINGLE_CPU_VP     0
```

Create Function **Statement**

You include a UDR in the system by executing a CREATE FUNCTION statement. This statement adds an entry in the SYSPROCEDURES system catalog. SYSPROCEDURES is searched when the database server resolves the implicit or explicit function calls within SQL statements.

The following statement shows the syntax of the CREATE FUNCTION statement:

```
CREATE [DBA] FUNCTION function_name(
   [parameter_list] )
RETURNING {SQL_type | REFERENCES [BYTE|TEXT]}
[SPECIFIC specific_name]
[WITH( [ { HANDLESNULLS | CLASS="vp_class" | [NOT]
   VARIANT | STACK=stack_size |INTERNAL | ITERATOR |
   PARALLELIZABLE | COMMUTATOR= function_name |
   NEGATOR=function_name | SELFUNC=function_name |
   PERCALL_COST=value } ] ]
EXTERNAL NAME 'path_name'
```

```
LANGUAGE C [PARAMETER STYLE INFORMIX] [ [NOT] VARIANT]
END FUNCTION
[DOCUMENT 'string' ] [ WITH LISTING IN
   'warningpath' ] ;

parameter_list: parameter [[, parameter]...] [, OUT
   parameter]
parameter: [parameter_name] { SQL_type | LIKE
   table_name.column_name | REFERENCES {BYTE | TEXT} }
   [DEFAULT default_value]
```

It is important to pay attention to the function modifiers available within the WITH() clause of the statement. Here is a short description of the ones you must know right away:

HANDLESNULLS: *By default, IDS.2000 functions do not process NULL values. If one or more arguments are* NULL, *the function will not be invoked and the return value will be set to* NULL. *If this is not the behavior that you desire, use the* HANDLENULLS *modifier. You will then have to include additional code within your function that will test for* NULL *values.*

VARIANT: *IDS.2000 assumes that a function either has side effects (e.g., updating a table) or returns different results when invoked with the same argument. Informix qualifies these functions as variant. Since the result may be different in each invocation of a* VARIANT *function, it is not possible to index its result. You should use the* NOT VARIANT *modifier when a function does not have side effects and returns consistent results. This allows the server to do additional optimization and, if needed, you can index the result of the function.*

PARALLELIZABLE: *This modifier tells the database server that the function can be executed in parallel within a query. Function parallelization has some restrictions that are checked at runtime. You can define a function as* PARALLELIZABLE, *but it may fail at runtime if the server tries to execute it in parallel. This is covered in more detail in Chap. 5.*

CLASS="vpclass": *In the previous section, we discussed ill-behaved functions. This modifier defined the class of virtual processor that will run the function. By default it assumes the CPU class. Looking back at our class definition in the previous section, we can define a function as running on the* MyClass *virtual processor by including*

`VPCLASS="MyClass"` *as a modifier. This modifier is also useful in debugging. If you create one extended virtual processor, you can then identify the exact virtual processor that runs your function and you can attach a debugger to this process for source-level debugging. We'll learn more about this in Chap. 12.*

The SQL statements used when extending IDS.2000, including the `CREATE FUNCTION` statement, are described in detail in Chap. 3.

Function Resolution

IDS.2000 provides the capability to create multiple functions with the same name. This is called function overloading. The parser resolves the function to the desired one by looking at the routine name, the type of routine, and the number and types of its arguments. Furthermore, a routine will not be considered if the user requesting it does not have execute permission.

The term *function signature* refers to the parameters used to determine which function is chosen. It is important to note that the return type is not included.

Operator Overloading

It is also possible to overload operators provided in the SQL syntax. Table 2–3 lists the operators and their function equivalent. Note that the operators `LIKE` and `MATCHES` can take two or three arguments. Table 2–3 lists their third argument within square brackets to indicate that they are optional. By implementing new versions of available operators for your user-defined types, you hide the particularity of your business processing within standard relational operations. The database server then decides at runtime which function will perform the requested operation by looking at the types of the values passed to the operator.

Table 2–3 IDS.2000 Operators.

Operator symbols	Implementation functions
"="	boolean = equal(arg1, arg2)
"<>", "!="	boolean = notequal(arg1, arg2)
">"	boolean = greaterthan(arg1, arg2)
"<"	boolean = lessthan(arg1, arg2)
">="	boolean = greaterthanorequal(arg1, arg2)
"<="	boolean = lessthanorequal(arg1, arg2)
LIKE	boolean = like(arg1, arg2 [, arg3])
MATCHES	boolean = matches(arg1, arg2 [, arg3])
"-"	<type> = minus(arg1, arg2)
"+"	<type> = plus(arg1, arg2)
"/"	<type> = divide(arg1, arg2)
"*"	<type> = times(arg1, arg2)
"||"	<type> = concat(arg1, arg2)
"+"	<type> = positive(arg1)
"-"	<type> = negate(arg1)

Built-in Functions Overloading

Some built-in SQL functions can be overloaded to support user-defined types. Table 2–4 lists the functions and their arguments.

Once again, the arguments within square brackets are optional. These functions are described in detail in the Informix SQL syntax manuals.

Table 2–4 IDS.2000 built-in functions.

<type>=root(arg1 [,index])	decval=round(arg1 [,digits])	<type>=sqrt(arg1)
<type>=trunc(arg1 [,digits])	floatval=exp(floatval)	floatval=logn(floatval)
floatval=log10(floatval)	decval=cos(arg1)	decval=sin(arg1)
decval=tan(arg1)	decval=acos(arg1)	decval=asin(arg1)
decval=atan(arg1)	decval=atan2(arg1, arg2)	

Library Loading and Unloading

IDS.2000 loads a dynamic library the first time one of its functions is invoked. The database server may decide to unload a library as it sees fit. This is important to remember; if your function initializes some static local variables, you may find yourself in a situation where the unloading and reloading of a library will discard these values. This could cause unexpected results. Furthermore, because this discard depends on server activities, your function could work for months before suddenly causing problems.

The loading and unloading of libraries has other interesting side effects. When you recreate the library to include fixes or changes, the library may have already been opened by the server. Replacing modules in a library that is in use should be avoided. If instead you create a new library, the new library won't get used until the server unloads the old one and has a need to load the new one. In the UNIX environment, a file is not removed from the system until the last file descriptor referencing it is closed. Externally, it looks as if the old library has been replaced with a new one with the same name in the same location. Internally, though, the database server is still using the old one. It is very easy to forget this fact and spend a significant amount of time trying to figure out why the new code is not working.

The database server log file keeps track of many events in the server, including the loading and unloading of dynamic libraries. You can review the latest events recorded in the log file with the command

```
onstat -m
```

The alternative is to know where the log file is and open it directly.

After replacing the dynamic library, you must make sure the database server unloads the old one and loads the new one. There are three ways to get this done. The first way is to bring down the database server and bring it back up. This can be disruptive, and this operation is reserved to the database administrator. The second way to unload a library is to remove all function definitions that include a reference to the dynamic library. The third way to do it is to execute the `ifx_replace_module()` function. This can be done either with an EXECUTE FUNCTION statement or within an SQL statement. This function is described in Chap. 3.

No matter which method you use, you should always check the database server log file to make sure your library has been unloaded. The library could have been kept in memory because one of your DROP FUNCTION statements failed or for unknown reasons.

A Simple Example

Lets assume we want to add `quarter()` functions to our database. This function will take a date as input and return a character string representing the quarter (VARCHAR(10)). The format of the string is four digits for the year, followed by the letter Q and one digit representing the quarter. The representation of the first quarter of 1999 is then 1999Q1.

Based on these requirements, the function prototype for the quarter function is:

```
mi_lvarchar
  *quarter(mi_date adate, MI_FPARAM *fparam);
```

The `quarter()` function returns a LVARCHAR pointer. This is the proper type for CHAR, VARCHAR, and LVARCHAR. It takes a `mi_date` as input. It also takes an additional argument of type MI_FPARAM. All UDRs always have this additional argument. Its use is described below. The mapping of SQL types and return values and arguments is covered in Chap. 4.

The function needs to be compiled and linked into a dynamic library. On the Solaris operating system, this can be done as follows:

```
cc -DMI_SERVBUILD -I$(INFORMIXDIR)/incl/public -c
  quarter.c
ld -G -o mylib.bld quarter.o
chmod a+x mylib.bld
```

The compilation requires the definition of the MI_SERVBUILD flag to indicate that the function will run in the server. It also includes the definition of the included directory of where to find the DataBlade API include files. The link line creates a dynamic library (-G option) called `mylib.bld` with only the `quarter.o` object in it. Finally, the access to the library is changed to add execution permission to the owner.

The Windows NT environment operates in a similar manner. The same operation looks like this:

```
cl -DNT -DMI_SERVBUILD -DGL_NT_STATIC -DNT_MI_SAPI
   -DWIN32
-I$(MI_INCLUDE)\public -O /Fo$quarter.obj /c quarter.c

link  /DLL /nologo /out:mylib.bld /def:mylib.def
   quarter.o $(INFORMIXDIR)\lib\sapi.lib
attrib +R $(BINDIR)\\$(PROJECT_TITLE).bld
```

The biggest difference between UNIX and Windows NT is the use of the `/def` option in the link command. This option defines a file that contains instructions for the linker. What we need is the definition of the function names included in the dynamic library. Otherwise, the symbol won't be found by the database server. In the previous case, the `mylib.def` file contains:

```
EXPORTS
quarter
```

The library can be located anywhere in the system. By convention, a directory should be created under `$INFORMIXDIR/extend`, and the library should be moved there. Let's assume that we call this directory `udrbook` and have a bin subdirectory. The function is created in the database with the following SQL statement:

```
CREATE FUNCTION quarter(date)
RETURNS varchar(10)
WITH (not variant, parallelizable)
EXTERNAL NAME
"$(INFORMIXDIR)/extend/udrbook/bin/mylib.bld(quarter)"
LANGUAGE C;
```

The function is defined as taking a date as input and returning a VARCHAR type of maximum length ten. An index could be created on the result of the quarter() function since the maximum length meets the requirements for index creation. If we had chosen to return an LVARCHAR, it would not be possible to index the result.

The function definition identifies two modifiers. The NOT VARIANT modifier tells the database server that the function always returns the same result with a given argument and does not have side effects, such as modifying some tables. The PARALLELIZABLE modifier indicates that the function meets the requirements to run in parallel if needed. The quarter() function does not handle NULLs (HANDLESNULLS modifier). This means that a NULL value is returned instead of being passed to the function for processing. This may not be the desired result. You may want to pass the NULL value and return "UNKNOWN" instead. This could help simplify some of your business processing.

The external name identifies the location of the function. The quarter name in parenthesis is optional because the name of the function is the same as the name within the library. Finally, we identify the language used to build the function as C. This opens the door for future language support. The first additional language supported is Java.

The last thing to do is to give execution permission to the appropriate users. In our case, we will give execution permission to everybody with the following statement:

```
grant execute on function quarter(date) to public;
```

At this point, the quarter function can be used in any SQL statements for this database as follows:

```
SELECT quarter(order_date), SUM(amount)
FROM orders
WHERE quarter(order_date) LIKE '1999Q?'
GROUP BY 1 ORDER BY 1;
```

The function helps eliminate rows at the scan level because it is used in the WHERE clause. It also simplifies identification of the business time period that is being analyzed.

The MI_FPARAM Argument

We saw that the quarter() function had one additional argument called the function parameter. It stores state information about the function as well as information about the arguments and the return value.

Table 2–5 lists the functions used to manipulate the MI_FPARAM structure. You can find their descriptions in the Appendix. These functions provide information about the number of arguments and return values, their scale, precision, length, and if they are NULL.

They all have a similar interface. They take an MI_FPARAM pointer as their first argument and the function argument number as the second argument.

If we were to handle NULLs within our quarter function, we would have to test if the argument is NULL with the following call:

```
ret = mi_fp_argisnull(fparam, 0);
```

Table 2–5 MI_FPARAM accessor functions

mi_fp_funcstate()	mi_fp_setfuncstate()
mi_fp_request()	
mi_fp_nargs()	mi_fp_setnargs()
mi_fp_arglen()	mi_fp_setarglen()
mi_fp_argprec()	mi_fp_setargprec()
mi_fp_argscale()	mi_fp_setargscale()
mi_fp_argisnull()	mi_fp_setargisnull()
mi_fp_nrets()	mi_fp_setnrets()
mi_fp_retlen()	mi_fp_setretlen()
mi_fp_retprec()	mi_fp_setretprec()
mi_fp_argscale()	mi_fp_setargscale()
mi_fp_rettype()	mi_fp_setrettype()
mi_fp_returnisnull()	mi_fp_setreturnisnull()
mi_fp_setisdone	
mi_fp_setfuncid()	

The argument number starts at zero, just like array addressing in C. The function returns MI_TRUE if the argument is NULL. The quarter() function can then take the appropriate action and return the string "UNKNOWN" as a result, instead of trying to calculate the quarter.

Other accessor functions are for iterator functions that will be covered in a later chapter. They include saving and retrieving state information (mi_fp_funcstate() and mi_fp_setfuncstate()), an indicator that shows the type of request for a specific invocation of an iterator function (mi_fp_request()), and an indicator to tell the calling function that all values have been returned (mi_fp_setisdone()).

Memory Allocation

One of the most common operations within UDRs is memory allocation. The DataBlade API manual documents five memory management routines: mi_alloc(), mi_dalloc(), mi_zalloc(), mi_free(), and mi_switch_memory_duration().

Each time memory is allocated, the allocation includes a memory duration. The Informix documentation defines two durations: PER_ROUTINE and PER_COMMAND. There is also a synonym of PER_FUNCTION for the PER_ROUTINE duration.

The PER_ROUTINE default memory duration is adequate for most situations. A function can allocate memory with this default duration for processing within the function or to return it to the caller as its return value. If the caller routine calls such a function a second time, the database server will collect any memory that was allocated with the PER_ROUTINE memory duration. In this case, the caller function must make a copy of the memory into a newly allocated buffer. The PER_ROUTINE memory allocation generally gets reclaimed at the next invocation of the function that allocated the memory.

The PER_COMMAND memory duration applies to the duration of the current SQL statement. It is useful for iterator functions, aggregation functions, and for some smart large-objects manipulation. We will cover these functions in later chapters.

The function `mi_switch_memory_duration()` is used to change the default memory duration. This can be useful if you want a `PER_COMMAND` duration when calling other DataBlade API functions that allocate memory without providing a duration option. This is the case when allocating a new `LVARCHAR` variable with the `mi_new_var()` API function.

The DataBlade Development Kit (DBDK)

In Chap. 1, we defined a DataBlade module as a packaging of functionality. Informix provides tools to facilitate the development, packaging, and distribution of DataBlade modules. It is called the DataBlade development kit and includes BladeSmith, BladePack, and BladeManager.

BladeSmith is a GUI tool running on Windows NT that helps you manage the development of DataBlade modules. You start by defining a project that is the container for your dataBlade module. Within this project, you can define different objects, including aggregation functions, casts, error messages, UDRs, and data types. The data types include collection, opaque, distinct, qualified, and row types. You can also define test data for opaque types and functions.

Once you have defined your types and functions, BladeSmith generates files such as function skeletons, makefiles, functional tests files, SQL scripts, messages files, and packaging files. The file generation includes options for tracing and debugging. You then need to modify the source code to add the desired functionality. If you make changes to your objects, the files can be regenerated with the code changes that you made.

The BladePack utility generates a distribution image of your DataBlade module. BladeManager can then be used to install your DataBlade module in the desired database.

The DataBlade development kit can greatly improve productivity in development and testing; I strongly recommend that you become familiar with it. This tool is constantly being improved, so make sure to follow its development.

Chapter 3

SQL Statements

IDS.2000 provides a set of SQL (structured query language) statements that allows for the definition of new functionality including, among other things, user-defined routines and new business types. The SQL statements include all the concepts of inheritance, function overloading, and polymorphism. They also provide mapping to the C implementation, which does not include any of these concepts.

This chapter presents the SQL statements used to create and remove the different objects you will encounter in your server-side programming. It explains what each object is, describes and explains its full syntax, and provides some examples.

Each object is presented with the complete syntax needed for creation and removal when appropriate. This has the advantage of showing all the possible choices in a single location instead of forcing you to consult separate sections of at least two manuals to cover everything.

The statements are presented and explained in alphabetical order. Each section contains all the information required to create and remove the object discussed.

Only the commands and their syntax, as they relate to user-defined routines in C, are covered here. The objects covered include

AGGREGATE	CAST	DISTINCT TYPE
FUNCTION	GRANT	OPAQUE TYPE
OPCLASS	PROCEDURE	ROW TYPE
ifx_replace_module()		

The last element covered, `ifx_replace_module()`, is a function provided by Informix. It is used to replace a shared library containing server-side functions with an updated one. Because it provides an essential functionality, it is discussed here as part of the statements that are needed for UDR programming.

Syntax Diagram Explanation

The syntax diagrams presented here are different from the Informix documentation. They follow only a few conventions, so they can be easily understood. The text following each diagram explains the statement in more detail. The main conventions are:

- **Uppercase:** Words in uppercase represent statement keywords. These words must be spelled exactly as shown, either in uppercase or lowercase.
- **Lowercase:** These words represent variables, such as function names, or lists of variables. Their meaning is explained in the text following the syntax diagram.
- **Optional section:** An optional section is presented within square brackets [. . .].
- **Multiple choices:** When multiple values are possible in a specific section, the choices are separated by vertical bars. If a default choice exists, it is shown in bold. { . . . } enclose the entire set of choices.

- Ellipses within square brackets represent a potential repetition of the previous argument within brackets.

AGGREGATE

Syntax

```
CREATE AGGREGATE aggregate_name WITH ( modifier_list) ;
modifier_list: modifier [ [, modifier] ...]
modifier: { INIT=function_name | ITER=function_name |
   COMBINE=function_name | FINAL=function_name |
   HANDLESNULLS }

DROP AGGREGATE aggregate_name ;
```

Description

A user-defined aggregate (UDA) is a function that operates on a set of values. The CREATE AGGREGATE statement adds an entry to the SYSAGGREGATES system catalog to identify the support functions that are used to perform the aggregation. The UDA uses the type information from the support functions to ensure that the values are well typed.

UDAs share the same named space as the user-defined routines. This implies that UDAs and UDRs cannot have the same name. Furthermore, the UDA name is a place holder that identifies a set of support functions that perform the aggregation. The aggregate function polymorphism is obtained through the support functions included in the definition of the UDA.

By default, NULL values do not participate in the aggregations. The modifier HANDLESNULLS must be included to add the processing of NULL values. Even if the NULL values are not part of the aggregation, the INIT function, if present, must handle NULLs. If the INIT function is not present, then the ITER function must handle NULLs.

The DROP AGGREGATE command removes the definition of the UDA from SYSAGGREGATES. It has no impact on the existence of the functions that provide the functionality.

Parameters Description

aggregate_name: *This is the name you give your aggregate function. This identifier must start with a letter or an underscore (_), followed by letters, digits, or underscore. For Informix-UDO version, before IDS.2000, the maximum length of the name is 18 characters. The IDS.2000 limit is set to 128 characters.*

modifier_list: *The modifier list is a set of modifiers separated by commas.*

modifier: *The* ITER *and* COMBINE *modifiers are required in the* CREATE *statement. However, both* ITER *and* COMBINE *can refer to the same function if the input type and the internal type used for processing are the same. The function names listed in the modifiers do not need to exist when the aggregation function is created. The names are resolved at execution time.*

function_name: *This represents the name of the function that implements the specified modifier. Only a name is provided. This means that IDS.2000 will resolve the function reference at run time, based on the type of the argument.*

INIT: *The* INIT *modifier identifies an initialization function. This function initializes the structure used by the other functions. This function is called with a* NULL *argument of the input column type. Therefore, it must be defined with the* HANDLESNULLS *modifier. It can also be defined with an additional argument that serves as an initialization parameter. The general function prototype is*

```
<state_type> = init_function(<column_type> [,
    <init_val>]);
```

ITER: *This is a required modifier. It identifies a function that merges a single value with a partial result. If there is no* INIT *function, the function defined by* ITER *must handle* NULL *values. The* ITER *function has this general prototype:*

```
<state type> = iter_function(<state_type>,
    <column_type>);
```

COMBINE: *The* COMBINE *function merges two partial results and returns an updated partial result. The* COMBINE *function may be the same as the* ITER *function if the state type is the same as the input type. The* COMBINE *function prototype is*

```
<state_type> = combine_function(<state_type>,
    <state_type>);
```

FINAL: *The* FINAL *modifier identifies a function that converts the internal result calculated in the aggregation into a result type. This modifier is not required if the state type corresponds to the result type. The final function prototype is*

```
<result_type> = final_function(<state_type>);
```

HANDLESNULLS: *By default,* NULL *values are not passed to an aggregation function. This modifier indicates that the aggregation function will get the* NULL *values. In this case, if the* INIT *function exists, it must be defined with the* HANDLESNULLS *modifier. If the* INIT *function is not defined, then the* ITER *function must be able to handle* NULL *values.*

Examples

Create an aggregate function percentTot() and identify all the modifier functions:

```
CREATE AGGREGATE percentTot
WITH (
INIT = percentTot_init,
ITER = percentTot_iter,
COMBINE = percentTot_combine,
FINAL = percentTot_final
);
```

Remove the percentTot() aggregation function:

```
DROP AGGREGATE percentTot;
```

Syntax

```
CREATE [{IMPLICIT | EXPLICIT}] CAST
( source_type AS target_type
[WITH function_name] );

DROP CAST ( source_type AS target_type );
```

Description

A cast function is used to convert one data type to another. You can use cast functions to convert unit of measures (meters to miles), currencies (yen to U.S. dollar), and the like. Casting allows you to tell the database server about variations on the environment strong typing.

The CREATE statement adds an entry to the SYSCASTS system catalog to make the cast available. The DROP statement removes the definition from the system catalog, effectively deleting it.

Parameters Description

IMPLICIT and EXPLICIT: *Casts come in two flavors: explicit and implicit. If the type of cast is not provided, it defaults to an explicit cast. An explicit cast must be part of an SQL statement to be invoked. An implicit cast will be invoked automatically by the database server when it encounters types that cannot be mixed while applying the system-defined casts.*

source_type: *The source type is any type available in the current database. It can be either a base type or an extended type.*

target_type: *The target type represents the resulting type of the conversion. The type must already exist in the database.*

function_name: *If both types have the same internal representation, the WITH clause is not needed. Otherwise, the cast is performed by the function identified in the WITH clause. The function is defined as taking an argument of* source_type *and returning a type* target_type.

Examples

Create an explicit cast to convert from `capital_expense` to `expense`. Note that `capital_expense` is a distinct type of `money`, so no conversion function needs to be declared in the `CREATE CAST` statement:

```
CREATE EXPLICIT CAST ( capital_expense AS expense);
```

Create an implicit cast from the `money` type to `capital_expense`:

```
CREATE IMPLICIT CAST (money AS capital_expense);
```

Create an explicit cast that converts miles to kilometers with the function `miles2km`:

```
CREATE CAST ( mile AS kilometer WITH miles2km );
```

The cast function can be used in two forms within a statement. To convert a miles column as kilometers within a `SELECT` statement you can use one of these two statements:

```
SELECT miles_col::kilometer FROM mytable;
SELECT CAST(miles_col AS kilometer) FROM mytable;
```

Remove the above three casts:

```
DROP CAST ( capital_expense AS expense );
DROP CAST ( money AS capital_expense );
DROP CAST ( mile AS kilometer );
```

DISTINCT TYPE

Syntax

```
CREATE DISTINCT TYPE distinct_type AS source_type ;

DROP TYPE distinct_type RESTRICT;
```

Description

A distinct type has the same internal representation as an existing type. This provides a way to implement strong typing and new behaviors for existing functions and operators through function overloading.

When you create a distinct type, IDS.2000 automatically creates two explicit casts. One from the distinct type to the source type, and another from the source type to the distinct type. If you would rather make one or both casts implicit, you must first drop the respective explicit cast.

You cannot create a distinct type from a SERIAL or SERIAL8 type.

The DROP TYPE statement removes a type from the database. The database server will automatically remove the two explicit casts that were created with the distinct type. You cannot drop a type if the database still contains reference to the type in the form of casts, columns, or functions whose definition references the type.

Parameters Description

distinct_type: *This represents the name of your new type. This identifier must start with a letter or an underscore (_), followed by letters, digits, or an underscore. For Informix-UDO version, before IDS.2000, the maximum length of the name is 18 characters. IDS.2000 defines a limit of 128 characters.*

source_type: *The source type is the name of an existing type. Your distinct type takes its internal representation from this type.*

Examples

Create a new type revenue that is based on the money type:

```
CREATE DISTINCT TYPE revenue AS money;
```

Remove the distinct type revenue:

```
DROP TYPE revenue RESTRICT;
```

FUNCTION

Syntax

```
CREATE [DBA] FUNCTION function_name( [parameter_list] )
RETURNING {SQL_type | REFERENCES [BYTE|TEXT]}
[SPECIFIC specific_name]
[WITH( [ { HANDLESNULLS | CLASS='vp_class' | [NOT]
  VARIANT | STACK=stack_size |INTERNAL | ITERATOR |
  PARALLELIZABLE | COMMUTATOR= function_name |
  NEGATOR=function_name |
SELFUNC=function_name | PERCALL_COST=value }  ] ]
EXTERNAL NAME 'path_name'
LANGUAGE C [PARAMETER STYLE INFORMIX] [ [NOT] VARIANT]
END FUNCTION
[DOCUMENT 'string' ] [ WITH LISTING IN 'warningpath' ] ;

parameter_list: parameter [[, parameter]...]
[, OUT parameter]

parameter: [parameter_name] { SQL_type |
LIKE table_name.column_name | REFERENCES {BYTE | TEXT} }
  [DEFAULT default_value]

DROP FUNCTION function_name [(parameter_list)] ;

DROP SPECIFIC FUNCTION specific_name ;

ALTER {SPECIFIC FUNCTION specific_name |
FUNCTION function_name( parameter_list) }
  WITH(alteration_list);

alteration_list: alteration [[, alteration]...]

alteration: {ADD modifier| MODIFY modifier|
MODIFY EXTERNAL NAME 'path_name'| DROP modifier_name}
```

Description

The CREATE statement defines a new function or operator. It adds entries to system catalogs including SYSPROCEDURES, SYSPROC-BODY, and SYSPROCAUTH. Operators are defined using specific function names including the following names:

LessThan	LessThanOrEqual	Equal	NotEqual
GreatherThanOrEqual	GreatherThan	Plus	Minus
Times	Divide	Concat	Positive
Negate			

A function or operator can be removed with the DROP FUNCTION statement. If a specific (unique) name was included in its creation, the DROP SPECIFIC FUNCTION statement and the specific name can be used instead.

The ALTER statement changes the definition of an existing function. You can add, modify, and drop any modifiers. The modifiers are the same that apply to the CREATE statement.

Parameters Description

DBA: *The* DBA *optional keyword indicates that the user who executes this function must have DBA privilege.*

function_name: *This specifies the name of the function. This identifier must start with a letter or an underscore (_), followed by letters, digits, or an underscore. For Informix-UDO versions, before IDS.2000, a name's maximum length is 18 characters. IDS.2000 defines a limit of 128 characters.*

parameter_list: *The parameter list identifies the type of each parameter that your function accepts. The last parameter can be defined with the* OUT *keyword. The* OUT *parameter is used for statement local variables (SLV). An SLV transmits a value from a function call in a statement to another part of the SQL statement.*

parameter: *The type of parameters are defined below as* SQL_type, Table_name.column_name, *and* defaultvalue. *One choice is* REFERENCES *for either* BYTE *or* TEXT. *This parameter type allows you to use a pointer to a* TEXT *or* BYTE *parameter. These types cannot be used directly. Only the* NULL *default value is allowed for this parameter type.*

parameter_name: *This is an optional parameter giving a name to the parameter.*

SQL_type: *A parameter can be of any type defined in the database except* SERIAL, SERIAL8, TEXT, BYTE, CLOB, *or* BLOB. *The types supported also include distinct type, opaque type, collection type, and named and unnamed row type.*

table_name.column_name: *A parameter type can be defined as being the same as the type of a column in a table.*

default_value: *Parameters can be given default values. A default value consists of a literal appropriate to the type of argument. Using a default value allows calling functions with fewer parameters than actually defined. If no default values are provided, a call with fewer parameters will end with an error.*

RETURNING: *The same comments apply to the return value as for the parameters described above.*

specific_name: *This identifier is a name that uniquely identifies the function in the database. The specific name can be used in the following SQL statements:* DROP, GRANT, REVOKE, UPDATE STATISTICS. *A specific name can be up to 128 characters long. Specific names make it easier to handle functions when the same function name is used with many signatures (overloaded).*

HANDLESNULLS: *By default, IDS.2000 assumes that functions do not process* NULL *values. If one or more arguments are* NULL, *the function will not be invoked and the return value will be set to* NULL. *If this is not the behavior that you desire, use the* HANDLESNULLS *modifier. You will then have to include additional code within your function that will test for* NULL *values.*

CLASS: *This modifier identifies the class of virtual processor (VP) that will execute this function. The default class is* CPU VP. *If your function is not well behaved, you need to have your system administrator create an extended virtual processor (EVP) and identify this EVP as the virtual processor to use for this function. For example, if my EVP is called* MyClass, *the* CLASS *modifier would be* CLASS='MyClass'.

VARIANT: *By default the database server assumes that a function may return different results from separate executions with the same argument(s) or that it has side effects such as modifying database tables or internal structures. A* VARIANT *function must be called for each set of values passed to it instead of caching results. Furthermore, since the result of the function varies* *between executions, the result of a* VARIANT *function cannot be indexed.*

STACK: *The default stack size provided in the server configuration parameter is 64 KB under Windows NT and 32 KB under UNIX operating systems. The stack size is given as a number of bytes. The stack is used to store variables declared in a function (automatic variables) and, among other things is used when calling other functions.*

INTERNAL: *This modifier indicates that an SQL or SPL cannot call the function directly. An* INTERNAL *function is not considered during routine resolution.*

ITERATOR: *This modifier indicates that the function returns a set of values.*

PARALLELIZABLE: *This modifier indicates that the function meets the requirements to run in parallel. If the function is found to violate the requirements at runtime, an error will be generated. The requirements are covered in detail in chapter 5.*

COMMUTATOR: *A commutator function takes the same arguments as the original function in reverse order and returns the same result. For example,* lessthan() *is a commutator function for* greaterthanorequal().

NEGATOR: *A negator function returns a Boolean complement of the original function. For example, the function* notequal() *is the negator of* equal().

SELFUNC: *This function is used to calculate the selectivity of the routine being created*

PERCALL_COST: *This integer value indicates the per-call cost of the function. The standard formula for calculating the cost is lines of code + (I/O operations × 100).*

path_name: *This parameter identifies the location of the dynamically loadable executable code. If the path name includes an environment variable such as* $INFORMIXDIR, *the variable value will be resolved by the server at runtime with whatever value is defined for that variable in the server's environment.*

LANGUAGE: *In the context of this book, the language is always C. Starting with IDS.2000, the Java language is also supported.*

string: *The* DOCUMENT *string is intended as a synopsis and description of the routine. It is stored in the* SYSPROCBODY *system catalog.*

warningpath: *This parameter identifies the file where compile-time warnings are sent. If this clause is missing, the compiler does not generate a list of warnings.*

Examples

Create a function `int2dec()` that takes an integer as an argument and returns a decimal value:

```
CREATE FUNCTION int2dec(int)
RETURNING dec
WITH (NOT VARIANT, PARALLELIZABLE)
EXTERNAL NAME
"$INFORMIXDIR/extend/udrbook/bin/mylib.bld(do2_dec)"
LANGUAGE C
END FUNCTION;
```

Alter the `int2dec()` function to add a cost of 10:

```
ALTER FUNCTION int2dec(int) WITH(ADD PERCALL_COST=10);
```

Remove the `int2dec()` function:

```
DROP FUNCTION int2dec(int);
```

GRANT

Syntax

```
GRANT USAGE ON TYPE type_name
TO { user_list [WITH GRANT OPTION] | role_name }
[AS grantor] ;

user_list: user [[, user]...]

GRANT EXECUTE ON
{ SPECIFIC specific_name |
  [{FUNCTION|PROCEDURE|ROUTINE}]
function_name ( parameter_list ) }
TO user_list [WITH GRANT OPTION]  [AS grantor] ;

parameter_list: parameter [[, parameter]...]
[, OUT parameter]

parameter: [parameter_name] { SQL_type |
LIKE table_name.column_name | REFERENCES {BYTE |
  TEXT} } [DEFAULT default_value]
```

Description

The GRANT function is used to authorize others to use your types and functions.

Parameters Description

type_name: *The name of the type.*

user_list: *This represents one or more users who are granted the privilege of using the type or function.*

user: *A user is a login name. You can put quotes around names. The optional* WITH GRANT OPTION *gives the users the privilege of authorizing others to use the type or function.*

role_name: *A role is a grouping of users under a specified identification. Granting permission to a role allows the users included in this role, or in any other roles that includes this one, the privilege to use the type or function.*

grantor: *This is a login name. This clause effectively changes the owner of the type or function from your login to the grantor. This clause changes the* SYSTABAUTH *table and therefore cannot be reversed once committed.*

specific_name: *This identifier is a name that uniquely identifies the function in the database. If the name was specified in the* CREATE FUNCTION *statement, this name can be used in the* GRANT *statement.*

function_name: *The function name specifies the name of the function. This identifier must start with a letter or an underscore (_), followed by letters, digits, or an underscore. For Informix-UDO version, before IDS.2000, a name's maximum length is 18 characters. IDS.2000 defines a limit of 128 characters.*

parameter_list: *The parameter list identifies the type of each parameter that your function accepts. The last parameter can be defined with the* OUT *keyword. The* OUT *parameter is used for statement local variables (SLV). An SLV transmits a value from a function call in a statement to another part of the SQL statement.*

parameter: *The type of parameters are defined below as* SQL_type, table_name.column_name, *and* default_value. *One choice is* REFERENCES *for either* BYTE *or* TEXT. *This parameter type allows you to use a pointer to a* TEXT *or* BYTE *para-*

meter. These types cannot be used directly. Only the NULL *default value is allowed for this parameter type.*

parameter_name: *This is an optional parameter giving a name to the parameter.*

SQL_type: *A parameter can be of any type defined in the database except* SERIAL, SERIAL8, TEXT, BYTE, CLOB, *or* BLOB. *The types supported also include distinct type, opaque type, collection type, and named and unnamed row type.*

table_name.column_name: *A parameter type can be defined as being the same as the type of a column in a table.*

default_value: *Parameters can be given default values. A default value consists of a literal appropriate to the type of argument. Using a default value allows calling functions with fewer parameters than actually defined. If no default values are provided, a call with fewer parameters will end with an error.*

Examples

The following examples show a grant type and a grant function respectively:

```
GRANT USAGE ON TYPE myopaquetype TO PUBLIC;

GRANT EXECUTE ON FUNCTION myopaquein(lvarchar) TO
    PUBLIC;
```

OPAQUE TYPE

Syntax

```
CREATE OPAQUE TYPE type_name (
   INTERNALLENGTH={length | VARIABLE}
[{MAXLEN=maxlen | CANNOTHASH | PASSEDBYVALUE |

ALIGNMENT=alignment]} ) ;

DROP TYPE type_name RESTRICT;
```

Description

An opaque type is an atomic data type that you define. It allows you to implement the proper representation for a specific business type. Because its content is unknown to the database server, you must define several support functions so that the database server can manipulate it. These functions are a subset of the following list: `input()`, `output()`, `receive()`, `send()`, `import()`, `export()`, `importbinary()`, `exportbinary()`, `assign()`, `destroy()`, and `lohandles()`.

The opaque type support functions are attached to the opaque type through a set of `cast` declarations. Opaque types are discussed in detail in Chap. 6.

The `CREATE OPAQUE TYPE` statement registers a new type in the `SYSXTDTYPES` system catalog. The `DROP TYPE` command removes the definition of the type. You cannot drop a type if the database still contains reference to the type in the form of casts, columns, or functions whose definition references the type.

Parameters Description

type_name: *This represents the name of your new type. This identifier must start with a letter or an underscore (_), followed by letters, digits, or an underscore. For Informix-UDO version, before IDS.2000, the maximum length of the name is 18 characters. IDS.2000 defines a limit of 128 characters.*

length: *This mandatory modifier indicates the length of the opaque type. If the type has a variable length, use the keyword* VARIABLE.

maxlen: *This modifier is used for variable length opaque types. It defaults to 2048 bytes. The maximum length of an opaque type is limited to slightly less than 32 KB for in-row representation, which is the maximum size of a row. Larger opaque types must use a smart-large object as their storage mechanism.*

CANNOTHASH: *This modifier specifies that the database server cannot use a hash function on this type. You must provide an appropriate hash function for the database server to evaluate* GROUP BY *clauses on this type. Without this modifier, the database server will use a hash function that applies to a stream of bytes without consideration for its meaning.*

PASSEDBYVALUE: *This specifies that an opaque type of four bytes or fewer is passed by value. By default, opaque types are passed by reference.*

alignment: *This value represents the memory alignment required by this type. The default value is four.*

Examples

The following statement creates a variable-length opaque type having a maximum size of 128 bytes:

```
CREATE OPAQUE TYPE vartype (INTERNALLENGTH=VARIABLE,
   MAXLEN=128);
```

The following statement creates a fixed-length opaque type of eight bytes:

```
CREATE OPAQUETYPE fixtype (INTERNALLENGTH=8);
```

The following statements remove the two previously defined types:

```
DROP TYPE vartype RESTRICT;
DROP TYPE fixtype RESTRICT;
```

OPCLASS

Syntax

```
CREATE OPCLASS opclass_name FOR sec_am_name
STRATEGIES (function_list) SUPPORT (support_fn_list);

function_list: function_name [[, function_name] ..]

support_fn_list: support_fn_name [[, support_fn_name] ..]

DROP OPCLASS opclass_name RESTRICT;
```

Description

The SQL keyword OPCLASS stands for operator class. An operator class defines a set of functions that are used by a secondary access method (index). The CREATE OPCLASS command creates a new operator class for a specific secondary access method. You need to create a new operator class for an existing secondary access method when you want a different sort order to apply data types that are supported by the current operator class.

Another way to provide similar functionality is to define a distinct type of an existing type and create new versions of the strategy and support functions that take the new type as argument.

The DROP OPCLASS statement removes the operator class from the current database.

Parameters Description

opclass_name: *The opclass name specifies a unique name for the operator class. This identifier must start with a letter or an underscore (_), followed by letters, digits, or an underscore. For Informix-UDO version, before IDS.2000, a name's maximum length is 18 characters. IDS.2000 defines a limit of 128 characters.*

sec_am_name: *This is the name of an existing secondary access methods. You can find the currently defined access methods for your database in the* SYSAMS *system table.*

function_list: *This represents a list of strategy functions. The strategy functions are used within an SQL statement. The optimizer can then decide if a particular index can be used. The list of functions defined for an operator class is found with the definition of the operator class in the* SYSOPCLASSES *system table.*

function_name: *The name of the strategy function. Remember that some names, like* lessthan(), *represent the name of an operator. If an operator name is used, the operator can be used in the SQL statement. Otherwise, the function name must be used.*

support_fn_list: *A support function is used by the secondary access method to build and search the index.*

support_fn_name: *This is the name of a support function required by the secondary access method.*

Examples

The following example, extracted from the Informix documentation, creates a new operator class for the b-tree access method. It then shows how an index could be created on a fictitious table using the new operator class. This example assumes that all the functions are already registered in the database and that the table customers exists:

```
CREATE OPCLASS abs_btree_ops FOR btree
STRATEGIES(abs_lt, abs_lte, abs_eq, abs_gte, abs_gt)
SUPPORT(abs_cmp);

CREATE INDEX c_abs_ix ON customers(cust_num
   abs_btree_ops);
```

The following statement removes the previously created operator class:

```
DROP OPCLASS abs_btree_ops RESTRICT;
```

PROCEDURE

Syntax

```
CREATE [DBA] PROCEDURE procedure_name( [parameter_list] )
[SPECIFIC specific_name]
[WITH(  [ { HANDLESNULLS | CLASS=vp_class |
STACK=stack_size |INTERNAL | PARALLELIZABLE } ] ]
EXTERNAL NAME 'path_name'
LANGUAGE C [PARAMETER STYLE INFORMIX] [ [NOT] VARIANT]
END PROCEDURE
[DOCUMENT 'string' ] [ WITH LISTING IN 'warningpath' ] ;

parameter_list: parameter [[, parameter]...]
[, OUT parameter]

parameter: [parameter_name] { SQL_type |
LIKE table_name.column_name | REFERENCES {BYTE | TEXT} }
   [DEFAULT default_value]
```

```
DROP PROCEDURE procedure_name [(parameter_list)] ;

DROP SPECIFIC PROCEDURE specific_name ;
```

Description

The CREATE statement defines a new procedure. It adds entries to system catalogs including SYSPROCBODY and SYSPROCAUTH. A procedure is similar to a function except that it does not return a value.

A function or operator can be removed with the DROP PROCEDURE statement. If a specific (unique) name was included in its creation, the DROP SPECIFIC PROCEDURE statement and the specific name can be used instead.

Parameters Description

DBA: *The* DBA *optional keyword indicates that the user that executes this function must have DBA privilege.*

procedure_name: *specifies the name of the procedure. This identifier must start with a letter or an underscore (_), followed by letters, digits, or an underscore. For Informix-UDO version, before IDS.2000, a name's maximum length is 18 characters. IDS.2000 defines a limit of 128 characters.*

parameter_list: *The parameter list identifies the type of each parameter that your function accepts. The last parameter can be defined with the* OUT *keyword. The* OUT *parameter is used for statement local variables (SLV). An SLV transmits a value from a function call in a statement to another part of the SQL statement.*

parameter: *The type of parameters are defined below as* SQL_type, table_name.column_name, *and* default_value. *One choice is* REFERENCES *for either* BYTE *or* TEXT. *This parameter type allows you to use a pointer to a* TEXT *or* BYTE *parameter. These types cannot be used directly. Only the* NULL *default value is allowed for this parameter type.*

parameter_name: *This is an optional parameter giving a name to the parameter.*

SQL_type: *A parameter can be of any type defined in the database except* SERIAL, SERIAL8, TEXT, BYTE, CLOB, *or* BLOB. *The types supported also include distinct type, opaque type, collection type, and named and unnamed row types.*

table_name.column_name: *A parameter type can be defined as being the same as the type of a column in a table.*

default_value: *Parameters can be given default values. A default value consists of a literal appropriate to the type of argument. Using a default value allows calling functions with fewer parameters than actually defined. If no default values are provided, a call with fewer parameters will end with an error.*

specific_name: *This identifier is a name that uniquely identifies the function in the database. The specific name can be used in the following SQL statements:* DROP, GRANT, REVOKE, UPDATE STATISTICS. *A specific name can be up to 128 characters long. Specific names make it easier to handle functions when the same function name is used with many signatures (overloaded).*

HANDLESNULLS: *This modifier indicates that the function can be passed* null *values. By default,* null *values are ignored.*

CLASS: *This modifier identifies the class of virtual processor (VP) that will execute this function. The default class is* CPU VP. *If your function is not well behaved, you need to have your system administrator create an Extended Virtual Processor (EVP) and identify this EVP as the Virtual Processor to use for this function.*

STACK: *The default stack size provided in the server configuration parameter is 64 KB under Windows NT and 32 KB under UNIX operating systems. The stack size is given as a number of bytes.*

INTERNAL: *This modifier indicates that an SQL or SPL cannot call the function directly. An* INTERNAL *function is not considered during routine resolution.*

PARALLELIZABLE: *This modifier indicates that the function meets the requirements to run in parallel. If the function is found to violate the requirements at runtime, an error will be generated.*

path_name: *This parameter identifies the location of the dynamically loadable executable code. If the path name includes an environment variable like* $INFORMIXDIR, *the variable value will be resolved by the server at runtime with whatever value is defined for that variable in the server's environment.*

LANGUAGE: *In the context of this book, the language is always C.*

string: *The* DOCUMENT *string is intended as a synopsis and description of the routine. It is stored in the* SYSPROCBODY *system catalog.*

warningpath: *This parameter identifies the file where compile-time warnings are sent. If this clause is missing, the compiler does not generate a list of warnings.*

Examples

Create a procedure upd_info() that takes an integer and a variable length character string as arguments:

```
CREATE PROCEDURE upd_info(int, varchar(30))
EXTERNAL NAME
"$INFORMIXDIR/extend/udrbook/bin/alib.bld(upd_info)"
LANGUAGE C
END PROCEDURE;
```

Remove the upd_info() function:

```
DROP PROCEDURE upd_info(int);
```

ROW TYPE

Syntax

```
CREATE ROW TYPE rowtype_name ( field_definition_list )
[UNDER supertype_name] ;

field_definition_list = field_definition
[ [, field_definition] ...]

field_definition = field_name data_type [ NOT NULL]

DROP ROW TYPE rowtype_name RESTRICT ;
```

Description

A row type is a sequence of one or more fields. Each field has a name and a data type. The CREATE ROW TYPE command creates a row type and gives it a unique name. This is called a named row type. The fields of a row type can be any data types except SERIAL and SERIAL8 in versions prior to IDS.2000. The types TEXT and BYTE can only be used in typed tables. They cannot be used for a row type that defines a field in a table.

Named row type allows the creation of type-inheritance hierarchy. Table inheritance can only be implemented if the tables are created with named row types.

The DROP ROW TYPE command removes an existing row type. The row type cannot be removed if it is used in a table or column, if a view is defined on the row type, or if the type is a supertype of another row type.

Parameters Description

rowtype_name: *Specifies the name of the row type. This identifier must start with a letter or an underscore (_), followed by letters, digits, or an underscore. For Informix-UDO version, before IDS.2000, a name's maximum length is 18 characters. IDS.2000 defines a limit of 128 characters.*

field_definition_list: *The field definition list identifies one or more fields that make up the row type.*

field_definition: *The row type definition allows for only the* NOT NULL *constraint.*

field_name: *Specifies a unique name for the field. This identifier must start with a letter or an underscore (_), followed by letters, digits, or an underscore. For Informix-UDO version, before IDS.2000, a name's maximum length is 18 characters. IDS.2000 defines a limit of 128 characters.*

data_type: *The data types supported include the built-in data types, user-defined types, and complex types. A field data type cannot be either* SERIAL *or* SERIAL8 *in versions prior to IDS.2000. Furthermore, if the row type is used to define a column in a table, it cannot include the types* BYTE *and* TEXT.

    The built-in data types include: CHAR, VARCHAR, LVARCHAR, DECIMAL (NUMERIC), MONEY, INT, SMALLINT, INT8, FLOAT,

DOUBLE PRECISION, SMALLFLOAT (REAL), TEXT, BYTE, CLOB, BLOB, DATE, DATETIME, *and* INTERVAL.

The user-defined types are distinct and opaque. The complex types include named row, unnamed row, SET, MULTISET, *and* LIST.

supertype_name: *This identifier is the name of an existing named row type. This places the named row type under this supertype, creating a type hierarchy. The named row type inherits all the fields defined in the supertype.*

Examples

The following example creates a row type retail_t. This row type inherits the fields from the loan_t row type:

```
CREATE ROW TYPE retail_t (
competitorINradius    int   NOT NULL,
market_size           float NOT NULL
) UNDER loan_t;
```

The following statement removes the previously created row type:

```
DROP ROW TYPE retail_t RESTRICT;
```

Shared Library Reload

Syntax

```
Error_code = ifx_replace_module("oldpath",
    "newpath", "language_name");
```

Description

After recreating a library containing server-side functions, you have to ensure that the database server will use the new version of the library. This can be done in three different ways. You can stop and restart the database server. You can drop and recreate all the functions. You can also execute this function to tell the server that it needs to reload the library.

Examples

The following statements ask the server to reload the specified library. Note that in the case of the SQL statement, you will want to make sure that only one row is returned; otherwise the function will be executed for each returned row.

```
EXECUTE FUNCTION
ifx_replace_module(
   '$INFORMIXDIR/extend/udrbook/bin/mylib.bld',
   '$INFORMIXDIR/extend/udrbook/bin/mylib.bld', 'c');

SELECT
ifx_replace_module(
   '$INFORMIXDIR/extend/udrbook/bin/mylib.bld',
   '$INFORMIXDIR/extend/udrbook/bin/mylib.bld', 'c')
FROM customer WHERE customer_id = 100;
```

Handling Data Types

Mapping the SQL types to arguments or return values of user-defined routines can be confusing. In addition to the base types such as integer, float, datetime, and numeric, we have to contend with complex types, including row and collection. The main decisions we need to make are what type we must use and whether it is passed by value or by reference.

This chapter covers every available type and explains how to handle each type as argument and as return value. The first section contains a description of the contexts encountered and an explanation of the manipulations required. The rest of the chapter consists of alphabetized reference material providing explanations and code example for each data type.

This material is designed as reference material. You may want to read the first few pages to get familiar with the content and come back to it when you write your user-defined routines to find information on the specific types you are dealing with.

Context Description

User-defined routines manipulate data types within three main contexts: argument passing, return values from SQL statement execution, and the return value of the function. The types of the function arguments are defined by the CREATE FUNCTION statement. For example:

```
CREATE FUNCTION do_int(val1 integer)
RETURNING INTEGER
WITH (NOT VARIANT)
EXTERNAL NAME
  "$INFORMIX/extend/udrbook/bin/chap4.bld(do_int)"
LANGUAGE C
END FUNCTION;
```

In this case, the C function do_int() is expected to take an integer as its argument. The function can then be used in an SQL statement such as:

```
SELECT do_int(int_col) from tab1;
```

The do_int() function knows what it received and handles it appropriately. In the case of an integer, the argument is passed by value. In other cases, it may be passed by value or by reference, depending on the type.

The second situation is when an SQL statement is executed in the user-defined routine. The statement result may be returned in two ways. It can be returned in internal format by specifying the MI_QUERY_BINARY flag or it can be returned as NULL terminated ASCII strings by specifying the MI_QUERY_NORMAL flag. The processing sequence is independent of the format of the return value. It is equivalent to the row type processing.

The return value format follows the same rules as the argument values. Depending on the type, it will either be a value or a pointer to that value.

The SQL type examples provided below include the three cases listed above. You will have to look at the appropriate entries when dealing with multiple data types in your server-side function. Table 4–1 provides a summary of the mapping between the SQL types and the DataBlade API types.

Table 4–1 SQL to DataBlade API mapping.

SQL Types	DAPI Types	Comment
BLOB	MI_LO_HANDLE *	
BOOLEAN	mi_boolean	Same as mi_integer
BYTE		This type is not supported in a UDR
CHAR(n) or		
CHARACTER(n)	mi_lvarchar *	
CLOB	MI_LO_HANDLE *	
DATE	mi_date	
DATETIME	mi_datetime *	
DEC or DECIMAL	mi_decimal *	Same as NUMERIC
DISTINCT	ALL	Use the type of the base type
DOUBLE PRECISION	mi_double_precision *	ANSI-compliant synonym for FLOAT
FLOAT(n)	mi_double_precision *	Same as DOUBLE PRECISION
INT or INTEGER	mi_integer	
INT8	mi_int8 *	
INTERVAL	mi_interval *	
LIST	MI_COLLECTION *	
LVARCHAR	mi_lvarchar *	

MI_DATUM

MI_DATUM is a DataBlade API type that serves as a generic representation of any type. It is used mostly in the manipulation of complex types, as in the case of the extraction of column values. The misunderstanding of this type is the cause of many errors in user-defined routines. For this reason, it will be covered for each SQL type in Table 4–1.

Table 4–1 *(continued)*

SQL Types	DAPI Types	Comment
MONEY	mi_money *	Same internal representation as DECIMAL
MULTISET	MI_COLLECTION *	
NCHAR(n)	mi_lvarchar *	
NUMERIC	mi_decimal *	ANSI-compliant synonym for DECIMAL
NVARCHAR	mi_lvarchar *	
"OPAQUE"	C structure or mi_bitvarying *	mi_bitvarying * is equivalent to mi_lvarchar *
REAL	mi_real *	ANSI-compliant synonym for SMALLFLOAT
ROW	MI_ROW *	
SERIAL	mi_integer	
SERIAL8	mi_int8 *	Same as int8
SET	MI_COLLECTION *	
SMALLINT	mi_smallint	
SMALLFLOAT	mi_real *	Same as REAL
TEXT		This type is not supported in a UDR
VARCHAR	mi_lvarchar	

The rest of this chapter describes each type and how it is handled as either a function argument or as a return value. A CREATE FUNCTION statement shows the SQL type as argument and return value. Then, the C implementation shows the argument type and the handling of it as a MI_DATUM. This last part is useful because a MI_DATUM is used in row processing and in SQL statement processing. This is why this section is introduced as row processing.

BLOB

A BLOB is a smart large object that stores binary data.

```
CREATE FUNCTION do_blob (blob)
RETURNING blob
. . .
```

Argument type: MI_LO_HANDLE * (pointer to a MI_LO_HANDLE)
Row processing:

```
MI_DATUM retbuf;
MI_LO_HANDLE *val;
. . .
val = (MI_LO_HANDLE *)retbuf;
```

Return value:

```
retbuf = (MI_DATUM)val;
```

or

```
return(val);
```

BOOLEAN

A BOOLEAN argument is treated as a mi_integer within a C
function. The difference resides in the declaration of the
function:

```
CREATE FUNCTION do_boolean (boolean)
RETURNING boolean
. . .
```

Please refer to the "INTEGER" section for a detailed description of
the DataBlade API type.

BYTE

The BYTE data type is the old way to store binary large objects. The DataBlade API does not support this type. You should convert these types to the BLOB type. IDS.2000 provides a casting function to convert from BYTE to BLOB.

CHAR(n) (CHARACTER(n))

All the character-based functions use the LVARCHAR type. The SQL definition of the user-defined routine impacts what the function will receive and return. The function will receive and return a fixed length LVARCHAR with the size defined in the function definition. The statement

```
CREATE FUNCTION do_char (char(10))
RETURNING char(10)
   . . .
```

defines a function that receives and returns a LVARCHAR containing ten characters. If the function returns a LVARCHAR containing more or less than ten characters, the result will be adjusted to the appropriate length. If the character length is not provided, a length of one is used.
Please refer to the "LVARCHAR" section for information on how to handle this type.

CLOB

A CLOB is a smart large object storing character data. When accessing a CLOB column, you receive a pointer to a MI_LO_HANDLE. You then use the handle to access the data either sequentially or randomly. See the "BLOB" section for information on how to handle this type.

DATE

A DATE is passed to a function as an integer value. The integer represents the number of days since December 31, 1899. The maximum valid value is 2958464. This represents December 31, 9999. The limit is imposed only as a validation and could be changed in the future. Considering that the maximum integer value is much higher, an integer will be sufficient for a long time. Given the following SQL definition:

```
CREATE FUNCTION do_date (date)
RETURNING date
  .  .  .
```

The UDR argument type is: mi_date
Row processing:

```
MI_DATUM retbuf;
mi_date  val;
  .  .  .
val = (mi_date)retbuf;
```

Return value:

```
retbuf = (MI_DATUM)val;
```
or
```
return(val);
```

The appendix lists the available functions that are used to manipulate the date type. Date types can be manipulated by DataBlade API functions and by ESQL/C functions. The mi_date type in the DataBlade API is the same as the long C type used in ESQL/C.

DATETIME

The DATETIME type is processed internally as a mi_datetime. This structure is the same as the dtime_t structure used by ESQL/C. The datetime functions and macros provided by ESQL/C can be used within a server-side function. Note that in the following definition the function argument and return value must be qualified with the precision of the datetime value:

```
CREATE FUNCTION do_datetime(datetime year to second)
RETURNING datetime year to second
. . .
```

Argument type: `mi_datetime *` **(pointer to a** `mi_datetime`**)**
Row processing:

```
MI_DATUM retbuf;
mi_datetime  *val;
. . .
val = (mi_datetime *)retbuf;
```

Return value:

```
retbuf = (MI_DATUM)val;
```

or

```
return(val);
```

DataBlade API and ESQL/C functions used to manipulate this type are listed in the Appendix.

DECIMAL (DEC)

The `DECIMAL` type is processed internally as a `mi_decimal`. This structure is the same as the `dec_t` structure used by ESQL/C. The `DECIMAL` functions and macros provided by ESQL/C can be used within a server-side function. For the following definition the function argument and return value does not need to be qualified with the size and precision of the `DECIMAL` value:

```
CREATE FUNCTION do_decimal (dec(10,2))
RETURNING dec(10,2)
. . .
```

Argument type: `mi_decimal *` (pointer to `mi_decimal`)
Row processing:

```
MI_DATUM retbuf;
mi_decimal *val;
. . .
val = (mi_decimal *)retbuf;
```

Return value:

```
retbuf = (MI_DATUM)val;
```

or

```
return(val);
```

The Appendix lists the functions that can be used to manipulate this type.

DISTINCT

A distinct type has the same internal representation as the type it is derived from. Look at the appropriate base type to find out how to handle your specific distinct type.

DOUBLE PRECISION

A DOUBLE PRECISION is an eight-byte floating-point value. The DataBlade API type `mi_double_precision` corresponds to a double C data type. A DOUBLE PRECISION value can have up to 16 significant digits.

```
CREATE FUNCTION do_double (double precision)
RETURNING double precision
. . .
```

Argument type: `mi_double_precision *` (pointer to `mi_double_precision`)

Row processing:

```
MI_DATUM retbuf;
mi_double_precision *val;
 . . .
val = (mi_double_precision *)retbuf;
```

Return value:

```
retbuf = (MI_DATUM)val;
```

or

```
return(val);
```

FLOAT(n)

The FLOAT data type is treated as a DOUBLE PRECISION. The precision value, *n* is an optional value that must be an integer between 1 and 14. SQL ignores this value. Please see the "DOUBLE PRECISION" section to see how to handle the FLOAT data type.

INTEGER or INT

An INTEGER value is passed by value. Both INTEGER and SMALLINT are treated the same within a C function. Given the following SQL definition,

```
CREATE FUNCTION do_int(integer)
RETURNING INTEGER
 . . .
```

The UDR Argument type is: `mi_integer`

Row processing:

```
MI_DATUM retbuf;
mi_integer val;
 . . .
val = (mi_integer)retbuf;
```

Return value:

```
retbuf = (MI_DATUM)val;
```

or

```
return(val);
```

INT8

An INT8 data type provides an eight-byte integer. It could require up to ten bytes of storage. If you try to insert a value that exceeds the range available to an INT8, the server will return an error and will not store the value.

```
CREATE FUNCTION do_int8 (int8)
RETURNING int8
 . . .
```

Argument type: mi_int8 * (pointer to mi_int8)
Row processing:

```
MI_DATUM retbuf;
mi_int8 *val;
 . . .
val = (mi_int8 *)retbuf;
```

Return value:

```
retbuf = (MI_DATUM)val;
```

or

```
return(val);
```

INTERVAL

The INTERVAL type is processed internally as a mi_interval. This structure is the same as intrvl_t used by ESQL/C. The interval functions and macros provided by ESQL/C can be used within a server-side function. Given the following SQL definition:

```
CREATE FUNCTION do_interval(interval day to day)
RETURNING interval day to day
. . .
```

The Argument type is: mi_interval * (pointer to a mi_interval)

Row processing:

```
MI_DATUM retbuf;
mi_interval  *val;
. . .
val = (mi_interval *)retbuf;
```

Return value:

```
retbuf = (MI_DATUM)val;
```

or

```
return(val);
```

LIST

The LIST data type is one of three collection types supported by IDS.2000. It stored an ordered list of values where duplicates are not allowed. Contrary to the other collection types, a LIST provides random access to its elements. The following function declaration takes a LIST and an integer as arguments. The integer argument represents an index in the list. The function returns the integer value at the given position. The first element of a list is at index position zero.

```
CREATE FUNCTION do_intcol(LIST(integer NOT NULL),
    integer)
RETURNING int
. . .
```

Argument type: MI_COLLECTION * (pointer to MI_COLLECTION)
Row processing:

```
MI_DATUM retbuf;
MI_COLLECTION *val;
. . .
val = (MI_COLLECTION *)retbuf;
```

Return value:

```
retbuf = (MI_DATUM)val;
```

or

```
return(val);
```

LVARCHAR

The LVARCHAR type is used for the following types: CHAR, VARCHAR and LVARCHAR. An LVARCHAR string should not be NULL terminated. Use the mi_get_varlen() to find the length of the data in an LVARCHAR. A function returning an LVARCHAR cannot be indexed because an LVARCHAR maximum length is defined as 2048 bytes. This exceeds the maximum field size for an index. If you need to index the string returned by a function, define it as returning a VARCHAR of less than 255 characters.

```
CREATE FUNCTION do_lvarchar (lvarchar)
RETURNING lvarchar
. . .
```

Argument type: mi_lvarchar * (pointer to mi_lvarchar)

Row processing:

```
MI_DATUM retbuf;
mi_lvarchar *val;
    . . .
val = (mi_lvarchar *)retbuf;
```

Return value:

```
retbuf = (MI_DATUM)val;
```

or

```
return(val);
```

MONEY

The MONEY type has the same internal data type as the fixed-point DECIMAL value. Instead of using mi_decimal in your server side function, you can use mi_money. This translates to the same type but is more appropriate for readability and documentation. You can use the functions provided by ESQL/C to manipulate this type. The types mi_decimal, mi_money, and dec_t are all equivalent. Note that the money qualifier in the following function declaration is optional:

```
CREATE FUNCTION do_money(money(10,2))
RETURNING money(10,2)
    . . .
```

Please see the "DECIMAL" section for more information on how to handle this type.

MULTISET

A MULTISET is a collection of unordered data. This collection type allows duplicates. The processing of a MULTISET is similar to the processing of a LIST except that the data is accessed sequentially.

Any indexing value in a MULTISET must be set to zero. Here is a declaration of a function accepting a MULTISET as argument:

```
CREATE FUNCTION do_mset(MULTISET(integer NOT NULL))
. . .
```

For processing information, please see the "LIST" section.

NCHAR(n)

The processing of NCHAR(n) values is similar to the processing of a CHAR(n) type. The NCHAR data type is provided for international support. A function handling this type as argument has the following declaration:

```
CREATE FUNCTION do_nchar (nchar(10))
RETURNING nchar(10)
. . .
```

See the "LVARCHAR" section for information on processing the NCHAR type.

NUMERIC

NUMERIC is an ANSI-compliant synonym for decimal. Instead of using mi_decimal in your user-defined routine, you can use mi_numeric. This translates to the same type and, as with the mi_decimal type, you can use the ESQL/C functions and the equivalent dec_t type to manipulate a numeric value. Here is an example of a NUMERIC function declaration:

```
CREATE FUNCTION do_numeric (numeric(10,2))
RETURNING numeric(10,2)
. . .
```

Please see the "DECIMAL" section for more information.

NVARCHAR

The processing of NVARCHAR(n) values is similar to the processing of a VARCHAR(n) type. The NVARCHAR data type is provided for international support. A function handling this type as argument has the following declaration:

```
CREATE FUNCTION do_nvarchar (nvarchar(10))
RETURNING nvarchar(10)
. . .
```

See the "LVARCHAR" section for information on processing the NVARCHAR type.

Opaque

Opaque is a generic term that applies to user-defined data types that are not based on existing database types. An opaque type comes in two flavors: fixed length or variable length. A function will receive and return a fixed length opaque type in the opaque type internal representation. The value will be passed either per value or per reference, depending on the definition. For a variable-length opaque type, it will be wrapped into a mi_bitvarying type variable. You then have to obtain a pointer to the data buffer in the mi_bitvarying structure and cast it to your internal opaque type structure to manipulate it. The mi_bitvarying type is equivalent to mi_lvarchar, so all the DataBlade API functions available to manipulate a mi_lvarchar also work for a mi_bitvarying. A function declaration for a function accepting a variable-length opaque type as argument looks like this:

```
CREATE FUNCTION do_opaque (my_opaque)
RETURNING my_opaque
. . .
```

The argument and return value my_opaque is an opaque type that you have previously created. In the case of a variable-length opaque type, we have the following processing:

Argument type: `mi_bitvarying *` (pointer to `mi_bitvarying`)
Row processing:

```
MI_DATUM retbuf;
mi_lvarchar *val;
MY_VAR_OPAQUE *myopaque;
. . .
val = (mi_lvarchar *)retbuf;
myopaque = (MY_VAR_OPAQUE *)mi_get_vardata(val);
```

Return value:

```
retbuf = (MI_DATUM)val;
```

or

```
return(val);
```

In the case of a fixed-length opaque type, the values are received and returned in their internal representation.

REAL

The REAL data type is a synonym for the SMALLFLOAT data type. Please see the "SMALLFLOAT" section to see how to handle this type.

ROW

A ROW type is either named or unnamed. A user-defined routine can either be declared as processing rows in general or as processing a specific named-row type. In the first case, the database server will resolve the function call to this function for any row type. In the second case, the database server will resolve the call to that function only if that specific named-row type is used. If your function accepts a generic row type, the processing should be generic to any row type. Otherwise, you should take advantage of the function-overloading feature to provide the specific processing and take advantage of better type checking from the database server.

```
CREATE FUNCTION do_row(row)
RETURNING row
. . .
```

Argument type: `MI_ROW` * (pointer to `MI_ROW`)
Row processing:

```
MI_DATUM retbuf;
MI_ROW *val;
. . .
val = (MI_ROW *)retbuf;
```

Return value:

```
retbuf = (MI_DATUM)val;
```

or

```
return(val);
```

SERIAL

A user-defined routine cannot be declared as accepting or returning a `SERIAL` data type. Use the `INT` data type instead. It will process the `SERIAL` type values.

SERIAL8

A user-defined routine cannot be declared as accepting or returning a `SERIAL8` data type. Use the `INT8` data type instead. It will process the `SERIAL8` type values.

SET

A SET is an unordered collection of elements. This means that, like a MULTISET, the elements can only be accessed sequentially. Furthermore, the elements of a SET must be unique.

```
CREATE FUNCTION do_set(SET(integer NOT NULL))
 . . .
```

For processing information, please see the "LIST" section.

SMALLINT

A SMALLINT value is passed to a C function as a mi_integer, which makes it identical to the C function handling an integer. The difference resides in the declaration of the function and the range of values handled:

```
CREATE FUNCTION do_smallint(val1 smallint)
RETURNING SMALLINT
 . . .
```

Please refer to the "INTEGER" section for a detailed description of the DataBlade API type.

SMALLFLOAT

The SMALLFLOAT data type corresponds to the float C type. It stores a single-precision value. Despite the fact that it is a four-byte value, it is still passed by reference.

```
CREATE FUNCTION do_sfloat(smallfloat)
RETURNING smallfloat
 . . .
```

Argument type: `mi_real *` (pointer to `mi_real`)
Row processing:

```
MI_DATUM retbuf;
mi_real *val;
. . .
val = (mi_real *)retbuf;
```

Return value:

```
retbuf = (MI_DATUM)val;
```

or

```
return(val);
```

TEXT

The TEXT data type is the old way to store character information in a binary large object. The DataBlade API does not support this type. You should convert these types to the CLOB type. IDS.2000 provides a casting function to convert from BYTE to BLOB.

VARCHAR

All the VARCHAR based functions use the LVARCHAR type. The SQL definition of the server-side function impacts what the function will receive and return. The function will receive and return a variable length LVARCHAR with a maximum size defined in the definition. The statement

```
CREATE FUNCTION do_varchar (varchar(5))
RETURNING varchar(5)
. . .
```

defines a function that receives and returns an LVARCHAR containing five characters. If the function returns an LVARCHAR containing at most five characters, the result will be truncated if it exceeds the defined maximum length. If the character length is not provided, a length of one is used.

Please refer to the "LVARCHAR" section for a detailed description of the DataBlade API type.

Computational Functions

The easiest way to take advantage of the IDS.2000 technology is to add functions that enable calculation or processing on existing data. These new functions may provide just enough functionality to cover the gap between two major operations, which would then allow the database server to do the processing instead of the old way—having to process in two phases or, worse, having to bring all the data into the application.

These functions take a number of values as arguments and return a result. We refer to this type of function as a computational function.

This chapter covers computational functions as building blocks for extensibility. It provides the right context to discuss some basic issues that are also found in more complex user-defined routines. The concepts covered in this chapter include function overloading, handling and returning NULL values, raising exceptions, and `mi_lvarchar` structure manipulation.

Functions Applications

The first applications of computational functions are to implement arithmetic operators, comparison operators, and IDS.2000 built-in-functions overloading. This constitutes a set of 32 functions that can be adapted to fit your business environment.

In many cases, adding a small amount of code within the server to process a value removes a larger amount of code from the application. It can also process the data in a more efficient way, providing significant performance improvement. Look for any situations where applications have to decide which row applies to the current problem or where applications retrieve data and need to sort it. Such situations can represent great opportunities to simplify applications while gaining performance.

Functions Parallelism

Multiple users can execute a user-defined routine simultaneously. This constitutes one level of parallelism and scalability, which may be all that is required—in the case of OLTP (on-line transaction processing) systems supporting a large number of users. There is another situation that requires a different level of parallelism.

Some applications require the execution of large SQL statements that can be divided into multiple tasks to be executed in parallel. This is very common in the case of decision support systems (DSS). The parallel execution of SQL statements can take advantage of multiple CPU resources. By adding CPUs, a system administrator can speed up the query processing. The IDS.2000 database server is designed to provide almost linear scalability when query processing involves multiple CPUs.

Since Informix-UDO 9.14, user-defined routines can execute in parallel if they follow certain restrictions. UDR parallelism is available to computational functions. The restrictions that apply to running UDRs in parallel pertain to a distinction between types of threads within the server. Any SQL-type processing must be executed in a primary thread, which correspond to the session thread. To run in parallel, a query is divided into multiple tasks executed by secondary threads. Based on this short explanation, the following restrictions apply in Informix-UDO 9.14:

- The UDR does not execute SQL statements.
- The UDR only executes thread-safe calls. This includes DataBlade API calls for data handling, sessions, thread and transaction management, function execution, memory management, exception handling, and callbacks.
- The UDR does not manipulate collections. These calls are not thread safe.
- The UDR does not accept or return complex arguments. The complex data types include row types and collections.

A UDR that doesn't violate any of these four restrictions qualifies as PARALLELIZABLE. When a query using it is executed, the database server can then decide if it should run the UDR in parallel. Of course, query parallelism also depends on the PDQ priority and the server rules on parallelism.

The Quarter Function

I have used this function as an example several times already in a previous chapter. It is a simple computational function that still demonstrates some important functionality. The function is added to a database with the following SQL statement:

```
CREATE FUNCTION quarter(date)
RETURNS varchar(10)
WITH(NOT VARIANT, PARALLELIZABLE)
EXTERNAL NAME
"$INFORMIXDIR/extend/udrbook/bin/chap5.bld(quar-
   ter)"
LANGUAGE C;
```

The following C code implements a quarter function where the fiscal year starts on January 1.

```
#include <mi.h>

mi_lvarchar *quarter(mi_date date,
  MI_FPARAM *fparam)
{
  mi_lvarchar *RetVal;          /* The return value.
  */
  short       mdy[3];
  mi_integer  ret, qt;
  char        buffer[10];

  /* Extract month, day, and year from the date */
  ret = rjulmdy(date, mdy);

  /* calculate the quarter */
  qt = (mdy[0] - 1) / 3;
  qt++;
  sprintf(buffer, "%4dQ%d", mdy[2], qt);
  RetVal = mi_new_var(strlen(buffer));
  mi_set_vardata(RetVal, buffer);

  /* Return the function's return value. */
  return RetVal;
}
```

The first line of this program declares an include file that
provides the definition of the types and functions from the
DataBlade API. In most cases, it is the only file you need to
include. Take for example the rjulmdy() function. This ESQL/C
function is declared in sqlhdr.h. This file is included by milo.h,
which is included by mi.h.

The quarter() function takes two arguments: An mi_date
value and a pointer to a MI_FPARAM structure. It returns a pointer to a mi_lvarchar type. One common error is to assume that
the arguments or the return value are passed by value when
they are passed by reference, and vice-versa. Chapter 4 provides
information on how to process all the different types available
within IDS.2000.

Even for a function as simple as the quarter function, we need
to make a design decision on the type of return value. The current implementation returns a mi_lvarchar structure that contains administrative information and a six-byte character string.

The `mi_lvarchar` structure is always used to return character data, as we saw in Chap. 4. The return value space utilization is offset by the intuitive use of this implementation. With a character string result, we can use all the SQL functions and operators that apply to character strings, including comparison functions and the `LIKE` operator.

Another approach is to return an integer representing the year and the quarter. The format could follow the following formula:

```
(year * 100) + quarter_number
```

For example, "199901" represents the first quarter of the year 1999. This representation is also convenient because it enables sorting through its integer representation and also allows the selection of a range of quarters.

This representation is slightly less intuitive than the character representation. For one thing, the `LIKE` operator cannot be used in a `SELECT` statement unless we decide to overload it for integer values. Overloading the `LIKE` operator should be done carefully. We have to make sure not to introduce a behavior that is inconsistent with the general use of an operator. Coming back to out integer representation, a range selection using `BETWEEN` must be used instead of the `LIKE` operator. The advantage of this representation is that it uses only four bytes of storage and can be passed by value. This reduces slightly the amount of processing required to manipulate a quarter value.

The `quarter()` function allocates two array variables: `mdy[3]` and `buffer[10]`. These are automatic variables allocated on the stack. If the function is rescheduled to run on a different virtual processor, the variables will still be available because the stack is allocated in shared memory. Defining the arrays outside the function body would make them global variables and would be a problem waiting to happen.

The first function called is `rjulmdy()`. This function comes from the ESQL/C API. This function defines the first argument as a long value. It is equivalent to our date value, which has a `mi_date` type. Table 5–1 lists the equivalences for SQL types, DataBlade API types, and C programming types.

Note that in Table 5–1, all the character types are listed as `LVARCHAR`. This is how the user-defined routine receives them.

Table 5–1 Types equivalence.

SQL type	DataBlade API type	ESQL/C type	ESQL/C server-side API
BLOB	MI_LO_HANDLE	ifx_lo_t	No
BOOLEAN	mi_boolean	boolean	No
CHAR	mi_lvarchar	void (pointer)	No, not for LVARCHAR
CLOB	MI_LO_HANDLE	ifx_lo_t	No
DATE	mi_date	long int	Yes
DATETIME	mi_datetime	dtime_t	Yes
DECIMAL	mi_decimal	dec_t	Yes
DOUBLE PRECISION	mi_double_precision	double	Yes, one function for conversion
FLOAT	mi_double_precision	double	Yes, one function for conversion
INTEGER	mi_integer	long int	Yes, one function for conversion
INT8	mi_int8	ifx_int8_t	Yes
INTERVAL	mi_interval	intrvl_t	Yes
LIST	MI_COLLECTION	ifx_collection_t	No
LVARCHAR	mi_lvarchar	void (pointer)	No
MONEY	mi_money	dec_t	Yes
MULTISET	MI_COLLECTION	ifx_collection_t	No
NUMERIC	mi_decimal	dec_t	Yes
OPAQUE	mi_bitvarying	void (pointer)	No
REAL	mi_real	float	No
ROW	MI_ROW	ifx_collection_t	No
SERIAL	mi_integer	long int	Yes, one function for conversion
SERIAL8	mi_int8	ifx_int8_t	Yes
SET	MI_COLLECTION	ifx_collection_t	No
SMALLINT	mi_smallint	short int	No
SMALLFLOAT	mi_real	float	No
VARCHAR	mi_lvarchar	void (pointer)	No, not for LVARCHAR

Informix does not define any of the ESQL/C LVARCHAR functions as running in the server. This is why Table 5–1 says "No" to ESQL/C server-side API. Keep in mind that ESQL/C provides a few functions to manipulate NULL-terminated character strings. This can be useful once you extract the data from an LVARCHAR.

Before we can use the quarter() function, we must compile the function into a dynamic library, as shown in Chap. 2.

Function Overloading

Our quarter() function handles a date argument. We may also want to use this function to handle the datetime type. Since the function signature is different, we can create a quarter() function that handles this additional case. The following SQL statement creates this function:

```
CREATE FUNCTION quarter(datetime)
RETURNS varchar(10)
WITH(NOT VARIANT, PARALLELIZABLE)
EXTERNAL NAME
"$INFORMIXDIR/extend/udrbook/bin/chap5.bld(quarterdt)"
LANGUAGE C;
```

Note that the SQL function here has the same name as the SQL function in the previous declaration; however, the C library member that is used to implement the functionality must have a different name. This fact sometimes confuses people because they keep thinking in object-oriented terms. The object-oriented features are provided at the SQL level. The database server identifies the function to execute by using the function name and its signature, so the same function name can be used to declare several functions as long as they have different argument types. The function's C implementation does not support overloading. This forces the UDR developer to think in two modes. In SQL, the developer thinks in object-oriented mode, but in C it is back to traditional programming with the traditional name space conflicts.

The function prototype of the new `quarterdt()` function contains a subtle difference from the `quarter()` function. Here is its declaration:

```
mi_lvarchar *quarterdt(mi_datetime *dt, MI_FPARAM *fp);
```

The argument type is now a `mi_datetime` pointer, whereas the `quarter()` function declared a `mi_date`. The `mi_date` is passed by value, but the `mi_datetime` is passed by reference.

A design decision must again be made about the implementation of the `quarterdt()` function. The first obvious solution is to implement the function independently from the previous implementation that handles a `mi_date` as argument. Another solution is to extract the date from the `mi_datetime` type and then call the `quarter()` function to perform the operation on the date. The second solution is appealing until we find that there is no function that converts from `datetime` to `date`. Since the `quarter()` function is so simple, it is easier simply to extract the needed information and perform the calculation independently from the other function. Here is a code fragment that converts a `datetime` to a `date`:

```
{
    dtime_t mydt;
    mi_date newdate;
    int ret;
    char buffer[30];

    mydt.dt_qual = TU_DTENCODE(TU_YEAR, TU_DAY);
    ret = dtextend(date, &mydt);

    ret = dttoasc(&mydt, buffer);
    ret = rdefmtdate(&newdate, "yyyy-mm-dd", buffer);
    . . .
}
```

The function could be simplified by simply using the `dttoasc()` function on the `mi_datetime` argument directly. The `dttoasc()` function comes from ESQL/C and takes a `dtime_t` pointer as the `datetime`. This type is equivalent to the `mi_datetime` type from the DataBlade API. Using `dttoasc()` could cause some problems if the datetime argument is defined with a precision merely year to year. Of course, it is hard to believe that would be the case. The proper processing should include the use of `dtextend()` to make sure we have the proper precision in our `datetime` argument.

Handling NULL Values

By default, a user-defined routine is not called with NULL values. If a NULL value is passed as one of its arguments, the database server simply returns NULL without calling the function. You can add the HANDLESNULLS modifier in the WITH() clause of the CRE-ATE FUNCTION statement to indicate that the function can process NULL values. The following is the declaration of the `quarter()` function that handles NULL values:

```
CREATE FUNCTION quarter(date)
RETURNS varchar(10)
WITH(NOT VARIANT, HANDLESNULLS, PARALLELIZABLE)
EXTERNAL NAME
"$INFORMIXDIR/extend/udrbook/bin/chap5.bld(quarter)"
LANGUAGE C;
```

In addition to indicating that the function can handle NULL values (HANDLESNULLS), this statement also declares that the function always returns the same value for a specific input value and that the function does not have side effects (NOT VARIANT). It also declares that it can run in parallel if needed (PARALLELIZABLE).

The DataBlade API does not define values to indicate a NULL as argument, so we cannot assume that any values for the date argument, will indicate that a NULL has been passed. Instead, we can find out the status of an argument by retrieving the argument indicator from the MI_FPARAM argument.

The function `mi_fp_argisnull()` returns a truth value indicating whether an argument is NULL or not. Its function definition is as follows:

```
mi_unsigned_char1 mi_fp_argisnull(MI_FPARAM *fp,
mi_integer argno);
```

The first argument is the MI_FPARAM pointer that is passed to
the function—in our case, the quarter() function. The second
argument is the argument position in the declaration. The position count starts at zero, so the indicator for the mi_date argument is at position zero.

The quarter() function could return the string "UNKNOWN"
when a date is NULL. We can do this by adding the following
code fragment at the beginning of the function:

```
if (MI_TRUE == mi_fp_argisnull(fparam, 0)) {
RetVal = mi_string_to_lvarchar("UNKNOWN");
Return(RetVal);
}
```

The rest of the quarter() function is the same as the code
shown in the preceding section.

Returning a NULL Result

In some cases, you may want to return a NULL value as the result
of a function execution. You need to tell the database server that
you are returning a NULL value. Once again, this is done with an
indicator in the MI_FPARAM argument.

The function used to indicate a NULL result is mi_fp_setre-
turnisnull(). Since we are dealing with a C function, the function still needs to return something. The returned value is
ignored. The quarter function can return a NULL value by issuing
the following statement before returning:

```
mi_fp_returnisnull(fparam, 0, MI_TRUE);
return(NULL);
```

The first argument to mi_fp_returnisnull() is the
MI_FPARAM pointer. The second argument represents the index
value of the return value. Since C functions only return one

value, this argument is always zero. The third argument represents a true or false value to which the return value is set. The choices are `MI_TRUE` (1) and `MI_FALSE` (0).

Raising Exceptions

IDS.2000 generates events when an unexpected condition occurs. These events, or exceptions, are either messages or errors. A message allows the SQL statement to complete while returning information to the caller. An error terminates the SQL execution and returns information about the cause of the error.

Your user-defined routine may need to deal with error conditions. In C programming it is customary to use status codes to indicate success or error. Since your routine executes in the context of a SQL statement, it is not possible to define your UDR as returning a status code, because the return value must be the result of the operation. Instead, you need to raise an exception that will indicate the severity of the error condition and give a specific explanation of the problem.

The database server already uses exceptions to indicate problems such as overflow, underflow, and division by zero. It is also used to report warnings that, for example, no rows are found or that the last row has already been returned. A user-defined routine generates exceptions using the `mi_db_error_raise()` API function. This function has the following syntax:

```
mi_integer mi_db_error_raise(MI_CONNECTION *conn,
    mi_integer msg_type, mi_char *msg, . . .);
```

This function declaration includes an ellipsis (...) at the end of its declaration that indicates a variable number of arguments. Its usage is better explained through simple examples. Let's start with a DISTINCT TYPE of INTEGER:

```
CREATE DISTINCT TYPE myint AS integer;
```

We can now create new operators for our distinct type. Let's create a divide operator for the `myint` type:

```
CREATE FUNCTION divide(myint, myint)
RETURNS myint
WITH (NOT VARIANT, PARALLIZABLE)
EXTERNAL NAME
"$INFORMIXDIR/extend/udrbook/bin/mylib.bld(divide)"
LANGUAGE C;
```

The divide() function is quite simple. It executes the division and returns the integer part of the result. Its first task is to test if the divisor is zero and generate an exception if it is:

```
mi_integer divide(mi_integer val1, mi_integer val2,
MI_FPARAM *fparam)
{
    mi_integer    ret;

    /* test for zero */
    if (val2 == 0) {
 mi_db_error_raise(NULL, MI_EXCEPTION,
  "divide by zero!", NULL);
 return(0);
    }

    /* do the division */
    ret = val1/val2;

    /* Return the function's return value. */
    return ret;
}
```

The first argument of mi_db_error_raise() is a connection pointer. This value can be set to NULL within a user-defined routine. If your function does not require a database connection for any other reason, you should use a NULL value as argument for performance reasons. The second argument is the message type. It can take one of three values: MI_MESSAGE, MI_EXCEPTION, and MI_SQL. We use MI_EXCEPTION in our example. This has the effect of aborting the function and the SQL statement. In other situations, we can use MI_MESSAGE to return a warning instead. Finally, the third argument is the text of the message.

This approach to raising exceptions has some drawbacks. Any change to the text of the message requires recompilation of the function. Furthermore, it cannot accommodate multiple languages for international support. This is where the MI_SQL message type comes in.

The MI_SQL message type works in conjunction with an SQL-STATE status value and the SYSERRORS table. The basic idea is that the SQLSTATE value is used to indicate the severity of the exception and to identify the message entry in the SYSERRORS table. Additional arguments can be passed to mi_db_error_raise() to serve as values to be replaced within the message. These values are passed in pairs, where the first value is a string to be replaced within the message and the second value is the value to replace it. This is best explained through an example.

Taking the same divide() function, we replace the exception statement with the following line:

```
mi_db_error_raise(NULL, MI_SQL, "U0U01",
                                 "divisor%d", 0, NULL);
```

This statement indicates that the "U0U01" is the SQLSTATE value. The additional argument indicates that found in the message is the string "divisor" and that it must be replaced by the next argument, which has a format of an integer ("%d"). The database server looks up the message in the SYSERRORS system catalog. Before we can use the divide() function, we need to insert our customized message by executing the following SQL statement:

```
INSERT INTO syserrors
    VALUES("U0U01", "en_us.8859-1", 0, 1,
           "bad divider, value: %divisor%");
```

The values inserted represent, respectively, the SQLSTATE value, the language locale of the message, the level, the sequence number, and the text of the message. Both level and seqno are documented as reserved for future use in the *Informix Guide to SQL: Reference.*[1] Make sure you use the value zero for level and the value one for seqno, or your message will not be

---

[1]*Informix Guide to SQL: Reference* (Menlo Park, CA: Informix Software, 1998).

displayed. Here is the output of the execution of an erroneous statement through dbaccess:

```
select '4'::myint / '0'::myint from systables
where tabid = 1;

(U0U01) - bad divider, value: 0
Error in line 1
Near character position 61
```

The SQL statement above executes the division for each row retrieved from SYSTABLES. This is just a trick to test the divide() function for our myint type.

We could support several client locales simultaneously by inserting additional entries in the SYSERRORS table. For example, a client in Montreal could have his environment variable CLIENT_LOCALE set to "fr_ca.8859-1" to indicate his preferred language environment. We can tailor the use of the divide() function simply by adding an entry in the SYSERRORS system catalog with the following SQL statement:

```
insert into syserrors
   values("U0U01", "fr_ca.8859-1", 0,1,
"mauvais diviseur, valeur: %divisor%");
```

In this environment, the error message displayed becomes

```
(U0U01) - mauvais diviseur, valeur: 0
Error in line 1
Near character position 61
```

SQLSTATE

The SQLSTATE value is divided into two sections: a two-character class followed by a three-character subclass. The only acceptable character values are digits and uppercase letters. Some meanings have already been assigned to the class. The currently defined values are described in the *Informix ESQL/C Programmer's Manual,*[2] Chap. 11. These codes are listed in Table 5–2.

---

[2]*Informix ESQL/C Programmer's Manual* (Menlo Park, CA: Informix Software, 1998).

Table 5–2 SQLSTATE class values.

Class Code	Value
00	Success
01	Success with warning
02	Not found or end of data
03 and higher	Error
07	Dynamic SQL error
08	Connection exception
0A	Feature not supported
21	Cardinality violation
22	Data exception
23	Integrity-constraint violation
24	Invalid cursor state
25	Invalid transaction state
26	Invalid SQL statement identifier
28	Invalid user-authorization specification
2B	Dependent privilege descriptors still exist
2D	Invalid transaction termination
2E	Invalid connection name
33	Invalid SQL descriptor name
34	Invalid cursor name
35	Invalid exception number
37	Syntax error or access violation in `PREPARE` or `EXECUTE IMMEDIATE`
3C	Duplicate cursor name
40	Transaction rollback
42	Syntax error or access violation
S0	Invalid name
S1	Memory allocation error message
IX	Informix-reserved error messages
U0	User-defined error returned by a user-defined routine

Some general rules apply to the use of class codes. As indicated in Table 5–2, any class code greater than "02" indicates an error. Informix has already defined a number of class codes. If you are putting together a commercial DataBlade module, you should contact the Informix DataBlade Development Partners Program Registry to reserve a name, prefix, and error codes to avoid conflicts with codes used by other DataBlade module providers.

`mi_lvarchar` **API Functions**

The `mi_lvarchar` structure is used to manipulate all character type values. It is also equivalent to the `mi_bitvarying` type that is used to handle variable-length opaque types. There are 13 API functions that operate on `mi_lvarchar` types. These functions are listed in `Table 5-3`. Their use seems very straightforward when you read their description (see Appendix), but questions remain concerning mainly the memory allocation and de-allocation. This section discusses the `mi_lvarchar` functions and explains exactly what all of them do.

Memory Allocation

A `mi_lvarchar` variable is allocated in two sections. One section is the `mi_lvarchar` structure itself, containing the different elements of its opaque structure. The second section is a data buffer. Both memory allocations are allocated based on the memory duration currently active.

Table 5–3 mi_lvarchar API functions.

`mi_get_vardata()`	`mi_get_vardata_align()`	`mi_get_varlen()`
`mi_lvarchar_to_string()`	`mi_new_var()`	`mi_set_vardata()`
`mi_set_vardata_align()`	`mi_set_varlen()`	`mi_set_varptr()`
`mi_string_to_lvarchar()`	`mi_var_copy()`	`mi_var_free()`
`mi_var_to_buffer()`		

The default memory duration is `PER_ROUTINE`. This memory duration is also referred to as `PER_FUNCTION`. If you require a different memory duration for your `mi_lvarchar` variable, you need to execute the `mi_switch_memory_duration()` before the `mi_lvarchar` variable is allocated. This function takes one argument, which is the memory duration. The return value is the previous memory duration. The return value can be saved so that you can restore the old memory duration when you are done with your memory allocation. For example, to change the default memory duration to `PER_COMMAND`, you need to execute the following command:

```
oldDuration = mi_switch_memory_duration(PER_COMMAND);
```

The `PER_ROUTINE` memory duration allocates memory for the duration of a single invocation of a user-defined routine. The memory is released the next time a specific thread of execution enters that UDR. This memory duration is sufficient for most user-defined routines.

The DataBlade API supports a memory duration that lasts for the duration of an SQL statement. This memory duration is called `PER_COMMAND`. It is necessary in iterator functions, in some cases of large objects within an opaque type, and for specialized processing using advanced DataBlade API features.

Other memory durations exist but are not documented. These durations are needed in some rare cases by some DataBlade modules provided by Informix or some of its partners.

mi_get_vardata()

This function returns the value of the data pointer of a `mi_lvarchar` variable passed as an argument. The function signature is

```
char *mi_get_vardata(mi_lvarchar *lvar);
```

The return value gives you direct access to the data buffer of the `mi_lvarchar` variable. The data buffer was allocated by a `mi_alloc()` operation and has a specific length. As with any other buffer manipulation, you must make sure to stay within its limits so as not to corrupt memory contents that are outside the buffer.

mi_get_vardata_align()

The mi_get_vardata_align() is complementary to mi_set_vardata_align(). It retrieves the data pointer inside a mi_lvarchar variable. The pointer value is then adjusted to fit the requested alignment. This means that a number of bytes located at the beginning of the buffer may not be accessible, depending on the alignment requested. The mi_get_vardata_align() has the following signature:

```
mi_char *mi_get_vardata_align(mi_lvarchar *lvar,
        mi_integer align);
```

Depending on where the memory was allocated, the pointer that is returned may have a value of up to align-1 bytes greater than the data pointer stored in the mi_lvarchar variable. When you use this function, you have to make sure that the data was set using the mi_set_vardata_align() function.

mi_get_varlen()

The mi_get_varlen() function returns the length of the data buffer stored in the mi_lvarchar variable as stored in the opaque part of the structure. It has the following signature:

```
mi_integer mi_get_varlen(mi_lvarhcar *lvar);
```

mi_lvarchar_to_string()

The mi_lvarchar_to_string() function copies mi_get_varlen() bytes from the content of the mi_lvarchar data buffer into a newly allocated buffer. It ensures that the buffer is NULL terminated before returning it to the requester. This function has the following signature:

```
mi_string *mi_lvarchar_to_string(mi_lvarchar *lvar);
```

mi_new_var()

You use the mi_new_var() function to allocate a new mi_lvar-char variable. This function has the following signature:

```
mi_lvarchar *mi_new_var(mi_integer len);
```

A mi_lvarchar variable is allocated with a data buffer of length len. If the function is called with a length of zero, mi_new_var() does not allocate a data buffer. Instead, it considers the data buffer pointer as a value instead of as a pointer. This can be useful when dealing with opaque types that are declared as passed by value. The restriction is that the data value length must be at most four bytes.

If the function is successful, it returns a pointer to a mi_lvar-char structure. If it fails, it returns NULL.

mi_set_vardata()

The mi_set_vardata() function has the following signature:

```
void mi_set_vardata(mi_lvarchar *lvar,
    mi_char *value);
```

This function copied the content of the value argument into the data buffer of the lvarchar variable. The mi_set_vardata() function uses the length of the mi_lvarchar data buffer as the number of bytes that must be copied. This means that the copy operation could truncate the input value.

mi_set_vardata_align()

The mi_set_vardata_align() function has the following signature:

```
void mi_set_vardata_align(mi_lvarchar *lvar,
    char *value, mi_integer align);
```

This function retrieves the data buffer pointer from the mi_lvarchar variable and calculates the next memory address that is on the requested alignment boundary as requested by the function's third argument (`align`). It then copies the value argument at the newly calculated data buffer address, having already used the length stored in the `mi_lvarchar` variable to determine how many bytes must be copied. This could lead to the truncation of the input value.

mi_set_varlen()

The `mi_set_varlen()` function sets the length element of the `mi_lvarchar` structure to the value passed as argument. The function signature is

```
void mi_set_varlen(mi_lvarchar *lvar, mi_integer len);
```

The `mi_set_varlen()` function does not take into consideration the real size of the data buffer. This could create some inconsistencies leading to errors. This function is useful in conjunction with the `mi_set_varptr()` function.

mi_set_varptr()

The `mi_set_varptr()` function replaces the value of the data buffer pointer in a `mi_lvarchar` variable with a new value passed as argument. Its signature is

```
void mi_set_varptr(mi_lvarchar *lvar, char *newdata);
```

The `mi_set_varptr()` function does not free the previous data buffer. When using this function, the standard sequence of operations should be similar to the following:

```
. . .
newData = mi_alloc(mysize);
. . .
oldData = mi_get_vardata(lvar);
if (oldData != NULL)
mi_free(oldData);
mi_set_vardata(lvar, newData);
mi_set_varlen(mysize);
```

At some point you allocate a new buffer, using the DataBlade API function `mi_alloc()`. Before replacing the data buffer in the `lvar mi_lvarchar` variable, you retrieve the current data buffer and free it with the `mi_free()` function. Finally, you set the new data buffer and reset the length in the `mi_lvarchar` variable to the length of the data buffer.

mi_string_to_lvarchar()

The `mi_string_to_lvarchar()` function creates a new `mi_lvarchar` variable that contains a copy of the character string that is passed as argument. The NULL value at the end of the character string is not part of the resulting `mi_lvarchar` variable. Its signature is as follows:

```
mi_lvarchar
  *mi_string_to_lvarchar(mi_string *astring);
```

The `mi_string` pointer argument is a NULL-terminated character string. A `mi_string` * argument is equivalent to a `char` * argument. Since the argument is read-only, the `mi_string_to_lvarchar()` function does not modify or manage the variable in any way. If the variable used as argument was allocated specifically to create the `mi_lvarchar` variable, it is still your responsibility to free up its memory once you are done with it.

The `mi_string_to_lvarchar()` function is a utility function that makes it easier to create a new `mi_lvarchar` variable. Otherwise, you would have to create a new variable of a specific size using `mi_new_var()` and then copy the string into it using `mi_set_vardata()`.

mi_var_copy()

The `mi_var_copy()` function makes an exact copy of the `mi_lvarchar` variable passed as argument. The original variable remains untouched. This can be useful when a function needs to return a `mi_lvarchar` variable that was created through another function call. Because of memory duration, the memory for the original `mi_lvarchar` variable could be released before a user-defined routine is done with it. By returning a newly created copy, the variable will be valid long enough for the receiver to complete its work with it. The signature of the `mi_var_copy()` function is

```
mi_lvarchar *mi_var_copy(mi_lvarchar *lvar);
```

mi_var_free()

The `mi_var_free()` function frees the memory allocated to both the data buffer and the `mi_lvarchar` variable passed as argument. Its signature is

```
mi_integer mi_var_free(mi_lvarchar *lvar);
```

mi_var_to_buffer()

The `mi_var_to_buffer()` function copies the content of the data buffer into a buffer passed as argument. Its signature is

```
void mi_var_to_buffer(mi_lvarchar *lvar,
  char *buffer);
```

This function is similar to `mi_lvarchar_to_string()` except that the content of the data buffer is copied as is instead of adding a NULL character at the end. This is useful when the `mi_lvarchar` variable contains an opaque type represented by a data structure.

The mi_lvarchar buffer length

Since it is possible to get and set the `mi_lvarchar` buffer length, we need to make sure we understand its use.

The buffer length can be retrieved and set using `mi_get_varlen()` and `mi_set_varlen()`. This value represents the size of the data buffer allocated with the `mi_alloc()` DataBlade API call. Should you decide to put in less data than the buffer can accommodate, the `mi_lvarchar` will nevertheless still be manipulated according to the buffer size.

The buffer length represents the memory allocated to the internal buffer. Reducing the size won't break your code, but any increase should be accomplished by way of a new buffer allocation and a copy of the old buffer content to the new one. The `mi_set_varptr()` DataBlade API call is used to replace the buffer of an existing `mi_lvarchar` structure. The old buffer should be freed using the `mi_free()` API call.

Chapter 6

User-Defined Types

A key to object-relational extensibility is its ability to define new data types that better suit the problem domain. These types include row types, collection types, distinct types, and opaque types. Opaque types are covered in detail in Chap. 7. This chapter covers the use of row, collection, and distinct types. Row types and collection types are part of what are called complex types. We will see how to define these types at the SQL level and how to manipulate them both at the SQL level and within a user-defined routine. These discussions will include how to insert the types into tables, receive them as arguments to functions, identify their characteristics, manipulate their content, and return them from user-defined routines.

Complex Types

Complex types include row types and collections. Row types can be named or unnamed. Unnamed row types are created within another declaration, such as a function argument or return value, or within a table declaration. Named row types are created with the CREATE ROW TYPE statement. They can be used as column types in table definitions and field types within other row types. They are also used to create typed tables that can be part of table hierarchies, which is how IDS.2000 supports single inheritance.

Collection types come in three flavors: LIST, SET, and MULTI-SET. Differences among them only slightly affect how they can be manipulated, as we will see later.

The ensuing sections discuss the characteristics and processing requirements of row types first, followed by collection types.

Row Types

A row type is similar to a table declaration insofar as it defines a number of fields with specific data types. A row type may be used to create a logical grouping that can be manipulated as a single-column element. It is also the foundation for table inheritance. A table inheritance is defined over tables that are typed using row types. A row type can also inherit fields from another row type if it has been defined under the other row type.

You can use row types either by creating a named row type or by declaring a named row-type column—or a table column—as a row type. In the case of a table column, the row type is unnamed. Consider the following statements:

```
CREATE ROW TYPE myrow (a int, b int, c int);
CREATE TABLE tab_row1 (col1 myrow, col2 int);
CREATE TABLE tab_row2 (col1 ROW(a int, b int), col2 int);
```

The first statement creates a simple named row type: myrow. The second statement shows how the myrow row type can be use as a column within a table. The third statement shows a simple table declaration that defines its first column as an unnamed row type.

In Informix-UDO, a row type definition can contain fields of any type except SERIAL, SERIAL8, BYTE, and TEXT. IDS.2000 now allows the inclusion of SERIAL and SERIAL8 in a row type. The only constraint available for the fields of a row type is the

NOT NULL constraint. This can be confusing since you can also apply the NOT NULL constraint to a table column that is a named or an unnamed row type. To illustrate this, we will use insert statements. First, let's look at an example of an insert statement that involves row types. Considering the table declaration above, we can insert values using statements such as:

```
INSERT INTO tab_row1
   VALUES("ROW(51, 61, 71)"::myrow, 11);
INSERT INTO tab_row2 VALUES("ROW(52, 62)", 10);
```

The first statement contains a row type value that is inserted in the column of type myrow. Note that the ROW declaration is in double quotes. This represents a literal declaration of a row value. The declaration can also be done using single quotes. The additional casting declaration ::myrow indicates that the unnamed row type should be converted to a named row type. Since the unnamed row-type fields match the ones in the named row type, this casting operation is optional. The second statement demonstrates that the insert syntax is similar for unnamed row types.

A row type can contain fields that are themselves row types. Let's modify the row type myrow to illustrate this capability and add some field constraints to flesh out our discussion of the NOT NULL constraint:

```
CREATE ROW TYPE myrow (
     a int                    NOT NULL,
     b ROW(x int, y int)      NOT NULL,
     c int                    NOT NULL
);
```

We changed the definition of the second column to be an unnamed row type. Let's issue some insert statements against the new tab_row1 table:

```
INSERT INTO tab_row1 VALUES(NULL, 10);
1 row(s) inserted.
```

This statement inserted a NULL as the value of the col1 column. This is a valid insert because the table column does not have a NOT NULL constraint.

```
INSERT INTO tab_row1
  VALUES("ROW(51, ROW(NULL, NULL), 71)"::myrow, 11);
1 row(s) inserted.
```

This time we inserted a value into the col1 column. Each field of that column is declared with the NOT NULL constraint. Note that the value inserted for the unnamed row field contains two NULL values but the row type itself is NOT NULL. This is an important distinction between a NULL value and a type that contains NULL values: The constraint applies to the unnamed row type, not its elements.

```
INSERT INTO tab_row1
VALUES("ROW(52, ROW(NULL, NULL), NULL)"::myrow, 11);
  292: An implied insert column (rowinput():
        rowinput: arg c) does not accept NULLs.
```

Here the value of the c field from the row type myrow is NULL. Since there is a NOT NULL constraint on the field the insert fails as the error message shows.

Inserting Row Types

The preceding insert examples are good illustrations of the insert syntax. Their syntax uses what is called a *row literal*. A row literal is a row expression between double quotes. It is also possible to insert a row type without the double quotes. This is called a *row constructor:* Numeric values are entered directly, character values are provided within single quotes, and so forth. The following row type illustrates all cases of insertion into a row type. Some column types are not present but can be deduced from the ones provided:

```
CREATE ROW TYPE alltypes (
    A       BOOLEAN,
    B       VARCHAR(20),
    C       CLOB,
    D       DATE,
    E       DATETIME year to second,
    F       DECIMAL,
    G       DOUBLE PRECISION,
```

```
      H          INT8,
      I          LIST(SET(INT, NOT NULL) NOT NULL),
      J          ROW(a INT, b INT)
);

CREATE TABLE tab_row3 (col1 alltypes);

INSERT INTO tab_row3 VALUES(
  ROW('t', 'Jacques Roy',
  FILETOCLOB('lotostring.sql', 'client'),
  '01/01/2000', '1999-12-31 23:59:59', 10.02,
     3.1415926,
  99999999999, "LIST{SET{1, 2, 3}, SET{4, 5, 6}}",
  ROW(1, 2))::alltypes
);
```

We first created a named row type and a table containing one column of that type. The interesting part is the INSERT INTO statement: The third column is defined as a character large object (CLOB). We used a utility function, FILETOCLOB, provided by the database server, to create a new large object based on a file system file. The first argument represents a file. It could be either an absolute path or a path relative to the current directory. The second argument indicates that the file comes from the client machine rather than the machine where the database server is running. In this case, the file is located on the client machine in the current directory.

The next few fields are standard SQL type inserts until we reach the collection type in field "I": That collection is a list of sets—two separate collection types. Note that the list value and each set of elements use braces to identify their boundaries. This is the standard syntax for collections. The list is enclosed in double quotes, which indicate a list literal as opposed to a list constructor. List constructors are implemented starting with IDS.2000.

The last field is an unnamed row where its insert is covered by a row constructor. We finish the statement by casting the row constructor to the named row type that we are inserting (::alltypes). The explicit cast is required so that the proper named row type can be generated.

Row Type Constraints

The only constraint available within a row type is the NOT NULL constraint. A table uses a row type in two ways: The row type is either a column type or the table type. When a row type is used as a column type, the only available constraint is again NOT NULL.

When a row type is used as a type for tables, each field in the row type is a column within the table. The standard constraint rules then apply.

```
CREATE TABLE a_tab OF TYPE myrow;
ALTER TABLE a_tab ADD CONSTRAINT (UNIQUE (a));
CREATE TABLE a_tab2 OF TYPE myrow (UNIQUE(a));
```

The first statement creates a table of type myrow. The second statement alters the table definition to add a unique constraint on the first column. The third statement effectively does the same thing as the previous two statements.

Row Type Indexing

It is not yet possible to index a row type or a row type field directly, although these restrictions will certainly be removed in the future. It is possible, however, to work around these restrictions by implementing user-defined routines that process the row type and return an indexable type. Then you can create an index on the result of this function. This type of index is called a *functional index.*

Row Type Processing

A user-defined routine can be defined as receiving either a specific named row type or a generic row type, no matter which type it is. Consider the following statements:

```
CREATE FUNCTION process_row(row)
RETURNING int
EXTERNAL NAME ". . . "
LANGUAGE C
END FUNCTION;
```

```
CREATE FUNCTION process_myrow(myrow)
RETURNING int
EXTERNAL NAME ". . . "
LANGUAGE C
END FUNCTION;
```

The first statement defines a function that can receive any row type. This function needs to identify the characteristics of the row type such as the number of fields and their types. It could go as far as returning an error if the row type does not follow some specific rules.

The second statement defines a function that processes a specific row type: myrow. This simplifies the processing since the function knows everything about the type. The database server makes sure that only the myrow row type is passed to the function. This type of function definition makes more sense because it is more specific and takes advantage of the strong typing feature of the IDS.2000 server.

Getting the Row Type Name

When you have a function that handles unnamed row types, you may want to verify that the row type is part of a set of named row types you can handle or that it has some specific characteristics.

The following code shows how to get the row type name from the row type argument:

```
mi_lvarchar *getrowname(MI_ROW *myrow,
  MI_FPARAM *fp)
{
  MI_TYPEID *tid;
  MI_TYPE_DESC *td;
  mi_string *str;

  tid = mi_fp_argtype(fp, 0);
  td = mi_type_typedesc(NULL, tid);
  str = mi_type_typename(td);
  return(mi_string_to_lvarchar(str));
}
```

The `mi_fp_argtype()` function returns a pointer to the type identifier of its first argument that is stored in the `MI_FPARAM` structure. From this type identifier, we get the type descriptor. The `mi_type_typedesc()` function requires a database connection as its first argument. This value can be set to `NULL` in user-defined routines. Once we have the type descriptor, we get the type name using the `mi_type_typename()` function. The return value is a pointer into the `MI_TYPE_DESC` structure. The values returned by these three functions should be considered read-only.

The name we get from `mi_type_typename()` is the name of the type that is passed as argument. If this type is a distinct type of a named row type, we get the distinct type name. This could go further. It could be a distinct type of another distinct type. We may end up with several levels of distinct types. Looking at the DataBlade API, we may think that the following code would get us to the original row type:

```
. . .
td2 = td;
while (td2 != NULL) {
   td = td2;
   td2 = mi_get_type_source_type(td);
}
```

This code loops until the source type returned is `NULL`. The `mi_get_type_source_type()` function returns `NULL` if the argument is not a distinct type. Unfortunately, this loop does not work; it becomes an infinite loop. You should use the following code instead:

```
while (MI_TRUE == mi_typeid_is_distinct(tid)) {
   td2 = mi_get_type_source_type(td);
   tid = mi_typedesc_typeid(td2);
   td2 = td = mi_type_typedesc(NULL, tid);
}
```

The real difference in this loop is that we ask the database server to give us a new type identifier `MI_TYPEID`. From this new type identifier, we can get a new type descriptor, `MI_TYPE_DESC`, for the base type of the current type. The loop ends once we find a type that is not a distinct type. This code can be useful if your user-defined routine needs to process a specific base type. This way you can also process any distinct type that is rooted in that specific base type.

Getting Other Information

The DataBlade API provides other functions to extract information from a row type. The API function names start with `mi_column`. The following code shows how to get the number of columns from a row type argument:

```
mi_integer getfldcount(MI_ROW *myrow, MI_FPARAM *fp)
{
  MI_ROW_DESC *rd;
  mi_integer cnt;

  rd = mi_get_row_desc(myrow);
  cnt = mi_column_count(rd);
  mi_row_desc_free(rd);
  return(cnt);
}
```

This time, we get a row descriptor from the row type argument. Getting a row descriptor is a relatively expensive operation. If you use this type of code in a loop that keeps retrieving the same row descriptor, you should move this operation outside of the loop to avoid the overhead. This is particularly important in iterator functions (see Chap. 8).

The row descriptor is then used to get the number of columns with the `mi_column_count()` API function. Consult the Appendix to see what other information you can access.

Accessing Row Fields

Since a row type is a complex structure, we need to use DataBlade API functions to extract its fields. Furthermore, we need to determine whether the value extracted is NULL. This is done with the API function `mi_value()`. Let's assume we want to extract the first field of the `myrow` row type:

```
MI_DATUM datum;
Mi_integer val, ind;
.  .  .
switch(mi_value(myrow, 0, &datum, &collen)) {
case MI_NULL_VALUE:
    ind = -1;
    break;
case MI_NORMAL_VALUE:
    ind = 0;
    val = (mi_integer)datum;
     break;
.  .  .
} /* end switch */
```

The `mi_value()` function used its second argument as the index to the row field to retrieve. This index value starts at zero. The field is retrieved into the function's third argument, a pointer to a `MI_DATUM` variable. In our case, we know that the first field of the `myrow` row type is an integer that is passed by value. Chapter 4 provides all the information necessary to cast to the proper data type from a `MI_DATUM` variable and vice versa.

The `mi_value()` function returns a status indicator that can take the following values:

- `MI_NORMAL_VALUE`: The value returned is a normal value, either a base type, an opaque type, or a distinct type of the previous two.
- `MI_NULL_VALUE`: The value returned is `NULL`.
- `MI_ROW_VALUE`: The value returned is a row type.
- `MI_COLLECTION_VALUE`: The value returned is a collection type (list, set, multiset).
- `MI_ERROR`: The `mi_value()` function returned an error.

In the preceding code we have only dealt with `MI_NORMAL_VALUE` and `MI_NULL_VALUE`. In a more general situation, the other values should be included.

Returning Rows

You can either return a row that you have received in one way or
another, or you can create a new row from values that are
passed to you. In the following example, we see how to create
and return a row of type myrow:

```
MI_ROW *cre8row(mi_integer one, mi_integer two,
    mi_integer three, mi_integer four, MI_FPARAM *fp)
{
    MI_TYPEID      *tid, *tid2;
    MI_ROW_DESC    *rd, *rd2;
    MI_ROW         *prow, *prow2;
    MI_DATUM       datums[3], datums2[2];
    mi_boolean     isnull[3], isnull2[2];

    tid = mi_typestring_to_id(NULL, "myrow");
    rd = mi_row_desc_create(tid);
    tid2 = mi_column_type_id(rd, 1);
    rd2 = mi_row_desc_create(tid2);

    /* Create an unnamed row type */
    datums2[0] = (MI_DATUM)two;
    datums2[1] = (MI_DATUM)three;
    isnull2[0] = MI_FALSE;
    isnull2[1] = MI_FALSE;
    prow2 = mi_row_create(NULL, rd2, datums2, isnull2);

    /* Create the myrow row type */
    datums[0] = (MI_DATUM)one;
    datums[1] = (MI_DATUM)prow2;
    datums[2] = (MI_DATUM)four;
    isnull[0] = MI_FALSE;
    isnull[1] = MI_FALSE;
    isnull[2] = MI_FALSE;
    prow = mi_row_create(NULL, rd, datums, isnull);
    return(prow);
}
```

This function takes four integer arguments as input and creates a myrow row type as its return value. We are using the
myrow row type as defined earlier:

```
CREATE ROW TYPE myrow (
    a int                       NOT NULL,
    b ROW(x int, y int)         NOT NULL,
    c int                       NOT NULL
);
```

The row type `myrow` includes two integers and an unnamed row type. This example shows two levels of row type creation: Level 1 creates the `myrow` row type; level 2, the unnamed row type included as the second field of the `myrow` row type.

We first need to get type identifier of the `myrow` row type with the `mi_typestring_to_id()` DataBlade API functions. This function takes two arguments. The first one is a connection to the database server. Since we are running in the server, we can pass a NULL value instead of opening a connection using the `mi_open()` function. Since opening a connection is relatively expensive, the use of a NULL value saves some processing. The second argument is the name of the type that we want the type identifier for.

Once we have the type descriptor, we can create a row descriptor with `mi_row_desc_create()`. A row descriptor contains the information on the row fields. Each new row creation requires its own row descriptor. If you create a second row with the same row descriptor, the first row will be overwritten. A row descriptor can be reused if the processing of the previous row is completed and that row is not needed anymore. Reusing row descriptors can provide some performance improvement. Of course, we have to make sure that the row descriptor is then created with the appropriate memory duration.

Since our row type contains another row type, we need to create a second row descriptor. The operation is the same as before except that this time we obtain the type identifier of the unnamed row type from the `myrow` row descriptor. The `mi_column_type_id()` function takes a row descriptor and an integer as the index of the field we are looking for. This index starts at zero.

The next step is to provide the data that is inserted in the row. Two elements are needed for each field: the field content and a status that indicates whether it is a true value or a NULL value. Since a row can contain different value types, the values are stored in an array of MI_DATUM. Depending on the value type, the value is stored as the value itself or as a pointer to it. This follows the same rules as those for passing arguments. Again, Chap. 4 covers the conversion from SQL types to MI_DATUM and vice versa in detail.

Finally, the row is created by calling mi_row_create():

```
MI_ROW * mi_row_create(MI_CONNECTION *conn,
            MI_ROW_DESC *rowdesc, MI_DATA coldata[],
            mi_boolean colisnull[]);
```

The mi_row_create() function takes four arguments: the database server connection, the row descriptor, the datum array, and an array of NULL value indicators. Each element of the indicator array corresponds to the datum element that is at the same relative position in the datum array. The first argument to the mi_row_create() function is a database connection that can be set to NULL. It is followed by the row descriptor, the array of values, and the array of indicators. Since one of the elements is also a row type, we had to create a row for that field and put it in the array. Once the myrow row is created, we can return the value to the caller.

Executing SQL Statements

Processing an SQL statement in a user-defined routine is very similar to manipulating a row type. This section completes the information on the row type processing while also covering the SQL statement execution.

We require a database connection to execute an SQL statement. This is similar to the execution of SQL statements from client applications. The difference is that this time the execution is kept inside the database server. The statement execution in the database server is equivalent to writing stored procedure in C. Since we are already in the server, we can obtain a connection by passing NULL parameters to the mi_open() API function:

```
MI_CONNECTION *conn;
  . . .
conn = mi_open(NULL, NULL, NULL);
```

In a user-defined routine, the `mi_open()` function must be called with the three `NULL` arguments. The arguments could be different when used in a client application. The DataBlade API provides a few choices when it comes to executing SQL statements. We can execute a statement based on a character string or first prepare the statement and then execute the prepared statement. The DataBlade API functions used with prepared statements are listed in the Appendix under the heading "Parameterized Queries and Cursors." In this section, however, we cover only the use of the `mi_exec()` API function to execute statements based on character strings.

When executing and processing SQL statements in the server, the general sequence of events is as follows:

- Obtain a database connection.
- Execute the SQL statement.
- Get the result.
- Obtain a row descriptor for the result.
- Loop:
  - Get a row,
  - Process each column,
  - Release column resources (if necessary).
- Release resources (row descriptor, connections, etc.).

We already saw how to obtain a database connection. This connection may be used for several purposes. Since opening a connection to the server is relatively expensive, you may want to pass it as a parameter *as needed* to other C functions that you use as subroutines rather than having each subroutine open its own connection.

The execution of the SQL statement is done with the `mi_exec()` API function. It takes three arguments: a database server connection, a character string representing the statement, and a control parameter that indicates whether each column of the result should be returned in binary format or in character format. The function returns an integer representing the status of the execution. Here are two statements showing the use of the `mi_exec()` function:

```
ret = mi_exec(conn, "select * from tab_row1; ",
              MI_QUERY_NORMAL);
```

```
ret = mi_exec(conn, "select * from tab_row1; ",
                MI_QUERY_BINARY);
```

The first statement requires the result to be returned in character format, while the second asks for the result in binary format. The return value of the `mi_exec()` function indicates whether the function executed properly (`MI_OK`) or failed (`MI_ERROR`). The next step is to obtain the query result. This is done with

```
ret = mi_get_result(conn);
```

The return value is a status that is one of the following:

- `MI_DML`: The statement is a data manipulation language statement, either `INSERT`, `SELECT`, `UPDATE`, or `DELETE`.
- `MI_DDL`: The statement is a data definition language statement such as `CREATE TABLE`.
- `MI_ROWS`: The statement produced rows of data that should be fetched.
- `MI_NO_MORE_RESULTS`: No more results are pending.

When we execute SQL statements, most of the time we know the format of the result. We could just hard code the processing. In more generic processing, though, we have to use the DataBlade API to obtain the information. To find out how many columns are part of the result, we do the following:

```
MI_ROW_DESC    *rd;
mi_integer      colCount;
. . .
rd = mi_get_row_desc_without_row(conn);
colCount = mi_column_count(rd);
```

The `rd` value is a row descriptor. From this value we can obtain information on the result, including the number of columns. The row descriptor is also used to obtain information on the type of the columns. The DataBlade API functions starting with `mi_column` are used for this purpose.

We are now ready to process the rows. Since multiple rows may be coming back, we must loop over the result, obtaining the rows until no more rows are returned. Once we have a row, we

```
```

have to loop over the columns to process them. The processing loop has the following form:

```
MI_DATUM datum;
mi_integer i, error, collen;
. . .
while (NULL != (row = mi_next_row(conn, &error)) ) {
  for (i = 0; i < colCount; i++) {
    switch(mi_value(row, i, &datum, &collen)) {
    case MI_NULL_VALUE:
        . . .
        break;
    case MI_NORMAL_VALUE:
        . . .
        break;
    case MI_COLLECTION_VALUE:
        . . .
        break;
    case MI_ROW_VALUE:
        . . .
        break;
    case MI_ERROR:
        . . .
        break;
    } /* end switch */
  } /* end for */
} /* end while */
```

The `while()` statement executes until no more rows are available from the statement execution. For each row, the `for()` statement processes every column. Note that the column indexing starts at zero. The key to this processing is that the `switch()` statement uses the `mi_value()` function.

The `mi_value()` function returns one of five values:

1. `MI_NULL_VALUE`: This value indicates that the specified field is NULL. The datum value then has no meaning.
2. `MI_NORMAL_VALUE`: The `mi_value()` function returns this indicator when the value is either a basic database type, an opaque type, or a distinct type of basic database type and opaque type. The type of the value returned depends

on whether the query was executed with MI_QUERY_NORMAL or MI_QUERY_BINARY. In the former case, the value returned is a NULL-terminated character string. In the later case, the result is in binary format. Chapter 4 describes the types that are used for each SQL type available.

3. MI_COLLECTION_VALUE: This value indicates that the data returned is a collection complex type. This case occurs even when the query is executed with the MI_QUERY_NORMAL control flag. Only the simple values included within the collection type will be represented as NULL-terminated character strings.

4. MI_ROW_VALUE: As with value 3, the returned value is in binary format no matter which control flag is used to execute the SQL statement. The simple values included within the row type will then follow the requirement of the control flag as already explained for value 2.

5. MI_ERROR: In any case of error, this indicator is returned.

When dealing with complex types, such as row types, you need to consider the possibility that the row you are processing may contain a field that is itself a complex type. If we want to process rows in a generic manner, we need to consider this possibility. Even if we know the exact structure of a row type, we may encounter a situation that requires a processing loop similar to the MI_DATUM loop shown above. It is a good idea to consider putting the processing loop in a separate function that can be reused in multiple situations. If we provide a function that returns a character representation of a row, we could define a recursive function that would call itself each time it encountered a row type.

Collection Types

IDS.2000 provides three different collection types: SET, MULTISET, and LIST. These three collection types provide different functionality. The two set types, SET and MULTISET, are by definition unordered. A SET contains unique values and a MULTISET allows duplicate values. The LIST collection type provides an ordered set of values where duplicates are allowed. These features have an impact on the way each collection type is handled.

For our discussion, consider the following table creation and insert statements:

```
CREATE TABLE tab_col (
   col1 LIST(integer NOT NULL),
   col2 SET(integer NOT NULL),
   col3 MULTISET(integer NOT NULL),
   col4 integer
);

INSERT INTO tab_col
       VALUES ('LIST{7, 8, 9}', 'SET{1, 2, 3}',
               'MULTISET{4, 5, 4}', 1);
```

The CREATE TABLE statement provides an example of the syntax used to create each type of collection with integer elements. The element type used in the collection definition can be any available type, including any collection type.

The INSERT INTO statement uses a literal representation. Here we use single quotes instead of the double quotes used in previous examples, because IDS.2000 accepts both. The advantage of having two ways to express a literal is that we can then use the double quotes within a literal expression. The collection's integer elements are listed within braces (not parentheses) in a literal representation of a row. A collection type must always be inserted in literal mode (within quotes) in a textual insert statement. This contrasts with the constructor mode available for row types (see subsection "Inserting Row Types").

Collection Type Constraints

It is not possible to insert a NULL value into a collection. This fact is made explicit by forcing the inclusion of the NOT NULL constraint with its element type. A collection contains a number of elements. It does not make sense to say that one element does not exist. If it does not exist, it is not there. So if no elements are there, the collection is empty. If NULL values were allowed, we would have collections with elements that do not exist.

A column within a table can have constraints applied to it. In the case of a collection column, however, IDS.2000 allows only the NOT NULL constraint. Furthermore, it is not possible to set a default value for collection columns.

Collection Type Indexing

A collection type contains a variable number of values. A column that is defined as a collection type cannot be indexed. A specific value within the collection could be extracted with a user-defined routine, and the result of the routine could be indexed. In general, however, this is not a viable solution. Hopefully, the indexing of collection functionality will be supported in future releases.

Supporting collection indexing is not a trivial task. A collection can be made of any types available within the database. This includes all the base types from the relational model; it also includes row types and collections. Toss in the opaque types (see Chap. 7) to see how difficult collection indexing can get.

Indexing problems are why several of the standard constraints are not available for collection processing. Constraints like PRIMARY KEY and REFERENCES require indexing, so we cannot expect to be able to use these within our schema for some time.

Collection Type Processing

All collection types are passed to user-defined routines as MI_COLLECTION type pointer arguments. The first discrimination among the three collection types occurs with the function definition in SQL. When a function is created, it must declare the specific type of collection it receives as argument or returns as return value. This means identifying a collection type as list, set, or multiset. In the C declaration, however, they all use the same type: MI_COLLECTION.

Consider the following function creation declarations:

```
CREATE FUNCTION getcolname(SET)
RETURNS lvarchar
  . . .
```

```
;
CREATE FUNCTION do_col(SET(integer NOT NULL))
RETURNING lvarchar
. . .
;
```

As we can see, a function creation statement may not specify the type of the elements included in the collection. This is useful when creating functions that deal with general features of collections. We can find out the type of the collection elements by extracting the type descriptor for the collection elements. The following code extract illustrates how to do it:

```
MI_TYPEID *tid;
MI_TYPE_DESC *td, *td2;

tid = mi_fp_argtype(fp, 0);
td = mi_type_typedesc(NULL, tid);
td2 = mi_type_element_typedesc(td);
```

Assuming that the collection is the first argument to the function using this code, we first get the type identifier for the collection. We use the type identifier to retrieve the collection type descriptor with the `mi_type_typedesc()` function. Finally, we retrieve the type descriptor for the collection elements with `mi_type_element_typedesc()`. Once we have the type descriptor, we can easily retrieve the type name (`mi_type_typename()`) or its type identifier (`mi_typedesc_typeid()`).

The DataBlade API provides eight functions for the processing of collections. The following code shows how a collection argument can be processed:

```
mi_lvarchar *do_col(MI_COLLECTION *val1,
   MI_FPARAM *pfparam)
{
   MI_COLL_DESC  *pcoldesc;
   mi_integer i, value, len;
   mi_string buffer[120], buf2[20];

   pcoldesc = mi_collection_open(NULL, val1);
```

```
buffer[0] = 0;
/* the 1st element is element 1 (not 0) */
for (i = 1; MI_END_OF_DATA !=
   mi_collection_fetch(NULL, pcoldesc,
   MI_CURSOR_NEXT, 0, (MI_DATUM *)&value, &len);
      i++) {
  if (i > 1)
    sprintf(buf2, ", %d", value);
  else
    sprintf(buf2, "%d", value);
  strcat(buffer, buf2);
}
mi_collection_close(NULL, pcoldesc);
return(mi_string_to_lvarchar(buffer));
}
```

This function extracts the elements from a collection and
returns a character string displaying all the elements separated
by a comma. The first step of the execution is to open the collection. This is done with the `mi_collection_open()` function. The
first argument represents a database collection. For a user-defined
routine, the connection descriptor can be NULL as shown in our
code.

Once the collection is opened, we loop over the extraction of
collection elements until the `mi_collection_fetch()` function
returns a value that indicates the end of the collection. The
`mi_collection_fetch()` function takes the following arguments:

- **Connection:** A connection to the database. Once again, a
  NULL value can be used.
- **Collection descriptor:** This represents the result of the
  `mi_collection_open()` call.
- **Cursor action:** This value identifies which element represents the starting point of the operation (see the next subsection for details).
- **Jump offset:** This represents the offset where to find the
  element to work on (see the next section for details).
- **Datum:** This is the address of the buffer that receives the
  return value.
- **Length:** This is the address of the integer that receives the
  length of the datum fetched.

When a collection is opened, the current position is set before the first element. Our processing loop uses a cursor action of `MI_CURSOR_NEXT` with a jump offset of zero. This means that the current position cursor is moved to the next element and the value is returned. It is easy to see that this goes on until we reach the end of the collection.

In this example, because we knew the type of the elements within the collection, we were able to simplify the processing loop. The `mi_collection_fetch()` function can return six different values. It would be better to test all the possible return values. This is similar to the row type processing. The six possible values returned by the `mi_collection_fetch()` function are `MI_NULL_VALUE`, `MI_END_OF_DATA`, `MI_ERROR`, `MI_ROW_VALUE`, `MI_COLLECTION_VALUE`, and `MI_NORMAL_VALUE`. The values are self-explanatory so we won't cover them any further.

Once we have processed all the collection elements, our loop exits. We then close the collection with `mi_collection_close()` and return the result. Since our result is in a NULL-terminated string, we can convert it to a `mi_lvarchar` type by using the `mi_string_to_lvarchar()` function. This is a convenience function that frees us from having to execute the multiple steps of extracting the string length, creating a `mi_lvarchar` variable of that length, and setting the value with the buffer. Since the `mi_string_to_lvarchar()` allocates memory, you should always keep in mind the current memory duration and when the `mi_lvarchar` structure should be released.

Cursor Action and Jump Offset

The code example in the preceding section can process any type of collection. It processes a collection sequentially by using the `MI_CURSOR_NEXT` cursor action value. There are seven possible cursor action values:

- `MI_CURSOR_NEXT`: Operate on the element after the current position.
- `MI_CURSOR_PRIOR`: Operate on the element before the current position.
- `MI_CURSOR_FIRST`: Operate on the first element.
- `MI_CURSOR_LAST`: Operate on the last element.

- `MI_CURSOR_ABSOLUTE`: Use the jump offset element to find the desired position relative to the beginning of the collection.
- `MI_CURSOR_RELATIVE`: Use the jump offset element to find the desired position relative to the current position in the collection.
- `MI_CURSOR_CURRENT`: Operate on the element at the current position.

With the exception of the `MI_CURSOR_ABSOLUTE`, all of these cursor actions can be used with all collection types.

The `MI_CURSOR_ABSOLUTE` cursor action only works with `LIST` collections and it requires a jump offset greater than zero because collection indexing starts at one. A `LIST` collection is an ordered set of values, whereas `SET` and `MULTISET` are unordered. It makes sense to request an element from a specific position in an ordered set. This can be done with either an absolute position or a position relative to the current cursor position. This is similar in concept to file positioning in operating systems (see `lseek()` and `fseek()` from the C library). The relative position accepts a jump offset of zero. This is equivalent to asking for the value at the current position.

The jump offset is used only with the cursor actions `MI_CURSOR_ABSOLUTE` and `MI_CURSOR_RELATIVE`. In any other cases, its value should be set to zero. The jump offset value must always be zero when dealing with `SET` and `MULTISET` collection types. Since these collection types are unordered, it does not make sense to provide a positioning offset.

Returning a Collection Type

A user-defined routine may return a collection. The following code shows a function that takes four integers as arguments and returns a collection:

```
MI_COLLECTION *cre8col(mi_integer one, mi_integer two,
        mi_integer three, mi_integer four,
        MI_FPARAM *fp)
{
    MI_TYPEID    *tid, *tid2;
```

```
                MI_COLLECTION  *col;
                MI_COLL_DESC   *colldesc;
                mi_integer     ret;

                tid = mi_fp_rettype(fp, 0);
                col = mi_collection_create(NULL, tid);
                colldesc = mi_collection_open(NULL, col);

                ret = mi_collection_insert(NULL, colldesc,
                                        (MI_DATUM)one,
                                          MI_CURSOR_NEXT, 0);
                ret = mi_collection_insert(NULL, colldesc,
                                    (MI_DATUM)two, MI_CURSOR_NEXT,
                                    0);
                ret = mi_collection_insert(NULL, colldesc,
                                    (MI_DATUM)three, MI_CURSOR_NEXT,
                                    0);
                ret = mi_collection_insert(NULL, colldesc,
                                    (MI_DATUM)four, MI_CURSOR_NEXT,
                                    0);
                ret = mi_collection_close(NULL, colldesc);

                return(col);
            }
```

This code is very simple. We first got the type of the return value as defined in the function creation statement. The type identifier allowed us to create the collection and open it. This is followed by four sequential insert statements, one for each argument passed to the routine.

Creating Complex Types

In the previous sections, we saw some examples of how to create complex types. There are at least three ways to get the information needed to create complex types. The easiest way is to use the type identifier from an argument or the return value as provided in the MI_FPARAM parameter. For example, if the collection type is fully defined in the return value, we can use something like the following:

```
MI_TYPEID      *tid;
MI_COLLECTION  *col;

tid = mi_fp_rettype(fp, 0);
col = mi_collection_create(NULL, tid);
```

We have seen this code several times in this chapter, as recently as the preceding subsection. If for any reason you cannot use the return value, it is possible to obtain a type identifier from a type name. If you decide to return a `myrow` named row type, you can create a new row, using code similar to the following:

```
MI_TYPEID      *tid;
MI_ROW_DESC    *rd, *rd2;
MI_ROW         *prow;
MI_DATUM       datums[ <number_of_entries> ];
mi_boolean     isnull[ <number_fo_entries> ];

tid = mi_typestring_to_id(NULL, "myrow");
rd = mi_row_desc_create(tid);
. . . (setup each entry)
prow = mi_row_create(NULL, rd, datums, isnull);
```

In the case of row types including complex types, additional work is required to create each field within the row type.

Finally, we can create a complex type based on the literal definition of the type:

```
MI_TYPEID      *tid;
MI_COLLECTION  *col;

tid = mi_typestring_to_id(NULL,
   "SET(integer NOT NULL)");
col = mi_collection_create(NULL, tid);
```

In this case, instead of passing a type name to the `mi_typestring_to_id()` function, we passed the literal definition of the type.

In general, we should expect to be able to use the first method and extract the type identifier from the MI_FPARAM parameter. However, if other situations arise, we are still able to create the required type using one of the two other methods.

MI_CONNECTION **Usage**

Many of the DataBlade API functions we have seen in this chapter require MI_CONNECTION pointer as their first argument. These functions were used to create complex types and to manipulate collections. Looking back, we notice that all the examples using these functions used a NULL argument instead of a MI_CONNECTION pointer. The *DataBlade API Programmer's Manual*[1] (at least in version 9.1) does not make any mention of this fact in the function descriptions.

Creating a connection to a database is an expensive operation. The DataBlade Development Kit (DBDK) automatically generates the code to open and close a connection in user-defined routines. You should always pay close attention to the need for database connections in the code you write or get generated by DBDK. Your user-defined routine may get called thousands of times in an SQL statement. This simple change of using a NULL connection can provide noticeable performance improvement.

Distinct Types

A distinct type takes its definition from a type that already exists in the database. It is not limited to the database-based types but can use any available type. Consider the following statements:

```
CREATE DISTINCT TYPE capitalExpense AS Money(10,2);
CREATE DISTINCT TYPE OperationalExpense AS
   Money(10,2);
```

---

[1]*DataBlade API Programmer's Manual* (Menlo Park, CA: Informix Software, 1998).

```
CREATE TABLE distinct_tab (
  col1  capitalExpense,
  col2  operationalExpense
);

INSERT INTO distinct_tab VALUES("10.00", "11.00");
INSERT INTO distinct_tab VALUES("20.00", "21.00");
```

We created two distinct types that are both based on the same base type. The database server automatically creates two explicit casts for each distinct type to cast to and from the base type. We then created a table using these types and inserted some values. Since the database server knows the base type, we can start working with these types right away without having to create additional functions. For example,

```
SELECT SUM(col1) FROM distinct_tab;

(sum)  $30.00

1 row(s) retrieved.
```

The SUM aggregate function uses the "+" operator to do its work. The database server looks for a "+" operator that takes two values of type capitalExpense. Since the server does not find the operator, it uses the base type operator instead.

Distinct types implement strong typing. Any attempt to mix it with either the base type or with another distinct type of the same base type results in an error:

```
SELECT col1 + "1.00"::money FROM distinct_tab;
  674: Routine (plus) can not be resolved.
```

This statement casts the "1.00" character string to a money type. We solve this problem by casting the string to capitalExpense. We may be tempted to create a "+" operator to remove the casting requirement. This has an interesting side effect that we will see later. First, let's see how to implement the operator:

```
CREATE FUNCTION plus(capitalExpense, Money)
RETURNS capitalExpense
```

```
WITH(NOT VARIANT, PARALLELIZABLE)
EXTERNAL NAME ". . ."
LANGUAGE C
END FUNCTION;
```

We saw in Chap. 2 that a "+" operator is implemented by creating a function with "plus" as its name. The implementation is very simple:

```
mi_money *plus(mi_money *val1, mi_money *val2,
               MI_FPARAM *fp)
{
  mi_money *retval;
  mi_integer ret;

  retval = mi_alloc(sizeof(mi_money));
  ret = decadd(val1, val2, retval);

  return(retval);
}
```

Since the distinct type is based on the `money` type, our function works with this base type. The `decadd()` function comes from ESQL/C and takes three `dec_t` types as argument. As we saw in Chap. 5, the `mi_money`, `mi_decimal`, and `dec_t` types are equivalent.

With this new function installed in the server, we can successfully perform the SELECT statement above. However, the following statement still fails because the database server cannot resolve the `plus()` routine:

```
SELECT "1.00"::money + col1 FROM distinct_tab;
```

We need to define an additional `plus()` function that reverses the types of its arguments. This new definition can use the same C implementation because the arguments are the same in the implementation.

Adding the `plus()` routine has an interesting side effect. The following statement now completes without error:

```
SELECT col1 + col2 FROM distinct_tab;
```

The database server sees that the arguments to one of the available `plus()` functions are `capitalExpense` and `money`. Since the `operationalExpense` type can be cast to `money`, it uses that `plus()` function to perform the operation.

In general, it is probably not a good idea to implement functions that mix the distinct type and the base type, because it allows for operations between any distinct types based on the same base type.

Distinct types provide a mechanism for strong typing in the server. It allows the system designer to implement specific operations in the design. Distinct types also better document the schema by having more specific types used. These types can match the business types closely. It is then easier to figure out what operations make sense. If we see the different expense types within the schema, we can easily deduce what we can do with the types. If we only had money types, we could be left wondering what these amounts really represent.

Opaque Types

Opaque types are an important part of the extensibility of IDS.2000. As the name implies, the database server does not know the content of an opaque type. We need to implement several functions to teach the database how to manipulate these new types.

This chapter covers the implementation of both fixed-size and variable-size opaque types. It discusses the implementation of support functions to convert from external representation to internal representation, as well as all the aspects of inserting, retrieving, and transferring to and from the client application.

Opaque types often require additional functions to implement basic relational operations. These functions are also discussed below.

Why Use Opaque Types?

Database vendors have years of expertise in storing and retrieving large amount of data. The hope is that efficient manipulation of data will result in better processing of business information. Database vendors are experts at implementing a specific database model. This does not make them experts in specific business domains.

Opaque types allow the business experts to implement the representation of their business data that makes the most sense in light of the processing required. This functionality puts the power back in the hands of the domain experts.

In many situations, system designers have to compromise their design to fit the relational model. This often complicates the design and negatively impacts performance. With the help of opaque types and other features provided by IDS.2000, the compromises are reduced. This results in faster application development, simpler design, and faster applications.

Domain experts have to come up with the best use of this technology and the proper representation of their business types. Opaque types can be used to provide transparent data compression, date and time implementations that take time zones and daylight savings time into consideration, and XML document support, among other things.

Elements of Opaque Types

The definition of an opaque type includes the opaque type characteristics and a set of support functions that augment the database server's capabilities so that it can manipulate the new type. Table 7–1 lists some support functions that can be created for an opaque type.

Table 7–1 Support functions for opaque types.

input/output	send/receive	import/export	importbinary/exportbinary
assign	destroy	lohandles	compare
equal	notequal	greaterthan	lessthan
greaterthanorequal	lessthanorequal	overlap	contains
within	union	size	inter
plus	minus	times	divide
positive	negative	concat	hash

An opaque type does not necessarily require all these support functions for its implementation. The minimum set of functions required includes input/output and possibly send/receive. Additional functions may be required, depending on the content of the opaque type. Furthermore, any processing inside the server requires additional functions.

Fixed and Variable-Size Opaque Type

Opaque types come in two general forms, fixed size and variable size, which must be processed in slightly different ways. Consider the following declarations:

```
CREATE OPAQUE TYPE myfix (
   INTERNALLENGTH=8, ALIGNMENT=4
);
CREATE OPAQUE TYPE myvar (
   INTERNALLENGTH=VARIABLE, MAXLEN=128, ALIGNMENT=4
);
```

The first statement creates a fixed-length opaque type. The database server then knows that a new type of name myfix is available and that it requires eight bytes of storage. This storage must be aligned on a four-byte boundary, which is the default alignment.

This definition provides enough information for the database server to manipulate, store, and retrieve this opaque type. All functions within the server can receive the myfix opaque type and pass it around.

The second statement creates an opaque type named myvar. The type is declared to be of variable length with a maximum size of 128 bytes. It uses the default alignment on a 4-byte boundary.

The myvar type is passed around using pointers, as is the myfix type. However, the database server does not know how to find the size of this type: Since it has been declared variable length, its size can vary from one value to another. Because the type is opaque, the database server has no means to find out the amount of storage that needs to be manipulated.

IDS.2000 solves this problem by wrapping the variable-length opaque type into a mi_lvarchar variable. A mi_lvarchar variable contains the size of its data portion. The database server can then use this information to manipulate the opaque type. This means that any variable-size opaque type must always by wrapped into a `mi_lvarchar` variable. Any functions that receive or return the opaque type in fact receive and return a `mi_lvarchar` that contains the opaque type.

Let's illustrate what we have just discussed with specific examples starting with the fixed-size opaque type. We can define a function that performs some transformations on the `myfix` opaque type and return a `myfix` opaque type:

```
CREATE OPAQUE TYPE myfix (
   INTERNALLENGTH=8, ALIGNMENT=4
);


CREATE FUNCTION myfixfn(myfix)
RETURNING myfix
WITH (not variant)
EXTERNAL NAME ". . ."
LANGUAGE C;
```

The C function receives a pointer to the internal representation of the `myfix` opaque type. The structure of the `myfix` opaque type and the `myfixfn()` function prototype is

```
typedef struct {
   int a;
   int b;
} MYFIX;

MYFIX *myfixfn(MYFIX *val1, MI_FPARAM *fp);
```

We defined a structure that includes two integers as the representation of the `myfix` opaque type. The `myfixfn()` function uses pointers to `MYFIX` structures to match the SQL declaration of the function.

For the variable-size opaque type `myvar`, the function creation statement is similar to that of the previous function:

```
CREATE OPAQUE TYPE myvar (
   INTERNALLENGTH=VARIABLE, MAXLEN=128, ALIGNMENT=4
);
```

```
CREATE FUNCTION myvarfn(myvar)
RETURNING myvar
WITH (not variant)
EXTERNAL NAME ". . ."
LANGUAGE C;
```

The difference between the two types is evident in the C declaration:

```
typedef struct {
  int len;
  char buf[1];
} MYVAR;

mi_lvarchar *myvarfn(mi_lvarchar *val1, MI_FPARAM
  *fp);
```

The MYVAR structure defined its first element as an integer and its second element as a character array with a length of one. This structure represents a standard C trick to implement a variable-size structure. We can define the real size of the array by allocating more memory than is required for the structure. The additional memory goes directly to the array buf.

The myvarfn() function takes a mi_lvarchar pointer as argument and returns a mi_lvarchar pointer result. The myvar opaque type is wrapped into the mi_lvarchar argument. The function can get to it using the following code:

```
MYVAR *pvar;

pvar = (MYVAR *)mi_get_vardata(val1);
```

The mi_get_vardata() function returns a character pointer to the data contained in the mi_lvarchar variable passed as argument. The result is cast to the MYVAR pointer type and can then be manipulated. This raises an interesting issue. The data pointer comes from the input argument. Input arguments should not be modified inside a function. This is a programming rule defined by Informix. If the data manipulation requires modification, a copy of the MYVAR content should be made.

Returning a variable-size opaque type involves the reverse process. A `mi_lvarchar` variable must be allocated to wrap the opaque type:

```
MYVAR *pvar;
Mi_lvarchar *retval;
.  .  .
retval = mi_new_var(sizeof(MYVAR) + pvar->len);
mi_set_vardata(retval, (mi_char *)pvar);
```

This code assumes that the `pvar` variable was initialized to the address of a `MYVAR` variable. The `mi_new_var()` function allocates a new `mi_lvarchar` variable. Its argument represents the size of the data buffer inside the variable. The `len` element represents the length of the character buffer, and we add the size of the structure to it. Once the variable is created, we copy the `MYVAR` variable by using the `mi_set_vardata()`. This function uses the size of the data buffer that was defined in the previous statement as the number of bytes to copy from its second argument.

With this covered, we can now go over the multiple support functions that can be implemented. We do not cover these functions alphabetically; for the most part we present them in the order they are required

Input and Output Functions

These functions perform the operations of converting the internal representation of the data to its external representation, and vice versa. The input function converts from character representation to the opaque type, and the output function converts from the opaque type internal representation to characters:

```
CREATE FUNCTION myfixinput(lvarchar)
RETURNING myfix
WITH (not variant)
EXTERNAL NAME ".  .  ."
LANGUAGE C;
```

```
CREATE FUNCTION myfixoutput(myfix)
RETURNING lvarchar
WITH (not variant)
EXTERNAL NAME ". . ."
LANGUAGE C;
```

The `myfixinput()` function takes an LVARCHAR argument. Any character type maps to this type. At this point it returns an opaque type that can then be stored by the database server. The second function provides the reversed conversion.

So far we have defined two functions that can do the necessary conversions, but the database server does not know that these functions were provided for this purpose. They could do additional transformations that are not appropriate for input and output functions. We tell the database server about their role by creating cast functions:

```
CREATE IMPLICIT CAST (LVARCHAR AS myfix WITH
    myfixinput);
CREATE EXPLICIT CAST (myfix AS LVARCHAR WITH
    myfixoutput);
```

We declare the cast from the literal representation to the internal representation implicit because the server cannot expect to be told explicitly about these conversions. The reverse operation is done explicitly because the default manipulation is in the internal format. Assuming that we provided C implementations for the input and output functions, we can now do the following:

```
CREATE TABLE fix_tab (
  col1  myfix
);
INSERT INTO fix_tab VALUES("2, 3");
SELECT * FROM fix_tab;
```

Since the opaque type has been created, we can create a table that contains a column of that type. The insert of a literal representation of the opaque type is successful because of the input function, and the select is successful because of the output function.

The myfix opaque type consists of two integer values. The previous example shows the literal representation of the opaque type as an integer followed by a comma, a space, and the second integer. This is a totally arbitrary representation that is decided during the implementation. We could have decided to use a space (or any other separator) between the integers. These implementation decisions are similar to any others (e.g., a datetime representation). Let's look at a simple implementation of the myfixinput() function:

```
MYFIX *myfixinput(mi_lvarchar *val1, MI_FPARAM *fp)
{
    MYFIX *ret;
    mi_string *buf;

    ret = (MYFIX *)mi_alloc(sizeof(MYFIX));
    buf = mi_lvarchar_to_string(val1);
    sscanf(buf, "%d, %d", &ret->a, &ret->b);
    return(ret);
}
```

After allocating space for a MYFIX variable, the function extracts the character string from the mi_lvarchar argument. Then it uses the sscanf() function from the C library to extract the two integers from the character string into the elements of the structure. The result is returned to the caller, most likely the database server.

This function is adequate for a demonstration but requires much more work to make it production grade. At minimum we should check the result of the sscanf() function to make sure it returned the appropriate number of values—two in this case. Otherwise, we should generate an exception (see Section "Raising Exceptions," Chap. 5). In many situations, we should write our own parsing function. The DataBlade Development Kit (DBDK) generates scanning functions. These functions are designed to handle more general situations, as in the case of GLS (global language support).

The output function does the reverse operation. The following shows a basic implementation:

```
mi_lvarchar *myfixoutput(MYFIX *val1, MI_FPARAM *fp)
{
```

```
mi_lvarchar *ret;
mi_string buffer[30];

sprintf(buffer, "%d, %d", val1->a, val1->b);
ret = mi_string_to_lvarchar(buffer);
return(ret);
}
```

This function uses a fixed length buffer that is created on the stack when the function starts executing. Since the maximum integer value needs ten digits for its representation, the buffer size is safe in this situation. It makes sense to use a fixed-size buffer in this case instead of dynamically allocating memory using `mi_alloc()`. It saves us some processing time otherwise required for allocating memory and then releasing the buffer memory once we don't need it anymore. The `sprintf()` function creates a character representation of the opaque type, and the resulting string is used to create a new `mi_lvarchar` variable. A pointer to the variable is then returned to the caller.

Import and Export Functions

If we were to create an input file and try to load it using the LOAD command from the dbaccess utility, we would get an error because of missing functions. The operations performed by LOAD and UNLOAD are referred to as *bulk copy*. When loading in bulk, there may be some conversion steps that can be preserved from one value to another, making the operation more efficient. The import and export functions have the following declarations:

```
CREATE FUNCTION myfiximport(impexp)
RETURNING myfix
WITH (not variant)
EXTERNAL NAME ". . ."
LANGUAGE C;

CREATE FUNCTION myfixexport(myfix)
RETURNING impexp
WITH (not variant)
EXTERNAL NAME ". . ."
LANGUAGE C;
```

These functions are very similar to the input and output functions. The difference is the use of `impexp` instead of `LVARCHAR` in the first of two function definitions. However, the C implementation still receives a `mi_lvarchar` pointer argument. We can consider `impexp` as a distinct type of `LVARCHAR`. This means that we can use the same C implementation to provide the bulk copy capability. The `EXTERNAL NAME` portion of the `CREATE FUNCTION` statements can refer to the same library member as the input and output functions. The function creation statements are still required because they identify functions with specific types of argument and return values. These functions are then used in the creation of casts to indicate that they are used in the bulk copy operations:

```
CREATE IMPLICIT CAST (impexp AS myfix WITH
    myfiximport);
CREATE EXPLICIT CAST (myfix AS impexp WITH
    myfixexport);
```

The import and export casts are defined as implicit and explicit, respectively, for the same reasons as the input and output casts. If we were to use the input and output functions in these casts, the cast creation would still work but a bulk copy operation would fail with an error claiming that no cast exists from `impexp` to `myfix`. This error occurs because no input function exists with the appropriate signature. This means that the `input()` and `output()` function implementations can be used to provide the `import()` and `export()` functionality but that we must still use `CREATE FUNCTION` calls with the proper signature so the server can resolve to the correct cast implementation.

Send and Receive Functions

We saw that the input and output functions perform conversions between client and server for literal values. The send and receive functions perform the conversion required between the client and the server when the opaque type is exchanged in binary mode. Continuing our example, we find the following function declarations:

```
CREATE FUNCTION myfixsend(myfix)
RETURNING sendrecv
WITH (not variant)
EXTERNAL NAME ". . ."
LANGUAGE C;

CREATE FUNCTION myfixrecv(sendrecv)
RETURNING myfix
WITH (not variant)
EXTERNAL NAME ". . ."
LANGUAGE C;
```

This time the type used for the conversion is sendrecv. This types ends up mapping to a mi_lvarchar in the C implementation. This means that the communication between a client and the server is always done through an LVARCHAR type container. Here is a very important point: Since a variable-size opaque type is already wrapped in an mi_lvarchar variable, there is no need to wrap it a second time. The use of a variable-size opaque type in the send and receive function is similar to the processing in any other user-defined routine. However, the fixed-size opaque type must be wrapped in a mi_lvarchar variable.

In addition, to make sure the opaque type is wrapped in a mi_lvarchar structure, the send and receive functions must take care of converting the data between machine types. Note the following:

```
int main(int argc, char **argv) {
   int i = 0x01020304;
   char *pbuf = (char *)&i;

   printf("bytes: %d, %d, %d, %d\n", (int)pbuf[0],
          (int)pbuf[1],(int)pbuf[2], (int)pbuf[3]);

   return(0);
}
```

This program sets the value of variable i so that we know the content of each byte. Then it displays the bytes from the beginning of the integer to its end. This function returns the following result on an Intel-based machine:

```
bytes: 4, 3, 2, 1
```

On a SPARC-based machine, the result is reversed. These two representations are referred to as big-endian and little-endian representations. The DataBlade API provides functions that handle this conversion. Before we look at the implementation, let's see the casts required for these functions:

```
CREATE EXPLICIT CAST (myfix AS sendrecv WITH
    myfixsend);
CREATE IMPLICIT CAST (sendrecv AS myfix WITH
    myfixrecv);
```

The casts show which functions must be used to perform the operations. A simple implementation of the myfixsend() is as follows:

```
mi_sendrecv *myfixsend(MYFIX *val1, MI_FPARAM *fp)
{
    mi_lvarchar *ret;
    MYFIX *pfix;

    ret = mi_new_var(sizeof(MYFIX));
    pfix = (MYFIX *)mi_get_vardata(ret);
    pfix->a = mi_fix_integer(val1->a);
    pfix->b = mi_fix_integer(val1->b);
    return((mi_sendrecv *)ret);
}
```

This function allocates a mi_lvarchar variable that has a buffer area the size of the MYFIX structure. It then obtains a pointer to the buffer area using mi_get_vardata() and casts it to a MYFIX pointer. The return values are set using the result of mi_fix_integer(). This function ensures that the correct byte ordering is used. The final result is returned to the caller, which transmits the information to the client.

The DataBlade API contains multiple functions that provide the proper conversion between machine types. When data alignment is also an issue, the DataBlade API provides additional functions. Table 7–2 lists the DataBlade API functions that relate to data conversion.

Table 7-2 Data conversion functions.

mi_fix_integer	mi_fix_smallint	mi_get_bytes	mi_get_date
mi_get_datetime	mi_get_decimal	mi_get_double_precision	mi_get_int8
mi_get_integer	mi_get_interval	mi_get_money	mi_get_real
mi_get_smallint	mi_get_string	mi_put_bytes	mi_put_date
mi_put_datetime	mi_put_decimal	mi_put_double_precision	mi_put_int8
mi_put_integer	mi_put_interval	mi_put_money	mi_put_real
mi_put_smallint	mi_put_string		

The receive function performs the opposite conversion. For completion, here is a simple implementation of the receive function for the MYFIX type:

```
MYFIX *myfixrecv(mi_sendrecv *val1, MI_FPARAM *fp)
{
  MYFIX *ret, *inval;

  ret = (MYFIX *)mi_alloc(sizeof(MYFIX));
  inval = (MYFIX *)mi_get_vardata(val1);
  ret->a = mi_fix_integer(inval->a);
  ret->b = mi_fix_integer(inval->b);
  return(ret);
}
```

This time we allocate a buffer for the MYFIX structure and populate it with a fixed-up value of the structure included in the mi_lvarchar variable passed as the function's first argument.

Importbinary and Exportbinary Functions

These functions are the binary counterparts of the import and export functions. As you may suspect, they can be implemented using the send and receive functions. Special caveats obtain due to the bulk copy nature of the operation (recall section, "Import and Export Functions"). Furthermore, they may provide additional support when dealing with smart large objects BLOB and CLOB). The function declarations for importbinary and exportbinary are

```
CREATE FUNCTION myfiximpbin (impexpbin)
RETURNING myfix
EXTERNAL NAME ". . ."
LANGUAGE C;

CREATE FUNCTION myfixexpbin (myfix)
RETURNING impexpbin
EXTERNAL NAME ". . ."
LANGUAGE C;
```

This time, we use the impexpbin type as the target of the processing. The cast functions are declared as follows:

```
CREATE IMPLICIT cast (impexpbin AS myfix WITH
   myfiximpbin);
CREATE EXPLICIT cast (myfix AS impexpbin WITH
   myfixexpbin);
```

The Compare **Function**

Now that we are able to insert and retrieve opaque types, the next step is to allow for operations on opaque types within SQL statements. The compare function provides a large amount of functionality that includes any comparison operation. The function must be called compare in the SQL declaration. The C implementation can have a different name, which is declared in the EXTERNAL NAME portion of the create statement. This statement is as follows:

```
CREATE FUNCTION compare(myfix, myfix)
RETURNING integer
WITH (not variant)
EXTERNAL NAME ". . ."
LANGUAGE C;
```

The function signature resolves the `compare` function during any SQL operations that require it. The return type is always an integer for any argument type. The return value represents three different possibilities. If the first argument is smaller than the second argument, a negative value is returned. If the values are equal, zero is returned. If the first argument is larger than the second argument, a positive value is returned.

Once the function is implemented, it is possible to issue SQL statements that include comparisons and the following operations: BETWEEN, ORDER BY, UNIQUE or DISTINCT, UNION, and any operation required in a b-tree index.

Comparison Functions

The comparison functions include `lessthanorequal()`, `lessthan()`, `equal()`, `notequal()`, `greaterthanorequal()`, and `greaterthan()`. These function names act as keywords that map to the related symbol. Consider the following statement:

```
SELECT col1 FROM fix_tab
WHERE col1 > '2, 3'::myfix ;
```

The WHERE clause uses the ">" symbol. The database server will look for a function of name `greatherthan()` that takes two arguments of type `myfix`. The create statement for this function would be:

```
CREATE FUNCTION greaterthan(myfix, myfix)
RETURNING boolean
WITH(not variant)
EXTERNAL NAME ". . ."
LANGUAGE C;
```

This definition format applies to all the comparison functions. Additional `greaterthan()` functions can be added to allow mixed-type comparisons. We see that the function returns a BOOLEAN type. As we saw in Chap. 4, the C implementation of the function uses `mi_boolean`, which is equivalent to `mi_integer`. It turns out that a return value of zero indicates a false result, and any other nonzero value represents a true result.

The definition above is not quite adequate. When the database server receives a SQL statement, it first parses the statement and analyzes it. Part of the analysis may include rewriting the query in a more efficient manner. The CREATE FUNCTION statement provides modifiers that identify the transformations that are allowed. These modifiers are COMMUTATOR and NEGATOR. The following statements illustrate the situation:

```
A > B ⟷ B < A
A > B ⟷ NOT (A <= B)
```

The first statement says that if A is greater than B, then B is less than A. So, lessthan is the COMMUTATOR function for greaterthan. The second statement says that if A is greater than B, it means that A is not less than or equal to B. The lessthanorequal() function is the NEGATOR of greater than. We can rewrite the CREATE FUNCTION statement as follows:

```
CREATE FUNCTION greaterthan(myfix, myfix)
RETURNING boolean
WITH (NOT VARIANT, COMMUTATOR=lessthan,
                   NEGATOR=lessthanorequal)
EXTERNAL NAME ". . ."
LANGUAGE C;
```

The functions lessthan() and lessthanorequal() don't need to exist when you create the greaterthan() function. They will be retrieved at execution time if the optimizer decides that it needs to rewrite the statement using the greaterthan() function.

Assign and Destroy Functions

The assign function is used to perform operations just before the element of the type it supports is saved to disk. This occurs in the case of INSERT and UPDATE statements. The destroy function provides the reverse operation when an element is removed in the case of DELETE and DROP SQL statements.

These functions are useful when an opaque type contains one or more handles to smart large objects (BLOB and CLOB). We cover these functions in details in Chap. 10 where we discuss large object manipulations. Assuming an opaque type names mylo, the function creation statements are as follows:

```
CREATE FUNCTION assign (mylo)
RETURNING mylo
EXTERNAL NAME ". . ."
LANGUAGE C;

CREATE PROCEDURE destroy (mylo)
EXTERNAL NAME ". . ."
LANGUAGE C;
```

Note that the destroy function does not return any value, so it is declared as a procedure instead of a function. The difference between a function and a procedure is that a function is expected to return a result whereas a procedure does not return any value. We will see detailed applications of these functions in Chap. 10.

Math Functions

The math functions cover plus(), minus(), times(), divide(), positive(), and negative(). These keywords map to the well-known arithmetic symbols. The unary "+" and "−" are referred to by the functions positive() and negative(). Here are two examples of function declarations:

```
CREATE FUNCTION minus(myfix, myfix)
RETURNING myfix
WITH (NOT VARIANT)
EXTERNAL NAME ". . ."
LANGUAGE C;

CREATE FUNCTION negate(myfix)
RETURNING myfix
```

```
WITH (NOT VARIANT)
EXTERNAL NAME ". . ."
LANGUAGE C;
```

The keywords `minus()` and `negate()` are overloaded to accept the opaque type `myfix` as argument. Of course this overloading does not apply for the name of the C functions. It is a good idea to prefix the name of the C function with some type name identifier. In this case, the C implementation names are `myfixminus()` and `myfixnegate()`. We can now issue SQL statements such as

```
SELECT col1, col1 - '1, 1'::myfix from fix_tab;
SELECT col1, -col1 from fix_tab;
```

The first `SELECT` statement uses the `minus()` operator with two `myfix` arguments, and the second one uses the unary operator `negate()` to resolve the operation.

All the other math functions use the same principle where a specific keyword is overloaded to provide the requested functionality.

The b-tree Functions

IDS.2000 provides a generic b-tree indexing implementation that can be used to create indexes over opaque types. A b-tree index may be selected by the optimizer when one or more of the following operations are involved: `lessthan()`, `lessthanorequal()`, `equal()`, `greaterthan()`, `greaterthanorequal()`. The BETWEEN operation could also end up using the index. Note that the `notequal()` function is not on the list. Its selectivity would most likely cause the optimizer to do a table scan instead of using the index. However, the query optimizer may rewrite a complex query and be able to rephrase it using `equal()`, thereby achieving the right selectivity to use the index.

The only function we need to implement to take advantage of b-trees is the `compare()` function. With it the database server is able to deduce any of the comparison functions. The `compare()` function returns a negative number if the first argument is smaller than the second. It returns zero when they are equal, and a positive number if the first argument is larger. With these three possible results, we can easily implement any of the comparison functions. Here are two examples using `notequal()` and `lessthan()`:

```
mi_integer myfixnotequal(MYFIX *val1, MYFIX *val2,
                         MI_FPARAM *fp)
{
  if (0 != myfixcompare(val1, val2))
    return(1);
  return(0);
}
mi_integer myfixlessthan(MYFIX *val1, MYFIX *val2,
                         MI_FPARAM *fp)
{
  if (0 > myfixcompare(val1, val2))
    return(1);
  return(0);
}
```

These functions illustrate how the `compare()` function can be used to implement the comparison operators. But there are other issues to consider: The `myfixcompare()` function implements the compare operation for the `myfix` type. As for any other function, it takes an additional argument that is a pointer to a `MI_FPARAM` structure. Our use here does not pass that additional argument. This is fine if the function does not use the structure during its execution. A second issue: This code assumes that `myfixcompare()` is part of the same dynamic library. This way the function can be resolved by name. If `myfixcompare()` is not in the same library, the execution will fail at runtime with an undefined symbol. It is possible to call functions that reside in different dynamic libraries, however. This is covered in Chap. 9 where we discuss the fastpath interface.

The r-tree Functions

IDS.2000 provides a new type of indexing method called an r-tree index. An r-tree is similar in structure to a b-tree except that instead of dividing indexed values into ranges of values that are distributed in a balanced way throughout a tree structure, it uses a concept of bounding boxes to delimit the values.

The IDS.2000 r-tree implementation is designed as an extensible facility. It requires two sets of functions. The first set, the support functions, are used to navigate the r-tree and retrieve values. The second set, the strategy functions, are the operations that appear in an SQL statement to tell the optimizer that the index can be used. The two sets of functions are packaged into what is called an operator class. An operator class defines the functionality used by an indexing method to store and retrieve values. The r-tree implementation defines a default operator class called `rtree_ops`.

The r-tree default operator class defines three support functions. They have the following signatures:

```
mi_integer Inter(UDT *val1, UDT *val2,
                 UDT *val3, MI_FPARAM *fp);

mi_integer Size(UDT *val1, mi_double_precision *val2,
                MI_FPARAM *fp);

mi_integer Union(UDT *val1, UDT *val2,
                 UDT *val3, MI_FPARAM *fp);
```

These function prototypes refer to the UDT type. This type represents the opaque type we want to index with an tree index. The `Inter()` function calculates the intersection of the first two values and returns the result in the third argument. The `Size()` function returns the size of the region covered by `val1` into the double precision argument `val2`. The `Union()` function returns the overall bounding box that includes `val1` and `val2`. The result is stored in the third argument.

The strategy functions defined in the `rtree_ops` operator class have the following signatures:

```
mi_boolean Contains(UDT *val1, UDT *val2,
  MI_FPARAM *fp);

mi_boolean Equal(UDT *val1, UDT *val1,
  MI_FPARAM *fp);
```

```
mi_boolean Overlap(UDT *val1, UDT *val2,
    MI_FPARAM *fp);

mi_boolean Within(UDT *val1, UDT *val2,
    MI_FPARAM *fp);
```

All seven of these functions return a BOOLEAN value indicating whether the condition has been met. To take advantage of r-trees, we need to implement an opaque type and the seven functions if you want to use the default operator class. It is also possible to define our own operator class. This is what the geodetic DataBlade does. Its operator class is defined as follows:

```
CREATE OPCLASS GeoObject_ops FOR rtree
STRATEGIES (Intersect, Equal, Contains, Inside,
    Outside)
SUPPORT (Union, Size, Inter);
```

Note that the geodetic DataBlade implements the same support functions but different strategies functions. Since this DataBlade has its own operator class, the index creation must identify the class; otherwise the default operator class will be used:

```
CREATE INDEX tab_ix
ON tab_name(colname GeoObject_ops)
USING rtree;
```

The operator class is identified with the column to be indexed. There is one more issue that needs to be addressed when using r-trees. As in the case of the geodetic DataBlade module, several data types must be used within a single index. Table 7–3 shows all the types implemented by the geodetic datablade.

Table 7–3 Geodetic types.

GeoObject	GeoCircle	GeoEllipse	GeoTimeRange
GeoBox	GeoPoint	GeoCoords	GeoLineseg
GeoString	GeoRing	GeoAltRange	GeoPolygon

If we index a column that contains a `GeoPoint`, we may want to select the rows that have their points within a specific region, let's say a `GeoCircle`. The geodetic DataBlade works around this issue by defining what we can consider a type hierarchy. All types are in fact `GeoObjects`. The type includes an indicator that specifies the exact type of the object. The geodetic implementation defines implicit casts for all types to `GeoObject`. This way all types can be compared.

Creating types and implementations using an r-tree index is quite involved. This subject is beyond the scope of this book. Luckily, Informix provides an example implementation with the *DataBlade Development Kit* (DBDK). This r-tree index implementation can be found in:

```
$INFORMIXDIR/dbdk/examples/indexes/dapi/rtree
```

This is a basic implementation that can be used as a starting point for your own implementation. Some additional functionality needs to be implemented along the way, but it is relatively minor. In a few days you can have a decent implementation ready to go. This way you can test the advantages of this indexing method through basic capabilities before you decide which production-grade product is the best fit for your environment.

Like and Matches Functions

Both functions, `like()` and `matches()`, provide wildcard matching capabilities. They are part of the SQL syntax and can be overloaded to support opaque types. Both functions can be defined with two or three arguments. One simple way to deal with this is to provide three arguments and give the third argument a default value:

```
CREATE FUNCTION like(myfix, lvarchar, char(1)
   default '\')
RETURNING boolean
WITH (not variant)
EXTERNAL NAME ". . ."
LANGUAGE C;
```

This declaration defines a function that takes an opaque type, a character string, and a character and returns a truth value about the match. The `matches()` function would have a similar declaration. This declaration handles SQL statements, such as

```
SELECT * FROM fix_tab WHERE col1 like '1%';

SELECT * FROM fix_tab WHERE col1 like '1%' ESCAPE 'e';
```

Since the first statement does not provide an escape clause, the default value is passed as the third argument. The second statement uses the value passed in the escape clause. Both statements resolve to the `like()` function described above.

Since we are using function overloading to provide support for our opaque type, we could decide to allow `like()` and `matches()` to support comparison of two opaque types with the following declaration:

```
CREATE FUNCTION like(myfix, myfix, char(1) default
    '\')
RETURNING boolean
WITH (NOT VARIANT)
EXTERNAL NAME ". . ."
LANGUAGE C;
```

This declaration does not make sense with the `myfix` type, but there can be business situations where comparing two elements of different types must be done according to specific rules. The same reasoning applies for any other operations between types.

Other Functions

IDS.2000 provides other functions that can be overloaded. They include the functions `concat()`, `sin()`, `sqrt()`, among other things. These functions are listed in Chap. 2. We can also implement functions that are specific to the subject domain. The key to all this added functionality is consistency with the original intent of the function. The final test of added functionality is that its meaning should be obvious when used in an SQL statement.

NULL **Values**

Note that all the functions discussed in this chapter do not handle NULL values. To do so, they require the HANDLESNULLS function modifier. When one of these functions receives a NULL value as argument, the database server skips the function execution and returns a NULL.

Iterator Functions

In some cases, you may need to have your user-defined routine return a set of values. You may want the UDR to extract the values out of a collection or out of an opaque type. Your UDR may have to extract values, too, simply because your function executes SQL statements, with must return a set of values. This type of function is called an iterator function.

The DataBlade API provides a way to write this type of function. This chapter covers the creation of iterator functions. We cover the API elements involved and the processing required within an iterator function. We also go over a few examples to illustrate the requirements in processing and memory utilization. Finally, we discuss the use of iterator functions within different processing contexts.

DataBlade API Elements

When an iterator function is executed, the database server calls the function multiple time in different contexts: initialization, processing, and cleanup. The function must find out which state it is in and remember where it left off at the last execution. The DataBlase API provides the following functions to accomplish this:

- `mi_fp_request(MI_FPARAM *fp)`
  This function takes the `MI_FPARAM` pointer that is passed in any user-defined routine execution and returns the state the execution is in. The possible values are: `SET_INIT`, `SET_RETONE`, `SET_END`, and `MI_ERROR`. The `SET_INIT` value indicates that the function is called to initialize its processing. The `SET_RETONE` value is used to ask for a value. The `SET_END` value is passed to the function to allow it to clean up any resources that were allocated during the processing. The `MI_ERROR` value is returned if the function terminates unsuccessfully. The `milib.h` include file defines an additional possible value, `SET_INVALID`, that does not appear to be used.
- `mi_fp_setisdone(MI_FPARAM *fp, mi_boolean val)`
  This DataBlade API function sets a value in the `MI_FPARAM` structure that indicates whether the function has returned all the values. If the value is set to `MI_FALSE`, the database server will call the iterator function again to ask for another value. If the value is set to `MI_TRUE`, the database server then knows that all the values have been returned. It will call the iterator function one more time with a request value of `SET_END`, to allow for any cleanup that may be required.
- `mi_fp_setfuncstate(MI_FPARAM *fp, void *mem)`
  This function saves information that can be retrieved from another invocation of the iterator function. The argument saved is in the form of a void pointer. The value saved can be either a pointer to the information or if a value as itself the information fits within four bytes.
- `void *mi_fp_funcstate(MI_FPARAM *fp)`
  The `mi_fp_funcstate()` returns the information that was saved in a previous call to the `mi_fp_setfuncstate()` function. The result must then be cast to the appropriate format, as we will see later.

Examples in the sections that follow illustrate how these API elements are used in an iterator function.

A Countdown Function

The following example implements an iterator function that returns integer values starting from the value of its first argument, down to zero. The declaration of an iterator function is similar to any other function except that it includes the `iterator` modifier:

```
CREATE FUNCTION do_iter0(INT)
RETURNING int
WITH (NOT VARIANT, ITERATOR)
EXTERNAL NAME
"$INFORMIXDIR/extend/udrbook/bin/chap8.bld(do_iter0)"
LANGUAGE C;
```

This function is executed with the EXECUTE FUNCTION statement. For example:

```
EXECUTE FUNCTION do_iter0(10);
```

The `do_iter0()` function is as follows:

```
#include <mi.h>
mi_integer do_iter0(mi_integer val1,
  MI_FPARAM *pfparam)
{
  mi_integer state, curval;

  state = mi_fp_request( pfparam );

  switch(state) {
    case SET_INIT:
        mi_fp_setfuncstate(pfparam, (void *)val1);
        break;
    case SET_RETONE:
        curval = (mi_integer)mi_fp_funcstate
        (pfparam);
        if (curval < 0 ) {
          mi_fp_setisdone(pfparam, MI_TRUE);
          break;
```

```
      }
      mi_fp_setfuncstate(pfparam,
        (void *)(curval - 1));
      return(curval);
   case SET_END:
      break;
   default: /* do any error processing required */
      break;
   } /* end switch */
   return(0);
}
```

The function source code starts as usual by including the `mi.h` file to incorporate all the function and type declarations needed. The iterator function follows a standard declaration where it takes an integer as input and returns an integer. There is no special argument needed for iterator functions. The standard `MI_FPARAM` pointer argument contains all we need in order to implement the iterator function.

The first thing the iterator function needs to do is get the type of request that is being performed by calling the `mi_fp_request()` function with the `MI_FPARAM` pointer as argument. The value returned is used in the `switch` statement to provide the proper processing.

The `SET_INIT` case provides the initialization of the function. In this case, we save the integer value in the `MI_FPARAM` structure. Since an integer is a four-byte value, we can save it directly—instead of having to allocate memory for it and also save the pointer to that memory location. The initialization is not expected to return a value that is part of the set. So the initialization is done and we break out of the switch statement and return zero.

The `SET_RETONE` case returns a value from the set. We first retrieve the value that was saved to find out where we are. We then test the value to find out if we are done. If so, we set the value indicating that the iteration is done using `mi_fp_setisdone()`. At this point, the value returned is not part of the return set. If we have a value to return, we first update the status value stored in the `MI_FPARAM` structure and then return the appropriate value.

Once we have indicated that the set of values is completed, the iterator function is called one last time with the `SET_END` request type. In this case, the function has nothing to do, so we simply return.

This iterator function could have returned NULL values by setting the NULL indicator to true using the mi_fp_returnisnull() function for a specific element of the set.

An Item Extraction Function

Most cases are more complex than the countdown example. The processing requires allocation of memory both to preserve the state of the execution and for the creation of the return values. To illustrate this type of processing, we will look at a function that takes a character string containing a list of items as input and returns each item separately.

Since we are dealing with character strings as input and output, we have a choice of definition for the function:

```
CREATE FUNCTION do_iter1(lvarchar)
RETURNS lvarchar
WITH (NOT VARIANT, ITERATOR)
EXTERNAL NAME
"$INFORMIXDIR/extend/udrbook/bin/chap8.bld(do_iter1)"
LANGUAGE C;
```

We could have chosen CHAR or VARCHAR as well. But because LVARCHAR allows for the processing and return of larger variable strings, we use this definition. The execution of the function goes as follows:

```
EXECUTE FUNCTION
do_iter1("Garden Hose;Work Bench;Garden Hose;Work
  Bench;");

(expression)

Garden Hose
Work Bench
Garden Hose
Work Bench
```

4 row(s) retrieved.

The do_iter1() function takes a character string of semi-colon-delimited fields and returns each field one at a time. The function source is

```c
#include <mi.h>

mi_lvarchar *do_iter1(mi_lvarchar *document,
                       MI_FPARAM *fparam)
{
  mi_lvarchar    *RetVal;          /* The return value.
  */
  mi_integer state, i, j;
  mi_string *bufstr;
  mi_string *input;
  mi_string *result;

  state = mi_fp_request(fparam);
  switch(state) {
  case SET_INIT:
        i = mi_get_varlen(document);
        input = mi_lvarchar_to_string(document);
        bufstr = (mi_string *)
                 mi_dalloc(i + 5, PER_COMMAND);
        strcpy(&bufstr[4], input);
        (*(int*)bufstr) = 4;
        mi_fp_setfuncstate(fparam, bufstr);
        return(0);
        break;
  case SET_RETONE:
        bufstr = (mi_string *)mi_fp_funcstate
           (fparam);
        i = *(int *)bufstr;
        if (bufstr[i] == ';')
            i++;
        if (bufstr[i] == 0) {
            mi_fp_setisdone(fparam, MI_TRUE);
            return(mi_string_to_lvarchar(bufstr));
        }
```

```
        for (j = i; bufstr[j] != ';' &&
            bufstr[j] != 0; j++);
        (*(int *)bufstr) = j;
        /* mi_fp_setfuncstate(fparam, bufstr); */
        result = mi_alloc(1 + j - i);
        strncpy(result, &bufstr[i], j - i);
        result[j - i] = 0;
        RetVal = mi_string_to_lvarchar(result);
        return(RetVal);
        break;
    case SET_END:
        bufstr = (mi_string *)mi_fp_funcstate
            (fparam);
        if (bufstr != NULL) mi_free(bufstr);
            return(0);
    default:
        break;
    } /* end switch */
    /* Return the function's return value. */
    return (0);
}
```

This function follows the same pattern as our countdown example: It retrieves the type of request before using a switch() statement to execute the proper operation. This time the input value is a reference to an LVARCHAR variable. This changes the way we save the input value for future processing.

The SET_INIT Section

The SET_INIT case prepares the environment for the processing. It extracts the length of the LVARCHAR variable and its character string. This time we need to allocate some memory to hold both the character string we are working on and information on where we are in the processing. We allocate enough space for an integer representing the current position, followed by enough memory to hold the NULL-terminated character string. The integer at the beginning of the buffer is set to four because it is the position of the first byte of the buffer.

The integer at the beginning of the buffer is initialized using the following statement:

```
(*(int*)bufstr) = 4;
```

Here is how it works. The variable `bufstr` is a pointer to characters. We first cast it to a pointer to integers. Since we don't want to set the pointer, we need to dereference the pointer with a "*" operation to get an integer to set. This operation provides the first integer in the array, that is, the integer is located in the first four bytes of the buffer. This could also have been expressed with

```
((int*)bufstr)[0] = 4;
```

This expression, however, can also access any integer element in the array pointed to by the integer pointer.

The memory allocation may be a little bit obscure. This shortcut can be better expressed by using a C structure:

```
struct processingState {
   int currentPos;
   mi_char buffer[1];
};
```

Assuming that the `bufstr` variable is a `processingState` structure, the memory allocation using this buffer and the initialization of the current position becomes:

```
bufstr = (struct processingState *)
            mi_dalloc(sizeof(struct processingState) + i,
                 PER_COMMAND);
bufstr->currentPos = 0;
```

The `mi_dalloc()` function is used to allocate memory using the PER_COMMAND duration. This way, the next time the database server calls the `do_iter1()` function, the memory is not released too early. The PER_COMMAND memory duration is valid for the duration of the SQL statement the function is in. The current position is initialized to zero because we can now address the buffer directly. This buffer declaration is a standard C trick to handle variable-size structures. This requires a little more explanation.

The buffer declaration in the `processingState` structure simply indicates that an array is allocated. In this case it happens to be for a length of one. Consider this:

```
struct processingState x;
.  .  .
if (x.buffer[2] == '\0')
.  .  .
```

Despite the fact that the buffer has a size of one, the `if` statement tests a character that is located in a memory location outside the variable. This code will compile and most likely run without problem, but potential intermittent problems may constitute a bug that could be very difficult to find.

When we allocate memory for a `processingState` structure, we can decide to allocate much more memory than the size of the structure. In theory this will simply be wasted memory. Since the memory follows the structure sequentially, it has the effect of allowing a larger size for the character buffer at the end of the structure. If we allocate an additional ten bytes, it is equivalent to having the following structure:

```
struct processingState {
  int currentPos;
  mi_char buffer[11];
};
```

We still have the choice to use only one byte in the buffer, but it is also appropriate to use up to eleven. In our code we allocate enough to accommodate the size of the character buffer that we want to process.

Without this C trick, we would have to use the following structure declaration:

```
struct processingState {
  int currentPos;
  mi_char *buffer;
};
```

It would force us to do an additional memory allocation with a PER_COMMAND duration. This is more expensive and also requires more work to manage it.

We can now return to the do_iter1() function. The next section of code handles the recurrent processing of the SET_RETONE case.

The SET_RETONE Section

The first thing that this section does is retrieve the pointer to the processing buffer that was allocated with a PER_COMMAND memory duration. Once the buffer is retrieved, we can initialize the current processing position. Due to the way the elements of the array are retrieved, the current position could be on the ";" separator character. The subsequent field starts at the next position.

The processing is simple: Find the position of the next separator, starting at the current position. The new position is saved into the processing buffer. Next, we allocate memory of appropriate size, copy the field into it, and create a new LVARCHAR variable based on that string. This variable is then returned to the caller.

Note that the mi_fp_setfuncstate() statement is commented out. In the countdown example, the SET_RETONE section always saved the variable with this function. In this item extraction there is no need to do so, because the value saved is a pointer to a memory buffer. This pointer does not change from iteration to iteration. Since it does not change, we don't need to update the value stored in the MI_FPARAM structure.

The iterator function meets its exit condition when it reaches the end of the buffer. Despite the fact that the function indicates that the iteration is done with the mi_fp_setisdone() function, the database server still expects to receive an LVARCHAR variable as a result of the execution. Here is an example of execution if we were to replace the LVARCHAR return value with a NULL value:

```
EXECUTE FUNCTION do_iter1(
        "Garden Hose;Work Bench;Garden Hose;Work
           Bench;");

(expression)
```

```
Garden Hose
Work Bench
Garden Hose
Work Bench

 9791: User Defined Routine (do_iter1) execution
   failed.
Error in line 1
Near character position 74
```

As we can see, all the values are returned properly but the statement still fails due to the end-of-iteration return value.

Each time a new field is retrieved, the do_iter1() function allocates a buffer and copies the field into it. That buffer is used to create an LVARCHAR variable. Once the LVARCHAR variable is created, the buffer is not needed anymore. A few things could be changed there, however.

The mi_alloc() function allocates memory with the default memory duration. The database server monitors memory and releases it at some point after the memory has exceeded its duration. Since we know that our buffer is not needed anymore, we could explicitly release that memory in our code so that the server can reuse it as soon as possible. This can be done with the mi_free() API function.

In some cases, say, in the do_iter1() function, it is possible to identify the maximum size of buffer that will be required. Since the buffer has a very short lifespan, we can avoid the overhead of memory allocation and release by using a variable that is allocated on the stack when the function is called. We could replace

```
mi_string *result;
```

with

```
mi_string result[64];
```

and remove the mi_alloc() statement from the iterator function. This can provide a significant performance improvement. This technique should be used only when the buffer size is relatively small. If you decide to use it for larger buffers, you may have to change the SQL declaration of your function to define a new stack size. The default stack size is 64 KB on NT systems and 32 KB on UNIX systems.

The SET_END Section

This section is used for cleanup activities. In the countdown example, nothing needed to be done. Since we allocated memory in only the SET_INIT section, we could simply return and let the database server release the memory when it sees fit. However, since we know that the memory is not needed anymore, it is a good idea to release the memory when we reach this section. This way the database server can reuse the memory sooner. This becomes important when large memory demands are made on the system via execution of large queries or a multitude of smaller queries, for example.

Iterator Limitations

Relational database servers provide aggregation functions. Assuming that we have an order table that contained a customer ID and order amount, it is possible to get the total amount of orders per customer by issuing an SQL statement such as

```
SELECT customerID, SUM(orderAmount)
FROM orders
GROUP BY customerID;
```

This type of operation could be seen as the opposite of what an iterator function does. Consider the following table and insert statements:

```
CREATE TABLE foo (
   id     serial,
   items  lvarchar
);
```

```
INSERT INTO foo
VALUES(0,
   "Garden Hose;Work Bench;Garden Hose;Work Bench;");
INSERT INTO foo
VALUES(0, "Metal Rake;Circular Saw;");
```

If we want to list all the items related to a specific id, it would be nice to be able to issue the following SQL statement:

```
SELECT id, do_iter1(items)
FROM foo;
```

We would expect this statement to return one row per item found and use the appropriate id for each of them. However, this statement returns the following error:

```
686: Function (do_iter1) has returned more than one row.
Error in line 2
Near character position 6
```

Hopefully, this limitation will be removed in future releases. This functionality could be very useful in processing more complex content. With increased popularity of the extensible manipulation language (XML), we may want to provide functions that will extract specific sections of the XML document and return the result as a set of rows, as shown in the example above.

The implementation of this feature has its limitations. The use of more than one iterator function in the select list of a SELECT statement is not possible. An SQL result set is by definition unordered. Using multiple iterator functions would result in multiple possible results. The possibilities include all join permutations of the iterator functions.

The next step would be to be able to use an iterator function in a join statement. We would have to be able to provide a name for the result. Otherwise it would be impossible to have a join condition in the WHERE clause.

Continuing this line of thinking, we can come up with other ideas for interesting functionality. It would then become an issue of submitting feature requests to Informix.

Limitations Work-Around

We have seen that we execute iterator functions through the EXECUTE FUNCTION SQL command. Any solution will have to use this method. It is always possible to do this in a client application, but this is not always an option. By providing a table view of the data coming from the server, we can then use off-the-shelf products to provide the appropriate user interface.

We need to provide a function that will execute the SQL statement and then return a set of row results. This means that we have an iterator function that calls another iterator function.

An SPL Solution

The basic solution is to execute an SQL Statement and call the do_iter1() function for each row, returning the values one at a time. This is a case where using the Informix stored procedure language (SPL) is very convenient, since user-defined routines can also be written in this language.

To accomplish the result expected by the SELECT id statement mentioned in the section "Iterator Limitations," we can use the following function:

```
CREATE FUNCTION iter()
RETURNING integer, varchar(30);
define aid    integer;
define adoc lvarchar;
define aitem varchar(30);

FOREACH SELECT id, items INTO aid, adoc FROM foo
  FOREACH EXECUTE FUNCTION do_iter1(adoc) INTO aitem
    RETURN aid, aitem WITH RESUME;
  END FOREACH;
END FOREACH;

END FUNCTION;
```

The first thing we notice is that an SPL function can return more than one value. In this case we return an integer and a character string of up to 30 characters. We then define a few variables that are used later in the function.

The processing consists of two loops. The outer loop executes for each row returned and the inner loop executes for each value returned by the `do_iter1()` function.

The outer loop executes the `SELECT id` statement and puts the result in the variables `aid` and `adoc`. These variables were defined earlier with the same types as the columns of table `foo`. For each row retrieved, the inner loop is executed.

The inner loop used the `adoc` variable as argument to the `do_iter1()` function. The result of the execution is put in the `aitem` variable. The second part of the inner loop returns the two values expected. The key to this processing is the `with resume` clause. This tells the database server to return control to this location after it has retrieved the return values. Control is then returned to this location, and the `do_iter1()` function is called once again to provide another value. This continues until `do_iter1()` is done. Then control returns to the outer loop to retrieve another row and the inner loop is called once again. Once all rows are processed, the function exits the outer loop and the processing is completed.

The execution of this function provides the following result:

```
(expression) (expression)

          1 Garden Hose
          1 Work Bench
          1 Garden Hose
          1 Work Bench
          2 Metal Rake
          2 Circular Saw
          3 Garden Hose
          3 Work Bench
          3 Garden Hose
          3 Work Bench
          4 Metal Rake
          4 Circular Saw


12 row(s) retrieved.
```

The variables used in the `iter()` function and the return value types must match exactly everywhere or errors will occur.

If, for example, the return value of the `do_iter1()` function is defined as an `LVARCHAR` instead of a `VARCHAR(30)`, the result of the execution can be either an execution error or a type mismatch error.

A C Solution

We can write a C user-defined routine that accomplishes a similar result. The solution is not quite as straightforward as the SPL one. This section discusses how this can be done. In the process it introduces additional features provided by the DataBlade API.

When the database server executes an iterator function, it manages information in the `MI_FPARAM` structure. This includes the `MI_SETREQUEST` value and the flag indicating that the set is done. The `mi_fp_request()` function retrieves the type of request that is being performed. The first time an iterator function is called, it receives a `SET_INIT` request. The function performs its initialization and returns. The database server then updates the request type and sets it to `SET_RETONE`. The `MI_FPARAM` structure is an opaque type that can only be manipulated by using API functions. The DataBlade API does not provide a function to set the request type. If we were to call an iterator function from another C function, the only request that the function would receive is `SET_INIT`.

If this problem were not enough, the DataBlade API does not provide API function to reset the `setisdone` flag either. If we were able to call an iterator function, we would have to create a new `MI_FPARAM` structure for each row sent to the iterator function for processing.

The solution is to ask the database server to execute the iterator function for us. This means that we execute an SQL statement to retrieve the rows from the database and then build another statement to execute the iterator function on the row data.

We declare this new iterator function as follows:

```
CREATE FUNCTION do_iter2(lvarchar)
RETURNS ROW (col1 integer, col2 varchar(30))
WITH (NOT VARIANT, ITERATOR)
EXTERNAL NAME
"$INFORMIXDIR/extend/udrbook/bin/chap8.bld(do_iter2)"
LANGUAGE C;
```

This is very similar to the `do_iter1` iterator function declaration. The difference is that the function is now declared as returning a row. Note that the row return type must be qualified with the field names and types.

The processing done in the `do_iter2()` function needs to keep track of several pieces of information. For this purpose we are using the following structure:

```
typedef struct info {
  MI_CONNECTION *conn;
  MI_ROW_DESC   *rd;
  MI_SAVE_SET   *ss;
  mi_integer    id;
} INFO;
```

Declaring this structure with a `typedef` is a convenience. We can now refer to a variable of this type as of type `INFO` instead of using `struct info` everywhere. This is only a convenience. Otherwise, `struct info` and `INFO` are equivalent. The `info` structure contains a connection to the database server, a row descriptor, a save set, and an integer. The database connection is used to submit our statements to the database. The row descriptor is needed to create a return row. We could retrieve the row descriptor each time we are ready to create a row. By keeping a copy of the row descriptor in this structure, we avoid having to retrieve the row descriptor each time we create a row.

This iterator function needs to execute SQL statements, retrieve rows, save state information, and create a return row, among other things. The variables used in the function are

```
MI_ROW     *aRow, *RetVal;
INFO       *stateInfo;
MI_MEMORY_DURATION oldDuration;
MI_TYPEID *tid;
MI_DATUM  datum1;
MI_DATUM  datum[2];
mi_boolean isnull[2];
mi_integer state, error, collen;
mi_string *pbuf, buffer[2000];
```

You can reference these definitions below in our discussion of the processing. As for an iterator function, `do_iter2()` first retrieves the type of operation that is requested and then executes a `switch()` statement to select the right processing section.

The SET_INIT Section

This section initializes the environment. It contains the following code:

```
case SET_INIT:
  oldDuration = mi_switch_mem_duration(PER_COMMAND);
  stateInfo = (INFO *)mi_alloc(sizeof(INFO));
  tid = mi_fp_rettype(fparam);
  stateInfo->rd = mi_row_desc_create(tid);

  /* save a pointer to the INFO structure so we can
     * retrieve it at the next iteration
     */
  mi_fp_setfuncstate(fparam, stateInfo);
  stateInfo->conn = mi_open(NULL, NULL, NULL);

  mi_exec(stateInfo->conn, STMT, MI_QUERY_BINARY);
  /* create a save set for the rows since we'll need the
     * connection to process each row later
     */
  stateInfo->ss = mi_save_set_create(stateInfo->conn);
  while (NULL !=
          (aRow = mi_next_row(stateInfo->conn, &error)))
  {
    mi_save_set_insert(stateInfo->ss, aRow);
  }
  /* setup to process the first row */
  aRow = mi_save_set_get_first(stateInfo->ss, &error);
  mi_value(aRow, 0, &stateInfo->id, &collen);
  mi_value(aRow, 1, &datum1, &collen);
  (void)mi_switch_mem_duration(oldDuration);
  pbuf = mi_lvarchar_to_string((mi_lvarchar *)datum1);
  error = mi_save_set_delete(aRow);
```

```
sprintf(buffer,
    "execute function do_iter1(\"%s\");", pbuf);
mi_exec(stateInfo->conn, buffer, MI_QUERY_BINARY);
break;
```

The first operation performed is to change the default memory duration to a PER_COMMAND duration. We save the previous memory duration so that we can restore it later. By changing the default memory duration, we ensure that any memory allocation done by other DataBlade API functions will use the desired duration. If we were to allocate a mi_lvarchar variable, this would ensure that the variable stays valid between iteration calls. Otherwise, the memory used by the mi_lvarchar variable could be reassigned to other purposes during the execution, potentially causing intermittent problems.

We allocate the memory for our INFO structure. Then we retrieve the type identifier of the return value. This is the type identifier of the return type as defined in the CREATE FUNCTION statement. With the type identifier, we can create a row descriptor, which is required for the creation of rows. We could have chosen to create the row descriptor in the SET_RETONE section. By creating the row descriptor in the SET_INIT section, we do this operation only once instead of having to do it for each row returned. We then save the pointer to the INFO structure in the MI_FPARAM structure and open a connection to the database server. We are not quite done with the initialization of the INFO structure.

The mi_exec() statement contains a reference to STMT. This identifier is a definition for the following SQL statement:

```
"SELECT id, items FROM foo;"
```

This is the same statement that is executed in the SPL example. Once the statement executes, we create a save set that allows us to retrieve rows and save them for future processing. We then loop on the result of the SQL statement execution and retrieve the rows into our save set. We need to retrieve all the rows into our save set because we need the database connection to execute the do_iter1() function as we will see below.

We are now ready to setup the execution of `do_iter1()`. We retrieve the first row out of our save set and extract the two columns. The `id` column is saved in the `INFO` structure because it is required in multiple iterations. The other column is retrieved as a `mi_lvarchar`. We restore the memory duration to its original and then obtain a `NULL`-terminated string from the `mi_lvarchar` variable representing the `items` field. Since we have restored the memory duration, the character string has that memory duration. We then remove this row from our save set because we are done with it.

The last two statements build an SQL statement for the execution of the `do_iter1()` function. The SQL statement is put into a character buffer and executed. A fixed-size character buffer is used for convenience. In theory we should calculate the size required and allocate it with `mi_alloc()`. When you know the size of the buffer required, it is more efficient to use an automatic variable instead of having to allocate it. Of course, this could lead to some problems if the buffer is not large enough.

The setup is completed for the `SET_RETONE` loop. The next section, `SET_RETONE`, can expect to be able to retrieve the values from the SQL statement execution and make decisions on the result.

The `SET_RETONE` Section

At this point in the processing, we know that we are iterating over the SQL execution of the `do_iter1()` function. Through the multiple calls, we need to process all the rows returned by that execution and then process to the next row from the `foo` table. The code is as follows:

```
case SET_RETONE:
  stateInfo = (INFO *)mi_fp_funcstate(fparam);
  while (NULL ==
        (aRow = mi_next_row(stateInfo->conn, &error))) {
    error = mi_query_finish(stateInfo->conn);
    if (0 == mi_save_set_count(stateInfo->ss)) {
      mi_fp_setisdone(fparam, MI_TRUE);
      isnull[0] = MI_TRUE;
      isnull[1] = MI_TRUE;
```

```
                RetVal = mi_row_create(NULL, stateInfo->rd,
                                        datum, isnull);
            return(RetVal);
        }
        aRow = mi_save_set_get_first(stateInfo->ss, &error);
        mi_value(aRow, 0, &stateInfo->id, &collen);
        mi_value(aRow, 1, &datum1, &collen);
        pbuf = mi_lvarchar_to_string((mi_lvarchar *)datum1);
        error = mi_save_set_delete(aRow);
        sprintf(buffer,
                "execute function do_iter1(\"%s\");", pbuf);
        mi_exec(stateInfo->conn, buffer, MI_QUERY_BINARY);
    }
    datum[0] = (MI_DATUM)stateInfo->id;
    isnull[0] = MI_FALSE;
    mi_value(aRow, 0, &datum[1], &collen);
    isnull[1] = MI_FALSE;
    RetVal = mi_row_create(NULL, stateInfo->rd,
                            datum, isnull);
    return(RetVal);
    break;
```

As usual, we first retrieve the pointer to our INFO buffer. Next, the while loop executes until we get a row from the execution of the do_iter1() function. As we'll see below, the code within the loop also contains an exit condition.

If the mi_next_row() function returns a NULL, it indicates that we are done with this current execution. We execute mi_query_finish() to close the query. The next step is to retrieve another row from our save set. If there are no more rows, as indicated by a count of zero returned by mi_save_set_count(), we indicate that the iteration is done and return a row with NULL elements. This returned row is required, as we saw earlier a related example where the do_iter1 function execution ended with error 9791 (see p. 187), even though the done flag is set to true. The database server discards this value.

If we get a row from our save set, we need to extract the column values and construct the next SQL statement to execute. This statement consists of the execution of do_iter1() with the items column content as argument. This is identical to the processing that was done in the SET_INIT section.

The `while` loop returns a row for the `do_iter1()` execution. We set the first value of the row with the value we saved in the `INFO` structure. This value represents the first column of the row from `foo` that we are processing. We extract the value from the execution and use it as the second column of the return value. Here we are assuming that the return value is not `NULL`. This is a proper assumption in this case. In other situations, we should add code to test for `NULL` values, as we saw in the earlier chapter on row processing.

The `SET_END` Section

The `SET_END` section cleans up after the execution. In this example, we allocate a structure to store a database connection handle, a row descriptor, and a save set, among other things. The `SET_END` section is as follows:

```
case SET_END:
    stateInfo = (INFO *)mi_fp_funcstate(fparam);
    mi_close(stateInfo->conn);
    mi_free(stateInfo);
    return(0);
```

The only thing we need to do is to close the connection and free the memory allocated to the `INFO` structure. We could use `mi_save_set_destroy()` to release the save set, but it is not necessary because closing the connection frees the save set.

We did not free the row descriptor. A row descriptor is attached to the row that it helped create. After the `SET_END` section is executed, the database server still expects to have a row descriptor. If we were to execute `mi_row_desc_free()`, the execution of the `do_iter2()` function would return all the rows and then generate the following error:

```
9791: User Defined Routine (rowoutput) execution
    failed.
Error in line 1
Near character position 1
```

Since we are at the end of the command execution, we know that the row descriptor will be scheduled to be free soon after the iterator function returns. The same can be said about the INFO structure. It is still a good idea to explicitly free memory you don't need anymore so that the server can reuse it as soon as possible.

Joining With an Iterator Function

At the time of this writing, it is not possible to join a table to an iterator function. The solution is to save the result of the function into a temporary table and then execute the join. A SELECT statement can create and populate a temporary table. It is not possible to do this with the EXECUTE FUNCTION. Using the count-down example, we can create a temporary table that could be used for a join with the following statements:

```
CREATE TEMP TABLE do_iter0_tab (
  a integer
);

INSERT INTO do_iter0_tab
  EXECUTE FUNCTION do_iter0(10);
```

A temporary table is visible only for the session that created it. There is no problem if several sessions use the same temporary table name. A temporary table exists for the duration of the session. This has the advantage that you can use it in multiple calls to the database from a client application (or from a session in the server). Once you are done with a temporary table, you may want to remove it in case future sequences of calls want to use the same temporary table name later.

Chapter

9

The Fastpath Interface

The fastpath interface is a facility that allows for the execution of UDR functions without having to go through the parser, optimizer, and executor. Fastpath locates the requested function and ensures that it is available in the server. It is a way to execute user-defined routines that reside in other dynamic libraries.

The DataBlade API does not allow for direct manipulation of dynamic libraries. The fastpath interface is the only direct mechanism to do this in a safe way.

Why Use Fastpath?

The first reason to use the fastpath interface is to access cast functions when manipulating data elements. This is particularly useful when functions need to deal with data types in a generic manner.

The second reason is to execute functions that manipulate types that have been implemented in other DataBlade modules.

Fastpath can be use to extend the functionality provided by a third-party DataBlade module without having access to the source code. This functionality could be added by creating a distinct type of the target type and implementing new functions that call the original accessor functions while providing added processing.

The Fastpath Functions

Informix defines eight functions in the fastpath implementation. These functions are listed in Table 9–1.

These functions allow us to retrieve function descriptors, execute the retrieved functions, and release the resources once we are done with the functions. Let's look at a few functions that illustrate the use of the fastpath interface.

The first thing to do is retrieve the function we want to use. It can be either a casting function or a user-defined routine. To retrieve a cast, we can use either mi_cast_get() or mi_td_cast_get(). These functions are basically the same, except that one takes MI_TYPEID pointer arguments and the other takes MI_TYPE_DESC pointer arguments. The mi_cast_get() function has the following signature:

```
MI_FUNC_DESC *mi_cast_get(MI_CONNECTION *conn,
            MI_TYPEID *fromTid, MI_TYPEID *toTid,
            mi_char *status);
```

The first argument is a connection to the database server. The two subsequent arguments represent the source and target type

Table 9–1. Fastpath functions.

mi_cast_get()	mi_fparam_get()	mi_routine_end()
mi_routine_exec()	mi_routine_get()	mi_routine_get_by_typeid()
mi_routine_id_get()	mi_td_cast_get()	

identifiers. The last argument is a status representing the type of result returned by `mi_cast_get()`. The possible values are:

- `MI_ERROR_CAST`: An error has occurred. In this case, `mi_cast_get()` returns a `NULL` value.
- `MI_NO_CAST`: Once again, the function returns a `NULL` value. The status indicates that there is no cast function available between the two types provided.
- `MI_SYSTEM_CAST`: This status indicates that the returned function descriptor represents a cast function that is provided by IDS.2000.
- `MI_NOP_CAST`: This status indicates that no conversion is required between the two types provided. For example, trying to get the casting function to convert between `VARCHAR` and `LVARCHAR` returns this status.
- `MI_UDR_CAST`: This status indicates that the cast is a user-defined routine. As far as I can tell, this status is never returned because it is superseded by one of the next two status values.
- `MI_EXPLICIT_CAST`: The function returned is a user-defined routine used as an explicit cast.
- `MI_IMPLICIT_CAST`: The function returned is a user-defined routine used as an implicit cast.

Once we have a function descriptor, we can execute the function with `mi_routine_exec()`. This function has the following signature:

```
MI_DATUM mi_routine_exec(MI_CONNECTION *conn,
            MI_FUNC_DESC *fn, mi_integer *error, . . .);
```

The first argument is a database connection. The second argument is a function descriptor that was retrieved previously with a function such as `mi_cast_get()`. The third argument is the return status of the execution. It is either `MI_OK` or `MI_ERROR`. The function declaration is followed by what is called an ellipsis (", . . ."). This indicates that the function can take a number of additional arguments of various types. This is where we pass the arguments to the function represented by the function descriptor.

A user-defined routine includes an additional argument that is a pointer to a `MI_FPARAM` structure. This argument is not part of the argument list passed through the `mi_routine_exec()` function.

The `mi_routine_exec()` function returns a value of type `MI_DATUM`. This value represents the result of the execution. It follows the same rule as any function argument or return values, as we saw in Chap. 4. For example, if the function returns a value of type `DOUBLE PRECISION`, it is returned as a pointer to a `mi_double_precision` type. The result should be cast to the proper type and stored in an appropriate variable.

We complete the fastpath call by releasing the resources that were allocated when getting the function descriptor. We use the `mi_routine_end()` function to do it. This function has the following signature:

```
mi_integer mi_routine_end(MI_CONNECTION *conn,
                          MI_FUNC_DESC *fn);
```

The arguments to this function are the same as the first two arguments to the `mi_routine_exec()` function: a database connection and a function descriptor. The return value indicates the success (`MI_OK`) or the failure (`MI_ERROR`) of the function execution.

This constitutes the main sequence of operations when using the fastpath interface. The next few sections look at the details and issues related to this interface.

Using System Casts

The `mi_cast_get()` function returns a status value that indicates the type of result it returns. One of these values is `MI_SYSTEM_CAST`. It indicates that the database server implemented the function that performs the requested operation. The Informix documentation does not appear to describe the arguments required for this function. Looking at user-defined casting operations, our first assumption could be that the function signature would be something like:

```
MI_DATUM *cast_function(Specific_type value,
    MI_FPARAM *fp);
```

It turns out, however, that Informix defined one function that performs all the possible system casts. That function effectively has the following signature:

```
MI_DATUM dosyscast(MI_DATUM value, mi_integer len,
                   mi_integer prec, MI_FPARAM *fp);
```

The MI_DATUM argument indicates that any type can be received. The second argument indicates the maximum length of the return value. Depending on the system cast function requested, the second argument is used to create the return variable. The third argument represents the precision of the result. The declaration of this function within SQL defines the first argument and the return value as a "pointer" type. This type is a generic type that accepts any argument. It is equivalent to the MI_DATUM used here.

A Casting Example

You may be in a situation where you need to convert different data types to their character representations. Instead of creating functions that handle specific conversions, you can use the fast-path interface to request the appropriate function as needed. This is more likely to be a function that is called internally by some other functions that may have an external declaration.

The following function is designed to be referenced through a CREATE FUNCTION SQL declaration. Multiple CREATE FUNCTION statements can reference this implementation and provide the desired conversion.

```
#include <mi.h>

mi_lvarchar *cast2lvar(MI_DATUM datum, MI_FPARAM *fp)
{
  MI_CONNECTION  *conn;
  MI_FUNC_DESC   *fn;
  MI_FPARAM      *castfp;
  MI_DATUM        new_datum;
  MI_TYPEID      *argtid, *rettid;
  mi_integer      ret;
  mi_char         status;
```

```
conn = mi_open(NULL, NULL, NULL);
argtid = mi_fp_argtype(fp, 0);
rettid = mi_fp_rettype(fp, 0);

fn = mi_cast_get(conn, argtid, rettid, &status);
if (NULL == fn) {
  switch(status) {
  case MI_ERROR_CAST:
  case MI_NO_CAST:
  case MI_SYSTEM_CAST:
  case MI_UDR_CAST:
  case MI_IMPLICIT_CAST:
  case MI_EXPLICIT_CAST:
        mi_db_error_raise(conn, MI_EXCEPTION,
           "Unable to find the casting function",
                NULL);
        break;
  case MI_NOP_CAST:
        return(datum);
        break;
  } /* end switch */
}
castfp = mi_fparam_get(conn, fn);
/* Execute the casting function */
if (status == MI_SYSTEM_CAST)
  new_datum = mi_routine_exec(conn, fn, &ret,
                               datum, 30, 0,
castfp);
else
  new_datum = mi_routine_exec(conn, fn, &ret,
                               datum, castfp);
mi_routine_end(conn, fn);
mi_close(conn);
return(new_datum);
}
```

This function declares its first argument as being of type
MI_DATUM. This is a generic type that accepts any value. The
argument follows the usual rules where, depending on the type,
it will be either the value itself or a pointer to the value. The second argument is the usual MI_FPARAM pointer. The return value

is a `mi_lvarchar` pointer because the function is used to cast any type to a string. The return value type is the same if the function is declared to return either a fixed-length character string (CHAR), a variable-length character string (VARCHAR), or the other variable-length character string (LVARCHAR).

The first thing the function does is to obtain a database connection. The result should be tested and an error should be generated if the connection is NULL. Then we need to get the type identifiers of the input type and the result type. The MI_FPARAM argument provides this information. With these two type identifiers, we are ready to obtain the casting function.

The `mi_cast_get()` function retrieves the function descriptor of the requested cast function from a valid database connection. If the function descriptor pointer returned is NULL it may indicate a problem. In this case, we have to test the status character to find out why. In most cases, an error must be generated when a NULL is returned. In the case of MI_NOP_CAST, no casting is required and the input value can be returned unchanged.

The `mi_db_error_raise()` function is used to generate an error exception. As we saw in Chap. 5, we could store the message in the SYSERRORS system catalog instead of putting the text of the message with the code. The error message shown here may be too generic since it does not identify the exact reason of the failure. It would be a good idea to add additional error messages for MI_ERROR_CAST, MI_NO_CAST, and MI_SYSTEM_CAST. Furthermore, the exact cast requested should be identified. We can extract the type name from a type descriptor obtained from the type identifier. The following code extract shows how it is done:

```
MI_TYPE_DESC *td;
mi_string    *pbuf;
. . .
td  = mi_type_typedesc(conn, argtid);
pbuf = mi_type_typename(td);
```

Note that the first argument to the `mi_type_typedesc()` function is a MI_CONNECTION pointer. A NULL value could be used in this case. Since we already have an open connection in our function, it can be used in this function call. After retrieving the type names for the two type identifiers, we can use these strings to improve the quality of our error message.

After obtaining the functions descriptor from `mi_cast_get()`, we obtain the `MI_FPARAM` structure for the cast function by using `mi_fparam_get()`, and we are ready to execute the function by calling `mi_routine_exec()`. The function call includes the first three required arguments representing the database connection, the function descriptor, and a location where to put the execution status. The fourth argument is the value to convert. In the case of a system cast, two additional arguments are required. In our case, we passed a constant value representing a maximum length of 30 characters and a precision of zero. The precision is not significant in the case of the conversion to a character string, but the length is. A maximum length of 30 should be sufficient to convert any base type to its character representation. Keep in mind that casting from one character type to another does not require a function execution, so we don't have to worry about converting a character string longer than 30 characters to a `LVARCHAR` type. The largest buffer size should be for a conversion of a `DATETIME YEAR TO FRACTION` value. Finally, we pass the `MI_FPARAM` structure as the last argument. It appears that the `MI_FPARAM` structure is not required, probably because it is not used by the casting function. However, it is good practice always to include it because it is part of a function implementation.

After the function execution, we release the resources allocated to the function descriptor, close the database connection, and return the result of the casting operation.

If we want to provide this capability as an internal function, we have to pass the type identifiers to the casting function or pass a `MI_FPARAM` structure that provides this information. It is likely that the calling function will have an open database connection. It should also be passed to the casting function to save the processing required to open the connection. The function signature of this internal function should be similar to this declaration:

```
mi_lvarchar *do_cast(MI_CONNECTION *conn, MI_TYPEID *src,
                     MI_TYPEID *dst, MI_DATUM val);
```

The `dst` target type is not really necessary because we know that the result must be a `LVARCHAR`. However, it saves us the processing within the casting function. If we were to use this function several times within our user-defined routine, this choice of interface would be appropriate. The body of this function is very similar to the one we just studied. It ends up being slightly simpler.

Calling an Informix Function

There are situations where you may want to call functions that are implemented in the database server. For example, you may want to get the square root of a double-precision value. According to the description of the function, you may think of including the following statement:

```
double result, arg;
. . .
result = sqrt(arg);
```

The user-defined routine including this statement will execute without error; unfortunately, the result will be invalid. The database server includes a sqrt() function, but there is no way to figure out what argument type it takes and what it returns. We don't even know if it really calculates the square root of its argument.

We know that the database server provides a sqrt() function. Using the fastpath interface, we can access that function and obtain our result. The process is similar to the one we saw in the casting example, except that this time we are getting the function with the mi_routine_get() function. To find the sqrt() function, we need to execute the following:

```
MI_CONNECTION *conn;
MI_FUNC_DESC  *fn;
. . .
fn = mi_routine_get(conn, 0, "sqrt(double precision)");
```

The mi_routine_get() function returns a function descriptor. It takes a database connection as its first argument. The second argument is a flag that must be set to zero. The third argument is a character string that represents the function signature.

Once we have the function descriptor, we can execute the function with the appropriate arguments:

```
MI_CONNECTION *conn;
MI_FUNC_DESC  *fn;
MI_FPARAM     *fnfp;
mi_double_precision val, *retval;
mi_integer status;
 . . .
retval = (mi_double_precision *)
         mi_routine_exec(conn, fn, &status, &val, fnfp);
```

The execution of the `sqrt()` function through the fastpath interface only requires an additional argument to the `mi_routine_exec()` function, and this is the value to operate on. Since the argument type is DOUBLE PRECISION, a pointer to the value is passed to the function. Similarly, the return value is a pointer to a DOUBLE PRECISION result. This is consistent with the way values are treated through the DataBlade API.

Calling Another User Function

The fastpath interface can be used to call functions that are provided by other DataBlade modules. We can use accessor functions to manipulate an opaque type and increase the functionality provided by the DataBlade module. We can also increase the functionality by creating a new type based on the existing one and thereby modify the processing. This is similar to doing type inheritance. This can be done by creating a distinct type of the original or by adding a row type in a row type inheritance model.

We saw in Chap. 1 an example of table inheritance. The example described a table inheritance for a bank where loans are divided into categories including manufacturing, telco, retail, healthcare, and financial services. The retail category is further divided into subcategories. With this hierarchy, we can create different functions for risk calculation, one function per category.

We implement a table hierarchy by first creating row types. These row types are organized in a hierarchy. The general creation is as follows:

```
CREATE ROW TYPE loans_t ( . . .);
CREATE ROW TYPE manu_t (. . .) UNDER loans_t;
CREATE ROW TYPE telco_t (. . .) UNDER loans_t;
CREATE ROW TYPE retail_t (. . .) UNDER loans_t;
CREATE ROW TYPE fnsrvc_t (. . .) UNDER loans_t;
CREATE ROW TYPE food_t (. . .) UNDER retail_t;
```

In addition to defining the fields of named row types, these statements define the hierarchy. In this example the food_t named row type is placed under the retail_t named row type in the hierarchy. This means that food_t includes its own fields but also gets the fields from the retail_t named row type. Since retail_t is under loans_t, food_t also includes the fields from loan_t.

We now create tables based on these named row types. This type of table is called a *typed table*. The creation statements are:

```
CREATE TABLE loans OF TYPE loans_t;
CREATE TABLE manu OF TYPE manu_t UNDER loans;
CREATE TABLE telco OF TYPE telco_t UNDER loans;
CREATE TABLE retail OF TYPE retail_t UNDER loans;
CREATE TABLE fnsrvc OF TYPE fnsrvc_t UNDER loans;
CREATE TABLE food OF TYPE food_t UNDER retail;
```

These statements define tables, their content, and their places in the hierarchy. If we needed to add constraints (e.g., primary key or referential integrity) the definition would have the following form:

```
CREATE TABLE manu OF TYPE manu_t (
  <add constraints here >
) UNDER loans;
```

With this table hierarchy in place, we can define functions that operate on specific row types. We can define functions that calculate the risk factor for each type of loan. For example, the riskf() function that handles the rows coming from the manu table has the following definition:

```
CREATE FUNCTION riskf(manu_t)
RETURNING double precision
WITH(NOT VARIANT)
EXTERNAL NAME ". . ."
LANGUAGE C;
```

Assuming that we have a complete set of riskf() functions that perform the risk factor calculation, we can now execute the following statement:

```
SELECT name, riskf(A) FROM loans AS A;
```

This statement assumes that the name column is defined in the loan_t named row type. The loans table is given an alias of A which is used as the argument to the riskf() function. This SELECT statement goes through all the rows from the hierarchy and passes the rows to the riskf() function. Depending on which table provides the information, the row returned will have a different row type. This way, the appropriate riskf() function will be called as needed so that the right calculation will take place. A riskf() function must be provided for all the named row types in the hierarchy, or the database server will generate the following error:

```
674: Routine (riskf) can not be resolved.
```

Even if no rows are retrieved from the loans table, a riskf() function taking a loans_t argument type must be there. We can also access a specific table without going further down in the hierarchy. Assuming that some rows were inserted into the loans table, we can retrieve the rows from only this table with the following SQL statement:

```
SELECT * FROM ONLY(loans);
```

This type of statement can be done on any table in the hierarchy. We can then work on specific types of loans (see Fig. 9–1). This provides an additional level of data partitioning.

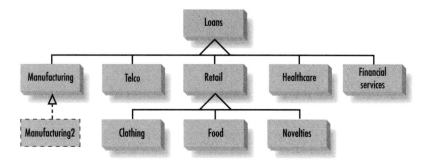

Figure 9–1. *Extending a table hierarchy.*

Let's say that we want to extend the table hierarchy, as shown in Fig. 9–1 with the dotted lines and boxes, to include a subclass of the manufacturing type (manu_t) and that we also want to implement a modified risk factor calculation that requires the use of the riskf() function from the manu_t type. The first step is to create a new named row type and table under the existing manufacturing type:

```
CREATE ROW TYPE manu2_t (. . .) UNDER manu_t;
CREATE TABLE manu2 OF TYPE manu2_t UNDER manu;
```

We then need to create a riskf() function that takes a manu2_t row type as input and returns a DOUBLE PRECISION result:

```
CREATE FUNCTION riskf(manu2_t)
RETURNING double precision
WITH(NOT VARIANT)
EXTERNAL NAME ". . ."
LANGUAGE C;
```

The implementation of this function needs to execute the riskf() function provided by the DataBlade module and also adjust the result based on additional information provided in the manu2_t named row type. Assuming an external name of riskmanu2(), the C implementation has the following signature:

```
mi_double_precision *riskfmanu2(MI_ROW *val1,
                                MI_FPARAM *fp);
```

The function returns a pointer to a DOUBLE PRECISION value. It takes a MI_ROW pointer as its first argument and the usual MI_FPARAM pointer as an additional argument. The MI_ROW pointer argument does not identify a specific row type. Any row type is received as a pointer to a MI_ROW structure. In this case, the SQL definition of the function declares that the row type is manu2_t. The function can process the row with this assumption.

Before we can get to calling the riskf() function that takes a manu_t argument, we need to cast the manu2_t row type to the manu_t row type. The following code shows how it can be done:

```
MI_CONNECTION       *conn;
MI_FUNC_DESC        *fn;
MI_FPARAM           *castfp;
MI_TYPEID           *tid, *tid2;
MI_DATUM            datum;
mi_integer          ret, collen;
mi_char             status;

conn = mi_open(NULL, NULL, NULL);

/* get the cast from manu2_t to manu_t */
tid = mi_fp_argtype(fp, 0); /* manu2_t */
tid2 = mi_typename_to_id(conn,
          mi_string_to_lvarchar("manu_t") );

fn = mi_cast_get(conn, tid, tid2, &status);
castfp = mi_fparam_get(conn, fn);

if (status == MI_SYSTEM_CAST)
  datum = mi_routine_exec(conn, fn, &ret, val1,
                          0, 0, castfp);
else
  datum = mi_routine_exec(conn, fn, &ret, val1,
                          castfp);
mi_routine_end(conn, fn);
```

We first get a connection to the database and then get the first argument type identifier, which is the `manu2_t` row type. We use the `mi_typename_to_id()` function to get the type identifier for the `manu_t` row type. This function takes the type name as a `mi_lvarchar` pointer. So we use `mi_string_to_lvarchar()` to convert the character string to the proper type.

We obtain the result of the `riskf(manu_t)` function by executing it through the fastpath interface:

```
mi_double_precision *riskf;
. . .
fn = mi_routine_get(conn, 0, "riskf(manu_t)");
castfp = mi_fparam_get(conn, fn);
riskf = mi_routine_exec(conn, fn, &ret, datum,
    castfp);
mi_routine_end(conn, fn);
```

We get the function descriptor by passing the function signature to the `mi_routine_get()` function, and we obtain the result of the calculation by executing the function through `mi_routine_exec()`. The argument of the function is the `manu_t` row that we got in the cast operation above. The result is a pointer to a DOUBLE PRECISION value.

The `manu2_t` row contains all the fields of the `manu_t` row type. We may want to pass the original `manu2_t` row as the argument to the `riskf()` function called through the `mi_routine_exec()` function. Despite the fact that we got a function descriptor by passing a specific function signature to `mi_routine_get()`, if we pass a `manu2_t` row as the argument to the function, the `riskf(manu2_t)` function gets called. This generates an infinite loop, because the function calls itself over and over through the fastpath interface. The database server allocates more and more memory to accommodate the execution, until it eventually runs out of memory and crashes.

Finding Functions Information

Before we can use any function, we need to find out the type and number of arguments and the type of the return value. Let's just take the `sqrt()` function: The Informix database server defines eleven different functions. These functions support the following SQL types: `INTEGER`, `SMALLINT`, `INT8`, `FLOAT`, `SMALLFLOAT`, `DECIMAL`, `MONEY`, `VARCHAR(1)`, `CHAR(1)`, `NVARCHAR(1)`, and `NCHAR(1)`.

Where can we get this information? We can find information about the available functions in several locations. The rest of this chapter covers how to find information on the functions defined in the database server.

Looking in `$INFORMIXDIR`

One way to find function definitions is to go to the Informix home directory and search some of the subdirectories. Any DataBlade module is installed under the "extend" directory. Every DataBlade module includes a set of files for installation. We can find information on all the types provided and all the functions created by looking at the `objects.sql` files. The location of all DataBlade module objects.sql files can be defined as

```
$INFORMIXDIR/extend/*/objects.sql
```

These files are set up to insert information into different tables. Here is an example of a definition of a function from the Large Object (LOB) Locator DataBlade module:

```
insert into sysbldobjects
    (bld_id, obj_kind, obj_signature, obj_owner,
        sequence,
     create_sql, create_can_fail, drop_sql,
        drop_can_fail)
values (
        "%SYSBLDNAME%", 5, "LLD_LobIn (lvarchar)",
        "%SYSBLDUSER%", 0,
        "create function LLD_LobIn (lvarchar) . . .",
        "f", "drop function LLD_LobIn (lvarchar);", "f"
);
```

This definition has been reformatted slightly, removing most of the `CREATE FUNCTION` statement. Any DataBlade module that is installed in your database server includes these definitions in full. However, it does not cover functions that were added to the database server using the CREATE FUNCTION directly; nor does it include system functions.

We can find additional function information in the "$INFORMIXDIR/etc" directory. This directory includes several files containing SQL statements. Several function creation statements can be found in these files. We can also find DROP FUNCTION statements that don't have CREATE FUNCTION counterparts. For example, in the file "boot911u.sql" we find several sqrt() function removal statements:

```
drop function informix.sqrt(integer);
drop function informix.sqrt(smallint);
drop function informix.sqrt(int8);
drop function informix.sqrt(float);
drop function informix.sqrt(smallfloat);
drop function informix.sqrt(decimal);
drop function informix.sqrt(money);
drop function informix.sqrt(varchar(1));
drop function informix.sqrt(char(1));
drop function informix.sqrt(nvarchar(1));
drop function informix.sqrt(nchar(1));
```

The "boot911.sql" file contains similar statements for a number of Informix built-in functions. This does not provide complete information, but it can be used with other methods to find out exactly which arguments a function receives and what it returns.

Looking in System Catalogs

The database server has a set of system catalogs that keep track of the casts, functions, and types available. The first one we'll look at is the SYSCASTS table. The definition of the SYSCASTS is shown in Table 9–2.

The database server does not include a table that describes the type of argument_type and result_type. These types are described in both *Informix Guide to SQL: Reference* and *Informix ESQL/C Programmer's Manual*. Table 9–3 lists the possible values and their meanings.

These values are also used to express the type of table columns. The column type is defined as being NOT NULL by

Table 9–2. SYSCASTS catalog table definition.

Column name	Type	Description
owner	char(8)	username of the owner of the cast
argument_type	smallint	Source data type
argument_xid	integer	Source extended ID type or zero
result_type	smallint	Result data type
result_xid	integer	Result extended ID type or zero
routine_name	char(18)	Routine name or blank
routine_owner	char(8)	Username of the routine owner or blank
class	char(1)	Type of cast: Explicit ('E'), Implicit ('I'), or System ('S')

Table 9–3. Type value description.

Value	Description	Value	Description
0	CHAR	256	CHAR NOT NULL
1	SMALLINT	257	SMALLINT NOT NULL
2	INTEGER	258	INTEGER NOT NULL
3	FLOAT	259	FLOAT NOT NULL
4	SMALLFLOAT	260	SMALLFLOAT NOT NULL
5	DECIMAL	261	DECIMAL NOT NULL
6	SERIAL	262	SERIAL NOT NULL
7	DATE	263	DATE NOT NULL
8	MONEY	264	MONEY NOT NULL
9	NULL		
10	DATETIME	266	DATETIME NOT NULL
11	BYTE	267	BYTE NOT NULL
12	TEXT	268	TEXT NOT NULL
13	VARCHAR	269	VARCHAR NOT NULL
14	INTERVAL	270	INTERVAL NOT NULL

Table 9–3. (continued).

15	NCHAR	271	NCHAR NOT NULL
16	NVARCHAR	272	NVARCHAR NOT NULL
17	INT8	273	INT8 NOT NULL
18	SERIAL8	274	SERIAL8 NOT NULL
19	SET	275	SET NOT NULL
20	MULTISET	276	MULTISET NOT NULL
21	LIST	277	LIST NOT NULL
22	ROW	278	ROW NOT NULL
23	COLLECTION	279	COLLECTION NOT NULL
24	ROWREF	280	ROWREF NOT NULL
40	Variable-length opaque type	296	Variable-length opaque type NOT NULL
41	Fixed-length opaque type	297	Fixed-length opaque type NOT NULL
4118	Named row type	4374	Named row type NOT NULL

adding 256 to the original value type. Assuming that we created a table baseType containing the columns value and description populated with the values listed in Table 9–3, we can issue the following statement to find out the available casts:

```
SELECT a.description source, b.description
   destination
FROM   syscasts, baseType a, basetype b
WHERE  argument_type = a.value
AND    result_type = b.value;
```

The fixed-length and variable-length opaque types, value 40 and 41, are used to represent BLOB, CLOB, BOOLEAN, LVARCHAR, and user-defined types. We can find out more information by using the columns argument_xid and result_xid when they have a value greater than zero. The description for these extended identifiers is found in the SYSXTDTYPES catalog table.

Table 9–4.   The SYSPROCEDURES system catalog.

Column name	Type	Description
procname	char(18)	Function name
owner	char(8)	Owner's name
procid	serial	Unique identifier
mode	char(1)	XDBA ('D'), Owner ('O'), Protected ('P')
retsize	integer	Compiled size (in bytes) of values
symsize	integer	Compiled size (in bytes) of symbol table
datasize	integer	Compiled size (in bytes) of constant data
codesize	integer	Compiled size (in bytes) of the instruction code
numargs	integer	Number of arguments
isproc	char(1)	Procedure ('t'), or function ('f')
specificname	varchar(128)	The specific name of the routine
externalname	varchar(255)	Location of the external routine
paramstyle	char(1)	Parameter style
langid	integer	Language identifier (from sysroutinelangs)
paramtypes	rtnparamtypes	List of parameter types
variant	boolean	True if the routine is variant
client	boolean	Reserved for future use
handlesnulls	boolean	True if the routine handles NULL values
iterator	boolean	True if the routine is an iterator function
percallcost	integer	Routine cost
commutator	char(18)	Commutator function for the routine
negator	char(18)	Negator function for the routine
selfunc	char(18)	Reserved for future use
internal	boolean	True if this is an internal function
class	char(18)	Virtual processor class used for this routine
stack	integer	Stack size required per invocation
parallelizable	boolean	True if the routine is parallelizable

The SYSCASTS table also contains the name of the routine used to perform the cast when it is not a system cast. As we saw earlier, the system casts are performed by the dosyscast() function. All these functions are found in the SYSPROCEDURES system catalog, which is described in Table 9–4.

We can find out the available routines and their arguments with a simple SQL statement:

```
SELECT procname, paramtypes
FROM sysprocedures;
```

Here is an example of the result of this statement when limiting it to dosyscast:

```
dosyscast pointer,integer,integer
```

The only thing missing from this SQL statement on the SYSPROCEDURES system catalog is the type of the return value. The SYSPROCBODY system catalog contains this information. SYSPROCBODY is described in Table 9–5.

We can find the create function statements in SYSPROCBODY rows that have a datakey value of 'T'. For example, we can find information on the dosyscast() function by issuing the following SQL statement:

```
SELECT procname, seqno, data
FROM      sysprocedures p, sysprocbody b
WHERE     p.procid = b.procid AND procname = 'dosyscast'
AND       datakey = 'T'
ORDER BY procname, seqno;
```

Table 9–5. The SYSPROCBODY system catalog.

Column name	Type	Description
procid	integer	Procedure identifier (from sysprocedures)
datakey	char(1)	Descriptor type: User document ('D'), procedure source ('T'), return value type list ('R'), procedure symbol table ('S'), constant data string ('L'), Interpreted instruction code ('P')
seqno	integer	Line number of the procedure
data	char(256)	Data of the specified type

The `seqno` column is needed because the statement sometimes spans more than one data element. In the case of `dosyscast()`, we get

```
Procname: dosyscast
Seqno   : 1
Data    : create dba function informix.dosyscast
                  (informix.pointer, int, int)
          returning informix.pointer
          external name '(dosyscast)'
          language C not variant;
```

Of course, the output is not formatted as nicely, but the information is there. It is possible to find more information on the arguments and return value types when they are other than base types. This information is found in the SYSXTDTYPES system catalog, described in Table 9–6.

Table 9–6. SYSXTDTYPES system catalog.

Column name	Type	Description
extended_id	serial	Unique identifier
domain	char(1)	Reserved for future use
mode	char(1)	Base opaque type ('B'), collection or unnamed row ('C'), distinct ('D'), named row type ('R')
owner	char(8)	Owner of the data type
name	char(18)	Name of the type
type	smallint	Type as in Table 9–3
source	integer	extended_id of the source type if it is a distinct type
maxlen	integer	Maximum length if it is a variable-length type
length	integer	Length if it is a fixed-length type
byvalue	char(1)	Passed by value ('T'). or by reference ('F')
cannothash	char(1)	Using default bit hashing function ('T'), or not ('F')
align	smallint	Type alignment (1, 2, 4, 8)
locator	integer	Locator (key) for unnamed row types

With these few system catalogs, we can find out all we need about the functions and data types. There is another way to get the information on user-defined routines quickly. We can write a user-defined routine that returns the information. The next section implements such a function.

Using a User-Defined Routine

The first thing we do when we use the fastpath interface is to retrieve a function descriptor. The DataBlade API provides an accessor function, mi_fparam_get(), that retrieves the MI_FPARAM argument for the function described by the function descriptor. The function signature is

```
MI_FPARAM *mi_fparam_get(MI_CONNECTION *conn,
                         MI_FUNC_DESC *fn);
```

This function takes two arguments. The first argument is a valid database connection and the second argument is a function descriptor. The MI_FPARAM structure contains information on the type and number of arguments and return values, as well as their precision and scale. We can put together a function that takes a function signature as argument and returns all that information. The function starts as follows:

```
mi_lvarchar *fninfo(mi_lvarchar *val1,
  MI_FPARAM *fp)
{
  MI_CONNECTION *conn;
  MI_FUNC_DESC   *fn;
  MI_TYPEID      *tid;
  MI_TYPE_DESC   *td;
  MI_FPARAM      *fnfp;
  mi_lvarchar    *retval;
  mi_string      buffer[2048], *pbuf;
  mi_integer     len, i;

  conn = mi_open(NULL, NULL, NULL);
  strcpy(buffer, mi_lvarchar_to_string(val1));
  fn = mi_routine_get(conn, 0, buffer);
```

```
if (fn == 0) {
  mi_close(conn);
  strcat(buffer, ": not found");
  return(mi_string_to_lvarchar(buffer));
}
fnfp = mi_fparam_get(conn, fn);
tid = mi_fp_rettype(fnfp, 0);
td  = mi_type_typedesc(conn, tid);
pbuf = mi_type_typename(td);
len = strlen(buffer);
sprintf(&buffer[len],
    "return value: %s(%d, %d)\n", pbuf,
        mi_fp_retprec(fnfp, 0),
mi_fp_retscale(fnfp, 0) );
```

After defining a set of variables, we open a connection to the database server. We then convert the `mi_lvarchar` argument into a string and copy it into our temporary buffer. That buffer is defined with length 2048, which is more than enough to contain all the information that we will return.

We retrieve the function descriptor by using the buffer containing the function signature. If `mi_routine_get()` returns a NULL value, no function with this signature exists. We indicate that the function was not found and return a `mi_lvarchar` variable based on the content of the buffer variable.

Using the function descriptor, we retrieve the MI_FPARAM structure for this function. The following three lines, starting with the `mi_fp_rettype()` function, retrieve the type name for the return value. We then add the type name, precision, and scale to our output buffer. What is left is to loop over the arguments and return the same information:

```
len = strlen(buffer);

for (i = 0; i < mi_fp_nargs(fnfp); i++) {
  tid = mi_fp_argtype(fnfp, i);
  td  = mi_type_typedesc(conn, tid);
  pbuf = mi_type_typename(td);
  sprintf(&buffer[len], "argument %i: %s(%d, %d)\n",
          i, pbuf, mi_fp_argprec(fnfp, i),
                  mi_fp_argscale(fnfp, i) );
```

```
        len = strlen(buffer);
    }
    retval = mi_string_to_lvarchar(buffer);
    mi_close(conn);
    return(retval);
}
```

The processing here is similar to the processing needed for the return value. The `mi_fp_nargs()` function gives us an exit condition for our loop. We retrieve the type identifier of the argument at the current position and process the type identifier the same way we processed the type identifier of the return value. The `sprintf()` function formats the result and puts it at the end of the buffer. The end-of-buffer position is recalculated, and we loop back to process the next argument. Once all the arguments are processed, we create a `mi_lvarchar` variable based on our buffer, close the connection, and return the `mi_lvarchar` result. Here is an example of the use of the `fninfo()` function:

```
execute function fninfo("cos(double precision)");
```

```
cos(double precision)
return value: float(0, 0)
argument 0: float(0, 0)
```

We reformatted the output to make it more readable. We can write a similar function to return information on casting function. We need to make only a few changes. First we add one argument:

```
mi_lvarchar *castinfo(mi_lvarchar *val1,
                    mi_lvarchar *val2, MI_FPARAM *fp);
```

Then we need to change the processing that retrieves the function descriptor. We first need to retrieve the type identifier from the type names provided as argument and use these type identifiers in the `mi_cast_get()` function that retrieves the function descriptor:

```
MI_TYPEID *tid, *tid2;
mi_char   status;
```

```
. . .
tid = mi_typename_to_id(conn, val1);
tid2 = mi_typename_to_id(conn, val2);
fn = mi_cast_get(conn, tid, tid2, &status);
. . .
```

The rest of the function is similar to the `fninfo()` function that we have seen before. The `castinfo()` function can then be used to retrieve information on casts:

```
execute function castinfo("integer", "double precision");

   cast from integer to double precision:
      return value: float(0, 0)
      argument 0  : integer(0, 0)
      argument 1  : integer(0, 0)
      argument 2  : integer(0, 0)
```

This type of information should make it easier to use functions properly on the first try. The fastpath interface is an important tool that reduces redundant code and enables the use of binary code from other sources.

Chapter 10

Smart Blobs and Multirepresentation

A row can store up to 32 KB of data, but it may not be sufficient to accommodate the size of your business type. For example, the travel industry may represent its rules as structures representing the specification of a main rule and a set of subrules. Since these variations can be numerous and complex, one approach could be to represent them internally as a hierarchy that can be processed efficiently with specialized algorithms. The representation of these rules may require more than 32 KB of storage.

With the current XML push, more and more businesses may represent their data in XML format. The more complex the data, the larger the XML representation will be. The representation size can easily exceed the row size limit.

IDS.2000 provides data types that solve the row size limitation. These types are called smart large objects and come in two flavors: binary large object, or BLOB, and character large object, or CLOB. This chapter introduces these data types and discusses their utilization: how to manipulate them as input to user-defined routines (UDRs) and how they are created as results to

UDR executions. This discussion culminates in the utilization of BLOBs and CLOBs in an opaque type, where they can be used either constantly as the storage mechanism of an opaque type or as a potential alternative, depending on the actual size of the opaque type.

What are Smart Large Objects?

Relational database systems have included the capability to store binary large objects, referred to as BLOBs, for many years. The Informix relational product implements BLOB versions. The type BYTE is used to store binary data, and the type TEXT is used for printable data. These types add the capability to store a large amount of data as an atomic element in a location separate from the row containing that element. Large objects allow for storage of large amounts of data. Furthermore, their specialized storage mechanism can be better tuned to the type of elements stored. The drawback is that these elements have to be retrieved as atomic elements. If we must operate on a two GB element stored as a BYTE, the entire element must be retrieved even if we need only a few hundred bytes from it.

IDS.2000 adds new types of large objects, dubbed smart large objects. IDS.2000 defines the maximum size of a smart large object as: 4 * (2 **40). This represents four TB of storage. Instead of giving access to the large object directly, smart large objects provide a handle for the content manipulation. A user-defined routine, or a client application, opens the handle to obtain a file descriptor. The large object file descriptor provides capabilities to position at specific locations within the large object and read an arbitrary number of bytes from its content. This way, the I/O operations are limited to the necessary ones, providing added performance. If the content of the smart large object is structured, most accesses will be limited to the needed data, which can provide significant performance benefits.

The DataBlade API supports only the smart large objects. The old-type BLOBs will be phased out over time. From now on, any reference to large objects actually refers only to smart-large objects.

Where Are Smart Large Objects Stored?

As we just saw, smart large objects are referenced through a large object handle: MI_LO_HANDLE. A MI_LO_HANDLE is a structure that uniquely identifies a specific large object. A large object is saved independently from a row. What is saved in the row is the 72-byte structure that identifies it. It is then possible to have multiple rows, even from different tables, point to the same large object by storing the MI_LO_HANDLE in multiple rows or tables.

The large object itself is stored in a specialized storage area called a smart blob space, or *sbspace*.

Defining Smart Blob Spaces

The Informix database products define storage areas to store system catalogs, indexes, tables, and so on. The general name for such a logical unit of storage is called a *dbspace* for database space. A dbspace defines contiguous storage areas called chunks. A *chunk* is a section of a disk drive or an entire disk drive. At the time of this writing, the chunk size was limited to 1,000,000 pages and the page size is usually two KB on UNIX systems and four KB on NT, so the chunk size is roughly limited to either two GB or four GB. A dbspace contains one or more chunks; however, the current version of IDS.2000 allows up to 2048 chunks in a given server.

An sbspace is a specialized dbspace that is used to store large objects. The database server must include at least one sbspace if large objects are to be used. The sbspace comprises a number of chunks that are used to store the large objects themselves but also includes metadata information about the large objects. IDS.2000 uses about 490 bytes of metadata information per large object.

The creation of an sbspace is a DBA task. However, it is good to know about the different characteristics that can be set at creation time. These characteristics include:

- Pagesize: An option is provided to set the size of a page for an sbspace. This option is currently ignored and the value one is used to represent one database page.

- EXTENT_SIZE: This value represents the size of the first extent that is allocated for a smart large. The default value is 16 KB.
- NEXT_SIZE: This is the next extent size used for space allocation to a large object. The default value is 16 KB.
- MIN_EXT_SIZE: This represents the minimum value that can be used for an extent size.
- LOGGING: IDS.2000 can log modified large objects. Even if logging is turned off, IDS.2000 still logs the metadata information. By default, logging is disabled.
- ACCESSTIME: This indicates whether the access time should be tracked. By default, the access time is not tracked.
- BUFFERING: This option indicates that the I/O should be done through the buffer pool or instead that the lightweight I/O, through private buffers from the session pool, will be used. The default value, off, enables lightweight I/O.
- AVG_LO_SIZE: This specifies the average size of the large objects that will be stored in this sbspace. The default value is 64 KB.
- MAX_IO_SIZE: This specifies the maximum size of I/O between client and server.

Several of these values can be overwritten either in the CREATE TABLE statement for a specific smart large object column or when creating a large object within a user-defined routine, as we will see later.

How to Find the Sbspaces

Your database administrator should be able to give you a list of the sbspaces available on your system. Here are two additional ways to find which sbspaces are available.

IDS.2000 contains a number of utility programs. One of them, onstat, provides multiple options to monitor system activities. Two options, -d and -D, are used to list storage information. Here is an extract of an execution of the onstat command:

```
onstat -d
. . .
Dbspaces
address   number flags fchunk nchunks  flags owner      name
c1e2108     1     1      1      1      N     informix rootdbs
c1e2480     2    8001    2      1      N S   informix sbspace
. . .
```

The sbspaces are identified by an additional `s` in the `flags` column. In this case there is only one sbspace, and it is named `sbspace`.

We can also retrieve the names of the sbspaces defined in the system by issuing the following SQL statement in the `sysmaster` database:

```
SELECT name FROM sysdbspaces WHERE is_sbspace = 1;
```

The result is one column of sbspaces names. These two methods can be useful reminders of the exact names of sbspaces; however, it is better to discuss their utilization with the appropriate responsible parties.

Creating Tables

IDS.2000 may define a default sbspace where to put smart large objects. This default location is defined in the configuration file "onconfig" with the parameter name `SBSPACENAME`. This way, it is possible to create a table that includes smart large objects with a statement such as

```
CREATE TABLE blobtab (
   col1 CLOB,
   col2 BLOB
);
```

This table defined one column, `col1`, as a character-based smart large object, and another one, `col2`, as a binary-based smart large object. Any insertion using default characteristics will put the smart large object in the database server default location using the defined characteristics of that sbspace.

It is possible to overwrite the default location where the smart large objects are stored and some of the characteristics used to store them by using the PUT statement in the CREATE TABLE statement:

```
CREATE TABLE blobtab (
   col1 CLOB,
   col2 BLOB
) PUT col1 IN (sbspace, sbspace2)
(EXTENT SIZE 4, NO LOG, HIGH INTEG, NO KEEP ACCESS TIME),
      col2 IN (sbspace2);
```

In this statement, we identify where each smart large object is to be stored by default. The first column, col1, will use two sbspaces, sbspace and sbspace2, in a round-robin manner when rows are inserted in blobtab. Some storage characteristics are set: The EXTENT SIZE is set to four KB, the smart large object data is not logged, it includes high-integrity features, and it does not keep track of the access time. The high-integrity feature uses pages that include page headers and trailers to detect incomplete writes and data corruption. The second column, col2, uses sbspace2 for storage with whatever characteristics the smart-blob space was created with.

The use of several sbspaces to store a smart-large object column can provide significant performance benefits. Accessing several rows then accesses several different smart blob spaces, which translates into simultaneous use of multiple disk drives.

Inserting Smart Large Objects

Since smart large objects are manipulated through MI_LO_HAN-DLES, it requires some programming intervention to insert and retrieve them. IDS.2000 provides four functions to accomplish this through SQL statements:

- FILETOBLOB: This function copies a file into a binary (smart) large object (BLOB). It takes at least two parameters, the path to the file to load and a string identifying whether the file is on the server or the client. It has two optional parameters that are used to identify the table and the column to which the storage characteristics are taken. The syntax is as follows:

```
FILETOBLOB(pathname, machine_location
[, table_name, column_name] )
```

- FILETOCLOB: This function is identical to FILETOBLOB except that it handles the creation of character large objects (CLOBs). The syntax is similar to that of FILETOBLOB.
- LOTOCOPY: The LOTOCOPY creates a copy of a smart large object and returns a handle to it. It can be used, for example, in an UPDATE statement where the update is done with a SELECT statement. This function takes either a BLOB or a CLOB column as input. It also has two optional parameters, table_name and column_name, that are used to overwrite the default storage characteristics. LOTOCOPY has the following syntax:

```
LOTOCOPY(BLOB_or_CLOB_column
[, table_name, column_name] );
```

- LOTOFILE: The LOTOFILE function is the reverse operation to FILETOBLOB and FILETOCLOB. It copies a smart large object to an operating system file, either on the server machine or on the client machine. It has the following syntax:

```
LOTOFILE(BLOB_or_CLOB_column,
pathname, machine_location);
```

To insert data into the blobtab table that was defined above, we can use FILETOBLOB and FILETOCLOB in a statement such as

```
INSERT INTO blobtab
VALUES(
  FILETOCLOB('/usr/informix/etc/onconfig',
  'server'),
  FILETOBLOB('/usr/informix/bin/onstat',   'server')
);
```

This statement takes well-known files that are part of the "$INFORMIXDIR" directory structure (assuming that directory is represented here as /usr/informix) on the server machine and copies them into smart large objects.

The Large Object API Functions

The DataBlade API provides a set of functions that are used to manipulate smart large objects. These functions are listed in Table 10–1. This may at first appear to represent a large number of functions to learn, but once we divide them into functional groups they are much less overwhelming.

Table 10–1 Smart-large object API functions.

mi_file_to_file()	mi_lo_alter()	mi_lo_close()
mi_lo_colinfo_by_ids()	mi_lo_colinfo_by_name()	mi_lo_copy()
mi_lo_create()	mi_lo_decrefcount()	mi_lo_expand()
mi_lo_filename()	mi_lo_from_file()	mi_lo_from_file_by_lofd()
mi_lo_from_string()	mi_lo_increfcount()	mi_lo_invalidate()
mi_lo_lolist_create()	mi_lo_open()	mi_lo_read()
mi_lo_readwithseek()	mi_lo_seek()	mi_lo_specget_estbytes()
mi_lo_specget_extsz()	mi_lo_specget_flags()	mi_lo_specget_maxbytes()
mi_lo_specget_sbspace()	mi_lo_specset_estbytes()	mi_lo_specset_extsz()
mi_lo_specset_flags()	mi_lo_specset_maxbytes()	mi_lo_specset_sbspace()
mi_lo_spec_free()	mi_lo_spec_init()	mi_lo_stat()
mi_lo_stat_atime()	mi_lo_stat_cspec()	mi_lo_stat_ctime()
mi_lo_stat_free()	mi_lo_stat_mtime_sec()	mi_lo_stat_mtime_usec()
mi_lo_stat_refcnt()	mi_lo_stat_size()	mi_lo_stat_uid()
mi_lo_tell()	mi_lo_to_file()	mi_lo_to_string()
mi_lo_truncate()	mi_lo_validate()	mi_lo_write()
mi_lo_writewithseek()		

About half the functions are used to get or set large object statistics and specifications. Other functions are used for smart large object creation, I/O, and handling. Finally, a few functions are provided to move large objects to and from operating system files. The next few sections cover these different function groups.

Large Object Structures

The DataBlade API provides three structures for manipulation of smart large objects.

- `MI_LO_HANDLE`: As its name implies, the `MI_LO_HANDLE` is a unique identifier to a smart large object. This is the structure we receive when retrieving a large object type.
- `MI_LO_SPEC`: The `MI_LO_SPEC` contains the storage characteristics that are used to create a smart large object or the characteristics extracted from an existing object.
- `MI_LO_STAT`: This structure describes the attributes of a smart large object.
- `MI_LO_FD`: The `MI_LO_FD` is a file descriptor. We obtain a file descriptor by opening a `MI_LO_HANDLE`.

These four structures allow the creation and manipulation of smart large objects. We will see in the next sections how they are used.

Processing a Large Object

A user-defined routine may receive a large object as argument. As mentioned before, the smart large object is represented by a `MI_LO_HANDLE`, so a user-defined routine receives a `MI_LO_HANDLE` pointer argument. The function definition of a user-defined routine taking a smart-large object as argument and returning a `LVARCHAR` is:

```
mi_lvarchar *do_clob(MI_LO_HANDLE *lo, MI_FPARAM *fp);
```

To process the smart large object, the user-defined routine must first obtain a `MI_LO_FD` by opening the `MI_LO_HANDLE`. The processing is illustrated in the following code:

```
mi_char buffer[120];
mi_integer len;
MI_CONNECTION *conn;
MI_LO_FD  fd;
. . .

/* open connection */
conn = mi_open(NULL, NULL, NULL);

/* Open the large object, get its size */
fd = mi_lo_open(conn, lo, MI_LO_RDONLY);

/* we can use the following test since MI_ERROR is < 0 */
while (0 < (len = mi_lo_read(conn, fd, buffer, 120)) ) {
   . . .
}
mi_lo_close(conn, fd);
mi_close(conn);
. . .
```

This code starts by obtaining a connection to the database server with the `mi_open()` API function. As we saw earlier, the NULL values default to the current environment. Once we have the database connection, we use it in the `mi_lo_open()` function to obtain an open file descriptor (`MI_LO_FD`) from the `MI_LO_HANDLE` that was passed as argument. The `while` loop reads the smart large object 120 bytes at a time into the buffer variable, until no more data is returned. Once the processing is done, we close the large object file descriptor and close the database connection.

The smart large object access functions are modeled after the UNIX file access functions. The DataBlade API includes ten functions for smart-large object I/O. Their usage is straightforward; however, the `mi_lo_open()` requires some attention because it impacts the way the large object is processed.

The `mi_lo_open()` syntax is

```
MI_LO_FD mi_lo_open(MI_CONNECTION *conn,
                MI_LO_HANDLE *lo, mi_integer flags);
```

The first argument is a valid database connection and the second argument is a handle to a large object. The third argument is a bitmask that indicates how the file descriptor will be handled. The possible values are:

- `MI_LO_APPEND`: Indicates that any write operation is done at end of file.
- `MI_LO_WRONLY`: Only write operations are allowed.
- `MI_LO_RDONLY`: Only read operations are allowed.
- `MI_LO_RDWR`: Both read and write operations are permitted.
- `MI_LO_RANDOM`: Indicates that the I/O will be random, so the system should not read ahead.
- `MI_LO_SEQUENTIAL`: Indicates that the I/O will be sequential, either forward or in reverse.
- `MI_LO_BUFFER`: Indicates that the I/O is going through the buffer pool.
- `MI_LO_NOBUFFER`: Indicates that the I/O does not use the buffer pool. This mode is referred to as lightweight I/O. The buffers are allocated out of the session pool.
- `MI_LO_TRUNC`: Truncates the large object.

These flags are mixed together to obtain the exact behavior desired. For example, we can open a large object for read/write that uses random access and has lightweight I/O thus:

```
fd = mi_lo_open(conn, lo,
                MI_LO_RDWR | MI_LO_RANDOM |
                  MI_LO_NOBUFFER);
```

The other API function used in the code example is `mi_lo_read()`. It takes a database connection, a large object file descriptor, a buffer, and the maximum length of the read. The result is either the number of bytes read or `MI_ERROR`. When the large object current position is at end of file, `mi_lo_read()` returns zero, indicating that no more data is available.

Other DataBlade API functions allow the user to set or to find the current position within the large object The read and write API functions also have a version that allows setting the current position before the operation is performed. The Appendix describes these functions.

Large Object Statistics

We can obtain large object statistics from a smart large object. The statistics include access time, creation time, modification time, reference count, size, and so on. Here is an example of how the statistics can be obtained:

```
mi_lvarchar *lostat(MI_LO_HANDLE *mylo, MI_FPARAM *fp)
{
  MI_CONNECTION *conn;
  MI_LO_FD      fd;
  MI_LO_STAT    *lstat;
  mi_integer    ret, atime, c_time, mtime, mutime,
     rcnt, uid;
  mi_int8       size;
  mi_char       buffer[512];
  mi_lvarchar   *retval;

  conn = mi_open(NULL, NULL, NULL);

  fd = mi_lo_open(conn, mylo, MI_LO_RDONLY);

  /* needs to be initialized to NULL or allocated */
  lstat = 0;
  ret = mi_lo_stat(conn, fd, &lstat);
  atime = mi_lo_stat_atime(lstat);
  c_time = mi_lo_stat_ctime(lstat);
  mtime = mi_lo_stat_mtime_sec(lstat);
  mutime = mi_lo_stat_mtime_usec(lstat);
  rcnt = mi_lo_stat_refcnt(lstat);
  ret = mi_lo_stat_size(lstat, &size);
  uid = mi_lo_stat_uid(lstat);

  sprintf(buffer, "Creation time: %s, ", ctime(&c_time));
  ret = strlen(buffer);
  sprintf(&buffer[ret], "access time: %s, ",
          ctime(&atime));
  ret = strlen(buffer);
  sprintf(&buffer[ret], "modif time: %s sec, ",
          ctime(&mtime));
  ret = strlen(buffer);
```

```
sprintf(&buffer[ret],
  "modif time: %d usec, ref count: %d, uid: %d, size: ",
    mutime, rcnt, uid);
ret = strlen(buffer);
ifx_int8toasc(&size, &buffer[ret], 30);

mi_lo_stat_free(conn, lstat);
mi_lo_close(conn, fd);
mi_close(conn);
retval = mi_string_to_lvarchar(buffer);
return(retval);
}
```

This function takes a MI_LO_HANDLE pointer argument and returns a LVARCHAR variable containing all the values available in the MI_LO_STAT structure. It first opens a connection to the database server and, with this connection, opens the large object handle to get a file descriptor.

The MI_LO_STAT pointer must be initialized to zero before the call to mi_lo_stat(); otherwise, the API function assumes that the pointer is valid and tries to populate it instead of allocating the structure first. The following few function calls simply extract the values from the MI_LO_STAT structure.

The MI_LO_STAT structure contains the creation time, access time, and modification time. These times represent the number of seconds since a specific epoch, which is in fact the way the operating system stores a calendar time value. Seeing the value as a number of seconds is not very useful because people don't process calendar time in these units. This function solves the problem by using a standard C library function, ctime(), to convert this value to a character string of the form

```
<day-of-the-week> <month> <day> <hh:mm:ss> <year>
```

The ctime() function takes a pointer to a time value as argument and returns a pointer to a statically allocated buffer containing the time as converted to a character string. This means that the function is not thread safe, since multiple calls to ctime() overwrite the buffer. This is why we call this function in separate statements. The UNIX environment provides an additional function, ctime_r(), that requires a buffer as argument and is thread safe.

Once we are done with the `MI_LO_STAT` structure, we free it up, close the large object handle, and close the database connection before creating and returning our string result.

Large Object Specifications

It is also possible to extract the large object specifications that contain where the large object is stored, the storage characteristics, and the flags that are set for it. The following function illustrates how this information can be extracted:

```
char *flagnames[] = {
        "LOG", "NOLOG", "DELAY_LOG",
            "KEEP_LASTACCESS_TIME",
        "NOKEEP_LASTACCESS_TIME", "HIGH_INTEG",
        "MODERATE_INTEG" };

mi_lvarchar *lospec(MI_LO_HANDLE *mylo, MI_FPARAM *fp)
{
  MI_CONNECTION *conn;
  MI_LO_FD        fd;
  MI_LO_STAT    *lstat;
  MI_LO_SPEC    *lspec;
  mi_integer    ret, i, val, extent, flags;
  mi_char       buffer[512], sbname[130], buf2[30];
  mi_int8       esize, maxsize;
  mi_lvarchar   *retval;

  conn = mi_open(NULL, NULL, NULL);
  fd = mi_lo_open(conn, mylo, MI_LO_RDONLY);

  lstat = 0;
  ret = mi_lo_stat(conn, fd, &lstat);
  lspec = mi_lo_stat_cspec(lstat);

  ret = mi_lo_specget_estbytes(lspec, &esize);
  extent = mi_lo_specget_extsz(lspec);
  flags = mi_lo_specget_flags(lspec);
```

```
ret = mi_lo_specget_maxbytes(lspec, &maxsize);
ret = mi_lo_specget_sbspace(lspec, sbname, 130);

ifx_int8toasc(&esize, buf2, 30);
sprintf(buffer, "est size: %s, ", buf2);
ret = strlen(buffer);
ifx_int8toasc(&maxsize, buf2, 30);
sprintf(&buffer[ret],
  "max size: %s, extent size: %d, flags: ",buf2,
extent);
ret = strlen(buffer);
for (i = 0, val = 1; i < 7; i++) {
  if (0 != (flags & val)) {
    sprintf(&buffer[ret], "%s, ", flagnames[i]);
    ret = strlen(buffer);
  }
  val *= 2;
}
sprintf(&buffer[ret], "sbspace name: %s", sbname);
mi_lo_spec_free(conn, lspec);
mi_lo_stat_free(conn, lstat);
mi_lo_close(conn, fd);
mi_close(conn);
retval = mi_string_to_lvarchar(buffer);
return(retval);
}
```

The lospec() function takes the same argument as the lostat() function we saw in the previous section. It also starts the same way by getting a connection to the database server and opening the large object handle. It even gets the MI_LO_STAT structure from the MI_LO_FD open descriptor. The MI_LO_SPEC is then obtained by using the mi_lo_stat_cspec() API function.

The following few calls extract information from the MI_LO_SPEC structure about the estimated byte size, the extent size, the creation flags, the maximum size, and the smart-blob space name. Both the estimated number of bytes and the maximum sizes are mi_int8 values, because the maximum size of a smart large object requires more than 32 bits to express it. We must then handle these values with the appropriate functions: in this case, ifx_int8toasc().

The rest of the function simply converts the `MI_LO_SPEC` information to character format. We do the conversion of the flags to a readable representation by using a predefined string array, `flagnames`, which contains the value for each flag. Once this is done, we make sure that all the structures are freed, the large object is closed, and the database connection is closed before we return the `LVARCHAR` result.

Creating a Large Object

To create a large object, we first need to create a large object specification (`MI_LO_SPEC`) that is then used to create the large object handle (`MI_LO_HANDLE`). We then open the handle to obtain a large object file descriptor (`MI_LO_FD`) and write into the large object. This process is best illustrated with an example. The following function takes the path name of a file and a location, and writes it to a large object. It returns a large object handle that the database server can insert into a row. This functionality is similar to the `FILETOCLOB` function provided with IDS.2000.

```
#include <mi.h>

MI_LO_HANDLE *cre8clob(mi_lvarchar *path,
                       mi_lvarchar *loc, MI_FPARAM *fp)
{
  MI_CONNECTION *conn;
  MI_LO_FD       fd;
  MI_LO_SPEC    *lspec;
  mi_integer    ret;
  mi_int8       size;
  mi_char       *pbuf;
  MI_LO_HANDLE *retval;

  conn = mi_open(NULL, NULL, NULL);
  lspec = NULL;
  ret = mi_lo_spec_init(conn, &lspec);
  ret = mi_lo_specset_extsz(lspec, 4);
```

```
    ret = mi_lo_specset_flags(lspec, MI_LO_ATTR_NO_LOG |
              MI_LO_ATTR_NOKEEP_LASTACCESS_TIME |
              MI_LO_ATTR_HIGH_INTEG);
    ret = mi_lo_specset_sbspace(lspec, "sbspace");

    retval = NULL;
    fd = mi_lo_create(conn, lspec, MI_LO_WRONLY, &retval);

    pbuf = mi_lvarchar_to_string(loc);
    if (strcmp(pbuf, "server"))
      flags = MI_O_SERVER_FILE;
    else
      flags = MI_O_CLIENT_FILE;
    flags |= MI_O_RDONLY;
    pbuf = mi_lvarchar_to_string(path);
    ret = mi_lo_from_file_by_lofd(conn, fd, pbuf,
                                    flags, 0, -1);
    mi_lo_spec_free(conn, lspec);
    mi_lo_close(conn, fd);
    mi_close(conn);
    return(retval);
  }
```

The function starts by opening a connection to the database server. It then creates a large object specification by calling `mi_lo_spec_init()`. The `MI_LO_SPEC` pointer is first initialized to `NULL` so that the function knows it does not contain a valid pointer. If the pointer is not initialized to `NULL`, an invalid pointer error will be returned.

We then initialize the specification values for the extent size, attribute flags, and the smart-blob space name. At this point, we are ready to create the large object. The `MI_LO_HANDLE` pointer must be initialized to `NULL` to indicate that it must be allocated.

Once the `MI_LO_HANDLE` is created, we get ready to transfer the content of the file argument to the large object by using `mi_lo_from_file_by_lofd()`. This function has the following signature:

```
  mi_integer mi_lo_from_file_by_lofd(MI_CONNECTION *conn,
            MI_LO_FD fd, mi_char *path, mi_integer flags,
            mi_integer offset, mi_integer amount);
```

The arguments are a database connection, an open large-object file descriptor, a file path name, and the indicators on how to open the file, where to start reading in the file, and the number of bytes to read (or –1 if the entire file should be read).

The `flags` argument provides several indicators on how to open and process the file. It also identifies the file location, and indicates whether it is on the machine where the database server is running or is located on the same machine as the client application. The possible values are as follows:

- `MI_O_EXCL`: Opens the file only if it exists.
- `MI_O_TRUNC`: Zeroes out the input file before reading it.
- `MI_O_APPEND`: Allows appending at the end of the file.
- `MI_O_RDWR`: Opens the file in read-write mode.
- `MI_O RDONLY`: Opens the file for read-only.
- `MI_O_TEXT`: Processes the file as text.
- `MI_O_SERVER_FILE`: Indicates that the file resides on the same machine as the database server.
- `MI_O_CLIENT_FILE`: Indicates that the file resides on the same machine as the client application.

Obviously some of these indicators do not apply to the function discussed here.

Before we call `mi_lo_from_file_by_lofd()`, we set the flags argument to the desired value by looking at the character string contained in the `loc` argument. We then retrieve the string contained in the path argument before copying the file into the newly created large object. Then we free the memory allocated to the `MI_LO_SPEC`, close the large-object file descriptor, and close the connection before returning the `MI_LO_HANDLE` pointer. After compiling the function we can use it, as in the following example:

```
CREATE FUNCTION cre8clob(lvarchar, lvarchar)
RETURNING CLOB
. . .

CREATE TABLE blobtab (
  col1 CLOB
);
```

```
INSERT INTO blobtab
VALUES(cre8clob('/jroy/book/code10/cre8.c',
   'client'));
```

In the `INSERT INTO` statement, the database server takes the result of the `cre8clob()` function, a `MI_LO_HANDLE` pointer, increments the reference count of the large object, and inserts it into a new row in the `blobtab` table.

A large object exists independently from any table row or any large object handles. Its existence depends only on its reference count. Once the reference count goes to zero, the large object is removed from the database. If we were to execute the following statement after the `INSERT INTO` statement above:

```
SELECT * FROM blobtab
INTO TEMP temptab;
```

the database would contain only one smart large object. The `SELECT INTO` a temporary table would copy the large object handle into the `temptab` table and increment the reference count of the smart large object. When the temporary table is dropped, the reference count is decremented to reflect the removal of one reference. In the current example, the database server handles the reference count, so we don't have to worry about this type of error. We will need to worry about the reference count later in this chapter.

Getting Row Specifications

In the previous example, we created a `MI_LO_SPEC` and manually set all the values. We also saw earlier that both `FILETOCLOB` and `FILETOBLOB` accept two optional arguments, a table name and a column name, to set the large-object creation specifications.

Instead of setting the specifications, we can retrieve them based on a table name and a column name. Once we have initialized a `MI_LO_SPEC`, we can execute the following statement to use the values included in the `CREATE TABLE` statement instead of setting the values:

```
ret = mi_lo_colinfo_by_name(conn, "blobtab.col1", lspec);
```

The arguments are a database connection, a column specification, and a pointer to a valid `MI_LO_SPEC`. The column specification has the following format:

```
[dbname[@servername]:][owner.]table.column
```

where

- `dbname`: database name
- `servername`: database server name
- `owner`: table owner name
- `table`: table name
- `column`: column name

Only the last two arguments are required, as illustrated in the example above. The DataBlade API provides another function, `mi_lo_colinfo_by_ids()`, which provides the same functionality by extracting the information from a `MI_ROW` pointer and a column number. We will see its usage later in this chapter.

Opaque Types and Large Objects

Opaque types may contain smart large object handles. Since the database server does not have access to an opaque type content, we must manipulate its content ourselves. Opaque types are covered in detail in Chap. 7. This section covers only the minimum required to discuss the handling of smart large objects.

A `MI_LO_HANDLE` object requires 72 bytes of storage. We can create an opaque type containing a large object reference with a statement such as:

```
CREATE OPAQUE TYPE myopaque (internallength = 72,
                            alignment = 8);
```

This constitutes a fixed-sized opaque type that, since its size is known, is manipulated directly by the database server. The opaque type implementation provides functions to convert between internal and external representations. It also provides two additional functions, assign and destroy, to provide processing when the opaque type is saved to disk and when it is removed.

The implementation of an opaque type containing a `MI_LO_HANDLE` can follow two strategies:

- Create the opaque type in the input function and increment the reference count in the assign function.
- Save the information about the input value in the input function and wait for the assign function to create the opaque type and increment the reference count.

We will cover the first option in this section and the second option in the section on multirepresentation. The following example simply takes a string as input and stores it in a large object within the opaque type. The input function is as follows:

```
typedef struct {
  MI_LO_HANDLE lo;
} myopaque;

myopaque *myoinput(mi_lvarchar *val, MI_FPARAM *fp)
{
  MI_CONNECTION *conn;
  MI_LO_FD      fd;
  MI_LO_SPEC    *lspec;
  mi_char       *data;
  mi_integer    ret, len;
  myopaque      *retval;
  MI_LO_HANDLE  *lo;

  conn = mi_open(NULL, NULL, NULL);

  data = mi_get_vardata(val);
  len = mi_get_varlen(val);

  retval = (myopaque *)mi_alloc(sizeof(myopaque));

  /* Create a large object */
  lspec = NULL;
  ret = mi_lo_spec_init(conn, &lspec);
  ret = mi_lo_specset_extsz(lspec, 4);
  ret = mi_lo_specset_flags(lspec, MI_LO_ATTR_NO_LOG |
          MI_LO_ATTR_NOKEEP_LASTACCESS_TIME |
          MI_LO_ATTR_HIGH_INTEG);
```

```
ret = mi_lo_specset_sbspace(lspec, "sbspace");
lo = NULL;
fd = mi_lo_create(conn, lspec, MI_LO_WRONLY, &lo);

/* write to the large object */
ret = mi_lo_write(conn, fd, data, len);

mi_lo_spec_free(conn, lspec);
mi_lo_close(conn, fd);
mi_close(conn);
memcpy(&retval->lo, lo, sizeof(MI_LO_HANDLE));
return(retval);
}
```

This function should be easy to follow considering what we covered earlier. Let's review briefly.

We create a structure for our opaque type that contains a MI_LO_HANDLE as its only element. After opening a connection to the database server, we retrieve the content and length of the LVARCHAR argument. We then allocate memory for the return argument, which is a myopaque structure.

The following section creates and sets a MI_LO_SPEC structure and creates a large object. Note once again that both the MI_LO_SPEC pointer and the MI_LO_HANDLE pointer are initialized to NULL so that the appropriate calls will allocate them. We then write the content of the argument to the large object, release the memory allocated to the MI_LO_SPEC, and close both the MI_LO_FD and the connection to the database server.

Before we return, we must copy the MI_LO_HANDLE into our opaque type structure. The opaque type is then returned to the database server.

Assuming that the context is an insert statement, the database server calls the assign function that takes a myopaque as argument before saving the opaque type to disk. The assign function is as follows:

```
myopaque *myoassign(myopaque *val, MI_FPARAM *fp)
{
  MI_CONNECTION *conn;

  conn = mi_open(NULL, NULL, NULL);
  mi_lo_increfcount(conn, &val->lo);
```

```
mi_close(conn);
return(val);
}
```

The key to this function is the call to `mi_lo_increfcount()`.
This function increments the reference count of a smart large
object described by the `MI_LO_HANDLE` pointer argument. Before
this call, the smart large object had a reference count of zero.
The `myoassign()` function ensures that the smart large object
becomes persistent. The functions are created in the database
server with the following statements:

```
CREATE FUNCTION myoin(lvarchar)
RETURNS myopaque
. . .


CREATE IMPLICIT CAST (lvarchar AS myopaque WITH
   myoin);

CREATE FUNCTION assign(myopaque)
RETURNS myopaque
. . .
```

The database server resolves the input function through the
implicit cast. The assign function is resolved by looking for an
`assign()` function with the proper signature. These two functions allow us to do the following:

```
CREATE TABLE myop (
   col1 myopaque
) ;
INSERT INTO myop VALUES("hello world");
```

To provide a minimum of functionality, we need to add an output function and the destroy function that is used in the case of
DELETE and DROP operations. The output function reads the
smart large object and returns its content in the proper external
representation. In our example, we simply stored a character string
in the smart large object. We only need to read and return it:

```
mi_lvarchar *myooutput(myopaque *val, MI_FPARAM *fp)
{
```

```
MI_CONNECTION *conn;
MI_LO_FD       fd;
mi_char        buffer[2048];
mi_integer     ret, len;
mi_lvarchar    *retval;

conn = mi_open(NULL, NULL, NULL);

fd = mi_lo_open(conn, &val->lo, MI_LO_RDONLY);
len = mi_lo_read(conn, fd, buffer, 2048);

retval = mi_new_var(len);
mi_set_vardata(retval, buffer);
return(retval);
}
```

This code opens a smart large object, reads its content, and creates a `mi_lvarchar` variable to return that content. For simplicity, this example assumes that the smart-large object content will never exceed 2048 bytes; otherwise, we would have to loop on the read operation until no more bytes are returned.

To handle the removal of this opaque type, we use the following `destroy()` function:

```
void myodestroy(myopaque *val, MI_FPARAM *fp)
{
  MI_CONNECTION *conn;

  conn = mi_open(NULL, NULL, NULL);
  mi_lo_decrefcount(conn, &val->lo);
  mi_close(conn);
  return;
}
```

The `destroy()` function decrements the reference count of the large object in the opaque type. If the reference count goes to zero, the database server will remove the large object from the system. The `output()` and `destroy()` functions are created with the following statements:

```
CREATE FUNCTION myoout(myopaque)
RETURNS lvarchar
```

```
. . .
CREATE CAST (myopaque AS lvarchar WITH myoout);

CREATE PROCEDURE destroy(myopaque)
. . .
```

Note that the destroy() function uses the CREATE PROCEDURE instead of the CREATE FUNCTION statement. A procedure is similar to a function except that it does not return a value. Since destroy() is defined as not returning anything, it must be defined as a procedure. With these functions in place we can issue SQL statements such as

```
SELECT col1 FROM myop;
DROP TABLE myop;
```

Additional functions are required for more complex SQL statements. Consult Chap. 7 for more information on support functions for opaque types.

Getting Row Context

The example above still defines the storage specification manually. This is somewhat problematic since the input function must know specific information about storage characteristics. The input() function relies on the existence of a smart blob space with a specific name.

In some SQL contexts, a user-defined routine can retrieve row context information through the MI_FPARAM structure. Two API functions provide this capability:

```
MI_ROW *mi_fp_getrow(MI_FPARAM *fp);
mi_integer mi_fp_getcolid(MI_FPARAM *fp);
```

The mi_fp_getrow() function returns a MI_ROW pointer that is the row context in which the function executes. The mi_fp_get-colid() returns the column number of this context. With these values, we can retrieve storage specifications by calling

```
mi_integer mi_lo_colinfo_by_ids(MI_CONNECTION *conn,
         MI_ROW *row, mi_integer colno,
         MI_LO_SPEC *lspec);
```

This function performs the same task as `mi_lo_colinfo_by_name()`. It retrieves storage specifications for a specific table column and stores the values in the `MI_LO_SPEC` provided as argument. We could find the storage characteristics by issuing the following statement:

```
ret = mi_lo_colinfo_by_ids(conn, mi_fp_getrow(fp),
                       mi_fp_getcolid(fp), lspec);
```

This statement assumes a context similar to that of the code example presented in the previous section.

The DataBlade API documentation defines `mi_fp_getrow()` as valid only when called from either `assign()`, `destroy()`, or `import()`. All these functions are always used in the context of a row: `assign()` and `destroy()` for storage and removal of rows to and from disk, and `import()` in the case of bulk copy. So, what about the `input()` function?

The `input()` function is used in the context of a row when doing inserts but can also be used in other situations. Consider the following SQL statement:

```
SELECT * FROM myop
  WHERE col1 = 'hello world'::myopaque;
```

Obviously, this statement does not make sense in the context of the `myop` table, which has only one column, but it is easy to see that this type of statement could be issued. In this case, the `WHERE` clause creates a `myopaque` type to resolve the clause. The character string is converted by calling the `myoinput()` function; the function does not have a row context to work with so a call to `mi_fp_getrow()` returns a `NULL` value instead of a `MI_ROW` pointer.

We could easily put together a hybrid solution that would test the return value of `mi_fp_getrow()` and then decide to use the row context or set specific values in the `MI_LO_SPEC` structure.

The SELECT statement above illustrates another issue with the creation of a large object within the input() function. The input function goes through all the trouble to create, open, and write a large object for the string in the WHERE clause, but the smart large object is discarded at the end of the statement because the reference count remains at zero. Furthermore, every comparison has to read two separate smart large objects. It would be more efficient to keep the temporary myopaque object in memory for the duration of the statement instead of going to a large object right away. This provides a strong argument for waiting until the assign() function execution before creating a smart large object. This also ensures that a row context is available to get the storage specifications. This approach is discussed in the next section within the context of multirepresentation opaque types.

The lohandles() function

IDS.2000 defines a function that allows the user of an opaque type to get a list of the MI_LO_HANDLE structures contained in the opaque type. The function is called lohandles(). As of IDS.2000, this function is not yet required in opaque type implementations; however, this can easily become a requirement for features such as data replication. The lohandles() function for our myopaque type is as follows:

```
mi_bitvarying *myolohandles(myopaque *val, MI_FPARAM *fp)
{
  MI_CONNECTION  *conn;
  mi_bitvarying  *retval;
  MI_LO_LIST     *lolist;

  conn = mi_open(NULL, NULL, NULL);

  if (mi_lo_validate(conn, &val->lo) != 0) {
    mi_close(conn);
    return(NULL);
  }
```

```
retval = (mi_bitvarying *)mi_new_var(
        sizeof(mi_integer) + sizeof(MI_LO_HANDLE));
lolist = (MI_LO_LIST *)
        mi_get_vardata((mi_lvarchar *)retval);
memcpy(lolist->lol_handles[0], val->lo,
    sizeof(MI_LO_HANDLE));
lolist->lol_cnt = 1;

mi_close(conn);
return(retval);
}
```

This function creates a `MI_LO_LIST` structure and wraps it into a `mi_bitvarying` structure since the `MI_LO_LIST` is a variable-size structure. Keep in mind that a `mi_bitvarying` structure is the same thing as a `mi_lvarchar` structure. The name difference gives an indication of the content of the data buffer within the structure. The `MI_LO_LIST` structure is defined in `milo.h`. It contains a count followed by an array of `MI_LO_HANDLE` structures.

In our case, we know that the `myopaque` type contains only one `MI_LO_HANDLE`, so we allocate enough space for the count and one `MI_LO_HANDLE`. The handle is copied from the opaque type to the `MI_LO_LIST`, the count is set, and we return the result after closing the database connection.

The SQL declaration for the `lohandles()` function is as follows:

```
CREATE FUNCTION lohandles(myopaque)
RETURNS lolist
EXTERNAL NAME ". . . /chap10.bld(myolohandles)"
LANGUAGE C;
```

Multirepresentation Opaque Types

As we just saw, using smart blob space to store opaque types requires more processing than an in-row representation. Furthermore, it has additional space overhead, including about

490 bytes for the metadata information and 72-byte in-row representation for the large object handle.

A business type representation may contain a variable amount of information, and its maximum size may exceed the row size limit. It is possible to include some logic in an opaque type to base the choice of where the data is stored on the amount of storage required. If the opaque type requires less than a specific limit, it is stored in row; otherwise, it is stored in a smart large object. This dual storage method is called *multirepresentation.*

The DataBlade API provides basic functionality for the implementation of multi-representation opaque types. Most of the support is included in the following type definitions:

```
typedef mi_integer MI_MULTIREP_SIZE;
#define MI_MULTIREP_SMALL  0
#define MI_MULTIREP_LARGE  1

#define mi_issmall_data(size)(!((size) &
  MI_MULTIREP_LARGE))
#define mi_set_large(size) \
        ((void)((size) |= MI_MULTIREP_LARGE))

typedef union
{
    void    * mr_data;
    struct _mr_lo_struct
        {
        MI_LO_HANDLE    mr_s_lo;
        void            * mr_s_pin_addr;
        } mr_lo_struct;
} MI_MULTIREP_DATA;

#define mr_lo              mr_lo_struct.mr_s_lo
#define mr_lo_pin_data  mr_lo_struct.mr_s_pin_addr
```

These definitions are found in the milo.h include file. A new type based on an integer type, MI_MULTIREP_SIZE, is provided to identify a structure as being either a large object or an internal structure. It also defines two values for the two possibilities, as well as testing macros, mi_issmall_data() and mi_set_large(), to test and set the type of representation of an opaque type.

The key to the multirepresentation support is the `MI_MULTI-REP_DATA` union. It stores either a pointer to the opaque type data or a `MI_LO_HANDLE` and `mr_s_pin_addr`, which is provided for backward compatibility for some Illustra DataBlade API calls. Since this book is about IDS.2000, it does not cover any backward compatibility calls. An additional two shorthand macros are also provided.

The `MI_MULTIREP_DATA` union is used in one DataBlade API function:

```
MI_LO_FD mi_lo_expand(MI_CONNECTION *conn,
        MI_LO_HANDLE **handle, MI_MULTIREP_DATA *data,
        mi_integer len, mi_integer flags,
        MI_LO_SPEC *lspec);
```

The `mi_lo_expand()` function creates a new smart-large object and copies the data into it. The function arguments are as follow:

- `conn:` a database connection.
- `handle:` a pointer to a pointer to a `MI_LO_HANDLE` that will be set to reference the newly created `MI_LO_HANDLE`.
- `data:` a `MI_MULTIREP_DATA` pointer argument that is used to extract the content for the smart large object.
- `len:` the length of the data element.
- `flags:` the open flags for the large object.
- `lspec:` the storage specifications for the large object.

We need to keep track of which representation is used for a specific instance of our opaque type. This requires additional information in the opaque type structure, including the length of the data and the type of storage used.

Since a multirepresentation type may contain a large object handle, we need to decide on our implementation strategy. When needed, we can either create the large object in the `input()` function or in the `assign()` function. In the following example, we use the latter method.

For our example, we will use the following opaque type definition:

```
CREATE OPAQUE TYPE mymulti (
  internallength = variable, alignment = 8
);
```

The `mymulti` opaque type is defined as a variable-size type. Since the maximum length is not defined, it defaults to 2048. This maximum size indicates that the opaque type will not exceed this size. The opaque type implementation decided how close to this limit it gets. It is a good idea to be consistent between the declaration and the implementation.

To support our implementation, we first create an enumeration type to keep track of the state of the data and the internal structure of the multirepresentation type:

```
typedef enum {
  MyUndefined = 0,
  MySmall,
  MyBuffered,
  MyLarge
}MyState;

typedef struct {
  mi_integer        len;
  MyState           state;
  MI_MULTIREP_DATA data;
} mymulti;
```

The `MyState` enumeration defines `MySmall` to indicate that we have an in-row representation and `MyLarge` for the use of a large object handle. The `MyBuffered` state refers to an intermediary representation where the large object creation is deferred until the `assign()` function is called.

The `mymulti` structure contains the length of the data, the type of representation currently used, and a `MI_MULTIREP_DATA` structure to support multirepresentation. The opaque type data could also require other structure definitions to facilitate its access. To keep the example as simple as possible, we limit the data to a simple character string, similar to the example in the previous section.

The `input()` function takes a `mi_lvarchar` pointer as input value and returns the opaque type wrapped into a `mi_bitvarying` structure. The `mi_bitvarying` type is the same as `mi_lvarchar`. It indicates that the content is in binary format. The `input()` function is as follows:

```
mi_bitvarying *myminput(mi_lvarchar *val, MI_FPARAM *fp)
{
  mi_char       *data;
  mi_integer    ret, fullen, len;
  mi_bitvarying *retval;
  mymulti       *mymval;
  mi_char *     buffer;

  data = mi_get_vardata(val);
  len = mi_get_varlen(val);
  fullen = sizeof(mymulti) - sizeof(MI_MULTIREP_DATA) +
           len;

  if (fullen > MYTHRESHOLD) {
    buffer = (mi_char *)mi_dalloc(len, PER_COMMAND);
    retval = (mi_bitvarying *)mi_new_var(sizeof
      (mymulti));
    mymval = (mymulti *)mi_get_vardata(retval);
    mymval->data.mr_data = buffer;
    mymval->state= MyBuffered;
  } else {
    retval = (mi_bitvarying *)mi_new_var(fullen);
    mymval = (mymulti *)mi_get_vardata(retval);
    buffer = mymval->data.mr_data;
    mymval->state = MySmall;
  }
  mymval->len = len;
  memcpy(buffer, data, len);

  return(retval);
}
```

The `myminput()` function starts by extracting the data portion of the first argument and also gets its length. It proceeds to calculate the size required to store the data. The calculation takes the size of the `mymulti` structure and subtracts from it the size of the `MI_MULTIREP_DATA` structure. This is the equivalent of getting the combined size of both the `len` and `state` elements. The length of the input argument is added to the result. The resulting value is the size required to represent the input value in row. We use this value to test our threshold for the choice of representation. The MYTHRESHOLD value is not defined here.

The first section of the if statement processes the input value, so the assign() function puts it in a large object. Since the large object creation is delayed and the data exceeds the threshold size, we need to create a buffer that can store the input data. A pointer to this buffer is saved in the opaque type, which then meets the size limitation requirement. When the opaque type is passed around, the database server makes sure that its content is copied when an older buffer is scheduled to be freed. This copying involves only the pointer to the data buffer, not the data itself. We need to allocate this buffer so that it remains available for the duration of the SQL statement. This is why we use the mi_dalloc() function with a PER_COMMAND memory duration. This way the pointer in the mymulti structure will always refer to a valid memory location. We then allocate a mi_bitvarying (mi_lvarchar) variable that will include the mymulti structure. We save the buffer pointer in the mymulti variable and set the state to MyBuffered to indicate that the value is in a temporary buffer, waiting to be written in a large object. Since the setting of the length and the copying of the input data into the appropriate buffer are the same for the MyBuffered and MySmall cases, we delay these operations to use common code.

When the length is within the threshold value, the data can be written directly into the mymulti structure. We first need to allocate a mi_bitvarying variable and extract its data area, which will contain a mymulti structure. We then set the buffer pointer to the beginning of the MI_MULTIREP_DATA structure. Since the mi_bitvarying variable was created with enough space for the in-row content, we know that the size will be appropriate for the copy, notwithstanding the size of the MI_MULTI-REP_DATA structure.

Once the appropriate setup has been done, we set the length and copy the input data into the designated buffer before returning the mi_bitvarying variable to the caller.

In the case of an insert statement, the database server calls the assign() function with the proper signature before saving the value to disk. The assign function is as follows:

```
mi_lvarchar *mymassign(mi_lvarchar *val, MI_FPARAM *fp)
{
```

```
MI_CONNECTION  *conn;
MI_LO_HANDLE   *lo = 0;
MI_LO_SPEC     *lspec = 0;
MI_LO_FD       fd;
mymulti        *mymval;
mi_integer     ret;
mi_char        *data;

mymval = (mymulti *)mi_get_vardata(val);

switch(mymval->state) {
case MyUndefined: /* should generate an error */
case MySmall:
    break;
case MyBuffered:
    conn = mi_open(NULL, NULL, NULL);
    data = mymval->data.mr_data;
    ret = mi_lo_spec_init(conn, &lspec);
    ret = mi_lo_colinfo_by_ids(conn, mi_fp_getrow(fp),
                        mi_fp_getcolid(fp),
                            lspec);
    fd = mi_lo_expand(conn, &lo,
            (MI_MULTIREP_DATA *) data, mymval->len,
            MI_LO_WRONLY, lspec);
    mi_lo_spec_free(conn, lspec);
    mi_lo_close(conn, fd);
    mi_free(data);
    mymval->state = MyLarge;
    memcpy(&mymval->data.mr_lo, lo,
            sizeof(MI_LO_HANDLE));
    mi_lo_increfcount(conn, &mymval->data.mr_lo);
    mi_free((mi_char *)lo);
    mi_close(conn);
    break;
case MyLarge:
    conn = mi_open(NULL, NULL, NULL);
    mi_lo_increfcount(conn, &mymval->data.mr_lo);
    mi_close(conn);
    break;
} /* end switch */
return(val);
}
```

The `assign()` function first extracts the `mymulti` structure from the `mi_lvarchar` argument. Then it must test the state of the `mymulti` opaque type to decide what must be done.

Two cases are simple. If the state is set to `MySmall`, there is nothing to do and we return the input value. If the state is `MyLarge`, we increment the reference count of the large object by using the `MI_LO_HANDLE` included in the `mymulti` structure.

When the state is set to `MyBuffered`, the `mymulti` structure contains a pointer to a data buffer. This data must be saved into a smart large object. The `assign()` function opens a database connection and allocates a `MI_LO_SPEC` structure. This structure is initialized by extracting the storage characteristics of the table column used to store the smart large object. The `mi_lo_expand()` creates a smart large object and copies the content of the data buffer into it. After freeing the `MI_LO_SPEC` structure and closing the large-object file descriptor, it frees the data buffer, sets the `mymulti` structure state to `MyLarge`, copies the `MI_LO_HANDLE` to `mymulti`, increments the smart-large object reference count, releases the previous copy of the `MI_LO_HANDLE`, and closes the connection.

Since the `assign()` function manipulates the smart-large object reference count, we have to make sure we provide the reverse operation so that, when a row or table containing `mymulti` columns are removed, the smart-large object reference count is decremented and the large object is removed from the database. The `destroy()` function is as follows:

```
void mymdestroy(mymulti *val, MI_FPARAM *fp)
{
  MI_CONNECTION *conn;
  mymulti       *mymval;

  mymval = (mymulti *)mi_get_vardata(val);

  if (mymval->state == MyLarge) {
    conn = mi_open(NULL, NULL, NULL);
    mi_lo_decrefcount(conn, &mymval->data.mr_lo);
    mi_close(conn);
  }
  return;
}
```

This function tests the state of the `mymulti` structure and decrements the smart-large object reference count if the `mymulti` structure contains one.

Any function that manipulates a `mymulti` opaque type must take into consideration the different states of the structure. For example, the output() function can be implemented as follows:

```
mi_lvarchar *mymoutput(mi_lvarchar *val, MI_FPARAM *fp)
{
  MI_CONNECTION  *conn;
  MI_LO_FD       fd;
  mymulti        *mymval;
  mi_char        *pbuf, buffer[2048];
  mi_integer     ret, len;
  mi_lvarchar    *retval;

  mymval = (mymulti *)mi_get_vardata(val);

  switch(mymval->state) {
  case MyLarge:
       conn = mi_open(NULL, NULL, NULL);
       fd = mi_lo_open(conn, &mymval->data.mr_lo,
                    MI_LO_RDONLY);
       ret = mi_lo_read(conn, fd, buffer, 2048);
       buffer[ret] = 0;
       pbuf = buffer;
       mi_lo_close(conn, fd);
       mi_close(conn);
       break;
  default:
       pbuf = mymval->data.mr_data;
  }
  len = strlen(pbuf);
  retval = mi_new_var(len);
  mi_set_vardata(retval, buffer);
  return(retval);
}
```

This function is a simplified version of what would normally be required. The simplification is based on the assumption that a buffer of 2048 bytes is sufficient to read any large object stored in a `mymulti` opaque type. A more realistic situation would include finding the size of the large object, and possibly looping over the large-object read operation.

All the SQL declarations are similar to the ones for the `myopaque` type seen previously. They are listed here for completeness:

```
CREATE FUNCTION myoin(lvarchar)
RETURNS myopaque
. . .


CREATE IMPLICIT CAST (lvarchar AS myopaque WITH
  myoin);

CREATE FUNCTION myoout(myopaque)
RETURNS lvarchar
. . .


CREATE CAST (myopaque AS lvarchar WITH myoout);

CREATE FUNCTION assign(myopaque)
RETURNS myopaque
. . .


CREATE PROCEDURE destroy(myopaque)
. . .
```

Large Object Storage Specifications Caveats

We saw earlier that we can retrieve the storage characteristic of a large object by looking at the row context. Consider the following table declaration:

```
CREATE TABLE mymu (
  col1 mymulti
) PUT col1 in (sbspace2, sbspace)
                (EXTENT SIZE 4, NO LOG, HIGH INTEG,
                 NO KEEP ACCESS TIME);
```

An insert test done with Informix-UDO 9.14 shows that only the smart blob space `sbspace` is used. However, the same test under IDS.2000 shows that both `sbspace2` and `sbspace` are used alternatively.

Distributing large objects over a number of smart blob spaces in a round-robin manner can provide significant performance improvement.

As of this writing, functions handling smart large objects could not be declared as running in parallel via the `PARALLELIZABLE` modifier. There are talks, however, about removing this restriction by the time IDS.2000 gets out of beta.

Aggregate Functions

One of the most powerful features of any relational database system is its ability to process a set of rows to produce a result. A function that processes a set of values is called an *aggregate function*. Since IDS.2000 is a superset of a relational database, it provides all the aggregate functions available in a standard relational database system and adds a few more. It also provides the ability to create new aggregate functions to better address business requirements.

IDS.2000 includes many features that impact the way aggregate functions are used. This chapter describes the available aggregate functions and presents examples how to use them. It also demonstrates how these functions can be extended to support new types. With this background in place, it proceeds with how to add new aggregate functions, followed by a few detailed examples.

IDS.2000 Aggregate Functions

IDS.2000 includes the following built-in aggregate functions:

- **AVG()**: This function returns the average of the set of numeric values passed into it as argument. No NULL values are included in the calculation. In addition to the column argument, the AVG() function can use the DISTINCT keyword or its synonym UNIQUE. Then duplicate values will be eliminated from the calculation. Consider:

```
CREATE TABLE myaggr ( col1 integer);

INSERT INTO myaggr VALUES(1);
INSERT INTO myaggr VALUES(1);
INSERT INTO myaggr VALUES(2);
INSERT INTO myaggr VALUES(2);
INSERT INTO myaggr VALUES(NULL);
INSERT INTO myaggr VALUES(3);
INSERT INTO myaggr VALUES(4);
INSERT INTO myaggr VALUES(5);

SELECT AVG(col1), AVG(DISTINCT col1) FROM myaggr;

        (avg)              (avg)

2.57142857142857 3.00000000000000
```

The AVG(col1) calculation uses all seven values where the AVG(DISTINCT col1) only uses five distinct values. Note that the NULL value is ignored in both cases.
- **COUNT()**: The COUNT() function is used to count either the number of rows in the set it receives or the number of non-NULL values in a specific column of the set. As for the AVG() function, COUNT() can use the keywords DISTINCT or UNIQUE on a specific column. Using the table created by the code above, we can issue the following SQL statement:

```
SELECT COUNT(*), COUNT(col1), COUNT(DISTINCT col1)
FROM myaggr;
```

```
        (count(*))              (count)              (count)
                 8                    7                    5
```

The result shows that the table contains eight rows, seven rows have a non-NULL col1 column, and these seven rows have five distinct col1 values. The COUNT(*) form provides better performance because it does not need to inspect a specific column for NULL values. In the case where the count is done on the entire table, IDS.2000 simply returns a stored row count, making for an instantaneous response.

- **MAX():** The MAX() function returns the largest value available in the set of rows selected.
- **MIN():** The MIN() function returns the smallest value available in the set of rows selected.
- **RANGE():** The RANGE() function returns the difference between the maximum and minimum value of the specified column in the set. This is equivalent to MAX() - MIN().
- **STDEV():** This function calculates the standard deviation of a set of values. A standard deviation is a standard statistical measurement that represents the spread of data. With the standard deviation, it is possible to calculate the percentile rank associated with any value. The standard deviation is the square root of the variance.
- **SUM():** This function adds the values of the set. If the DISTINCT keyword is used, the operation applies only to distinct values, as we saw for AVG() and COUNT().
- **VARIANCE():** The variance is a basic measurement used in statistics. It is expressed:

```
(SUM(val ** 2) - (SUM(val)**2)/N)/(N - 1)
```

Where val represents a specific value and N represents the number of values in the set.

Aggregate Functions Use

Aggregate functions allow us to keep the data in the database server and get only the result of the calculation. Significant performance benefits result from not having to transfer all the rows to a client application. We also get the advantage of having the database server perform the aggregation. The database server can read the separate dbspaces in parallel and perform the calculation in parallel via algorithms that have been tuned over many years. If the database server calculates the aggregation, a client application won't have to. The result is less code to write and maintain in the application.

The syntax of a SELECT statement using aggregate functions can be expressed as

```
SELECT [column[, column...],] aggr_function(column)
FROM table-list
[WHERE conditions]
[GROUP BY column-list]
[HAVING aggregate-conditions]
[ORDER BY column-list]
```

This is not quite a formal definition, but hopefully it conveys the possibilities of this type of statement. For example, assuming that a table contains orders with a date, we can return the list of days where there were more than ten orders in descending order with the following statement:

```
SELECT order_date, count(*)
FROM order_table
GROUP BY order_date
HAVING count(*) > 10
ORDER BY 2 DESC;
```

We see that the GROUP BY clause identifies the column to use in the grouping for the aggregate function. This syntax can be limiting, however. For example, if we want to know the number of orders received for each quarter of the year, we need to execute several SQL statements with the following form:

```
SELECT 'Quarter 1', count(*)
FROM order_table
WHERE order_date BETWEEN '1/1/99' AND '3/31/99';
```

With IDS.2000, on the other hand, it is possible for user-defined routines to provide the row grouping. By providing a function that returns the quarter from a date, we can find out the counts for each quarter of the year with a statement akin to

```
SELECT quarter(order_date), count(*)
FROM order_table
WHERE quarter(order_date) like '1999Q%'
GROUP BY 1;
```

With this statement, the order table needs to be processed only once instead of four times. This functionality can lead to interesting solutions. Imagine that you have demographic information for all your customers. You may want to find out the quantity of each product that is sold to specific age groups. To make things simple, we assume that we have an age value in our table. What we need is a function that can identify which age group a specific age belongs to. Since we want flexibility, we can define two additional arguments: the starting age and the size of the range. The function would have the following signature:

```
CREATE FUNCTION bucket(int, int, int)
RETURNING varchar(10)
   .  .  .
```

Here is an example of its execution:

```
EXECUTE FUNCTION bucket(45, 20, 10);

(expression)

40-49
```

The bucket() function takes the age (45) with a starting age of 20 and a range of 10, and it returns the age group of the first argument. This function can then be used in a SQL statement similar to this one:

```
SELECT product, bucket(age, 20, 10), count(*)
FROM order
GROUP BY 1, 2
ORDER BY 1, 3 DESC;
```

This statement groups the rows by product and age group. It orders the result in descending order using the product and the count. The numbers used in GROUP BY and ORDER BY represent the position of the columns in the SELECT statement. This is required when user-defined routines or aggregate functions are referenced in these clauses.

The bucket() function is very simple, and it gives the information needed to the database server to complete the processing without the help of a customized client application. Significant performance benefits accrue because we don't have to send all the data to the client or issue several SQL statements that increase the processing load. The bucket() function can also be used with a WHERE clause to limit our processing to specific groups:

```
WHERE bucket(age, 20, 10) IN ('20-29', '30-39', '40-49')
```

We can also index the result of the bucket() function execution to speed up processing. Finally, the database server may execute the aggregation in parallel, giving us the benefits of multithreaded execution without having to deal with it in any of our code—all this because we added a simple bucket() function implemented as follows:

```
mi_lvarchar *bucket(mi_integer age, mi_integer start,
                    mi_integer size, MI_FPARAM *fp)
{
  mi_char buffer[10];
  mi_integer low, high, i;

  low = 0;
  high = start - 1;

  while (age > high) {
    low = high + 1;
    high += size;
```

```
    }
    sprintf(buffer, "%d-%d", low, high);

    return(mi_string_to_lvarchar(buffer));
}
```

The function starts by setting a range for the group below the starting age. It then moves from group to group until it finds the right group for the age argument. It then formats a string representing the age group and returns it.

The function could be modified to take a birth date and calculate the age. The `rtoday()` function retrieves today's date. It can be used to calculate the age with the following statements:

```
mi_integer today, age;
. . .
rtoday(&today);
age = (today - birthdate)/365.25;
```

A more accurate `age` calculation could be used, but this one should suffice in virtually all cases. If we calculate the age within the `bucket` function, the result of the execution will vary from day to day. This means that the function is VARIANT. The implication is that the result of the function cannot be indexed.

The grouping technique can be applied to other measurements—salary range, profit margins, and so on. It could also be used for nonnumerical values. It could, for example, be used to identify major competitors while it groups all the others together.

The use of grouping functions is a simple way to take advantage of the extensibility of IDS.2000. It can simplify application code and enhance process performance.

Extending Built-In Aggregate Functions

Aggregate functions operate on some IDS.2000 built-in data types. They also work on distinct types defined from the supported built-in types. IDS.2000 provides ways to extend aggregate functions to support any new types you may create, including row types. This functionality also applies to distinct types if you want

Table 11–1 *Aggregate support functions.*

Aggregate	Required support function
AVG()	plus(UDT, UDT), divide(UDT, integer)
COUNT()	None
MAX()	greaterthanorequal(UDT, UDT)
MIN()	lessthanorequal(UDT, UDT)
RANGE()	lessthanorequal(UDT, UDT), greaterthanorequal(UDT, UDT)
STDEV()	plus(UDT, UDT), minus(UDT, UDT), times(UDT, UDT), divide(UDT, UDT)
SUM()	plus(UDT, UDT)
VARIANCE()	plus(UDT, UDT), minus(UDT, UDT), times(UDT, UDT), divide(UDT, UDT)

to change the calculation method. Table 11–1 shows the support functions required to implement the built-in aggregate functions.

The UDT argument listed in the required functions is the type we want to support. We covered the implementation of support functions in Chap. 7. When an aggregate function is called with a user-defined type, it looks for the specific set of support functions that handles this user-defined type. If the functions are found, the aggregation can proceed and a value is returned; otherwise, the aggregate function fails.

The COUNT() function does not require any support function, because it only needs to test if a non-NULL value exists. In the case of the aggregate functions AVG(), STDEV(), and VARI-ANCE(), the type of the return value is determined by the return type of the divide() support function.

How Do Aggregate Functions Work?

At first glance, it is easy to assume that an aggregate function reads a row, processes the row, repeats until there are no more rows, and then returns the result. IDS.2000 provides parallel execution of queries, and this parallelism also applies to the execution of aggregate functions.

Parallel execution of SQL statements depends on several factors. The first is the partitioning of tables. A table can be defined over multiple dbspaces. The rows are stored in the dbspace either in a round-robin manner or according to an expression rule that determines which dbspace to use for each row. The number of dbspaces involved in a query defines the maximum level of workable parallelism.

IDS.2000 includes several configuration parameters that define the amount of system resources available for parallel execution. One of these parameters, MAX_PDQPRIORITY, defines the maximum level of parallelism available to a specific session. A client session can set its level of parallelism, PDQPRIORITY, either by setting it as an environment variable or by executing the SET command.

When parallelism is used, the aggregation execution is divided so that multiple partial results can be calculated in parallel. The partial results are then combined to produce the final result.

Parallel processing impacts how the aggregation is done. For example, a COUNT() aggregation counts in the parallel execution, but it does a SUM() in the combine level. The result of the aggregation is then identical whether it is run in parallel mode or is serialized.

Aggregate function execution represents another advantage of delegating execution to the server: We benefit from multithreaded processing without having to create multiple threads in our client application.

The User-Defined Aggregate Model

The user-defined aggregate implementation model takes into consideration the parallel execution of SQL statements in IDS.2000. It divides the aggregation operation in two logical levels. The lower level processes the data from the appropriate set of rows, and the upper level processes the partial results generated by the parallel execution of several lower level aggregate operations.

The aggregation model adds one more feature. It provides an additional step for any initialization required by the user-defined aggregate function. The user-defined aggregate model is illustrated in Fig. 11–1.

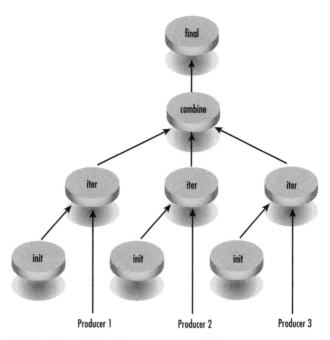

Figure 11–1 *User-defined aggregate model*

As shown in Fig. 11–1, the implementation of a user-defined aggregate function requires up to four user-defined routines. These functions are:

- **INIT:** The INIT function is not required. If present, its first argument is a NULL value of the type supported by the aggregate function. It may have a second argument that can be used as an initialization parameter. Since the first parameter is a NULL value, the INIT function must be declared as handling NULL values. This is done by adding the HANDLESNULLS modifier in the function declaration.
  The INIT function returns a type that is appropriate for the processing of the aggregation. This is the type that is used by the ITER function. We will see more about this type, a <STATE> type, later.
- **ITER:** The ITER function must always be present in a user-defined aggregate. It takes two arguments. The first

argument is a <STATE> type and the second argument is a value to process. If the INIT function is not present, the ITER function will be called once with a NULL value to perform initialization. In this case, the ITER function must be declared with the HANDLESNULLS modifier.

- **COMBINE:** The COMBINE function merges two partial results into a new partial result. When the <STATE> type happens to be the same as the type of the column on which the aggregation is performed, the ITER function can be used as the COMBINE function.
- **FINAL:** The final function takes the <STATE> type result returned by the combine function and converts it to a FINAL type. If the return type is the same as the <STATE> type, the FINAL function may be omitted.

With these functions in place, we can define a user-defined aggregate. Before we get to that, however, we need to discuss the use of the <STATE> type.

The <STATE> Type

When a SUM() aggregate function executes, it adds all the values of a specified column. In this case, the column type is the same as the result type. Furthermore, the only partial result processed in the aggregation is a partial summation. All of these values have the same types. This is not the case when the AVG() aggregation is performed.

The AVG() aggregate function must keep track of a summation as well as a count of values that participated in this summation. These two values constitute the state of the calculation at any particular point in the operation. This can be represented by a structure containing two values. This structure must be defined as a UDT and used in the ITER, COMBINE, and FINAL functions. Since this structure, the <STATE> type, is not the appropriate result, the FINAL function converts it to the appropriate value. In the case of AVG(), it divides the total by the count and returns the result.

Defining a User-Defined Aggregate

An aggregate function is defined as a set of functions used to perform the different steps of the aggregation. This is similar to a CAST definition that identifies the function that will perform the cast. In an aggregate function, its support functions are identified with the keywords INIT, ITER, COMBINE, and FINAL. We covered the SQL syntax for the creation of an aggregate function in Chap. 3.

To create our own version of the AVG() aggregate function, we would issue the following SQL statement:

```
CREATE AGGREGATE myavg
WITH (INIT=myinit, ITER=myiter, COMBINE=mycombine,
      FINAL=myfinal);
```

This statement identifies the names of the support functions that are used to perform the aggregation. Since the HANDLESNULLS modifier is not used, the aggregation does not consider NULL values as part of the calculation. When myavg is called, IDS.2000 finds a myinit() function that takes an argument of the same type as the column type. If no function is found, the aggregation fails because this type cannot be processed.

The return type of the FINAL function determines the return type of the aggregate function. The next section looks at the implementation of the support functions.

A Simple Example: MYAVG()

The myavg() function execution starts by finding the INIT function that has the proper function signature. An INIT function has the following general syntax:

```
<state_type> = init_function(<column_type>
                                    [, <init_value>]);
```

The function can be defined with an initialization value: <init_value>. We will see an example of its use in a later section. The first argument has the type that we want to process in the aggregate. The `myavg()` function processes integers. This argument is always a NULL value. The `init_function` returns a type that is used internally during the aggregation. In the case of the `myavg()` function, we define the `<state_type>` as

```
typedef struct {
  float total;
  int   count;
} myavg_state;
```

We need to declare this type within IDS.2000. This is done with the following statement:

```
CREATE OPAQUE TYPE myavg_state(INTERNALLENGTH=8);
```

The `myinit()` function needs simply to allocate and initialize this structure:

```
myavg_state *myinit(mi_integer val, MI_FPARAM *fp)
{
  myavg_state *retval;

  retval =
  (myavg_state *)mi_alloc(sizeof(myavg_state));
  retval->total = 0;
  retval->count = 0;

  return(retval);
}
```

The call to `mi_alloc()` uses the current memory location that should be, by default, PER_ROUTINE.

Since we are dealing with a fixed-length opaque type, we can return the pointer to the `myavg_state` structure directly instead of having to wrap it in a `mi_lvarchar` variable. The myinit() function is created in SQL with the statement

```
CREATE FUNCTION myinit(integer)
RETURNING myavg_state
WITH (NOT VARIANT, PARALLELIZABLE, HANDLESNULLS)
EXTERNAL NAME ". . ."
LANGUAGE C;
```

The next function we must define is the `myiter()` function. It takes a `myavg_state` and a value, and it returns a `myavg_state` pointer. The general syntax of an ITER function is

```
<state_type> = iter_function(<state_type>,
   <column_value>);
```

The `myiter()` function code is as follows:

```
myavg_state *myiter(myavg_state *state,
                    mi_integer val, MI_FPARAM *fp)
{
  myavg_state *retval;

  retval = (myavg_state
  *)mi_alloc(sizeof(myavg_state));
  retval->total = state->total + val;
  retval->count = state->count + 1;

  return(retval);
}
```

This code takes the values from the `state` argument, adds the new value to the total, and increments the count. The new `myavg_state` is then returned. The `myiter()` function is declared as follows in SQL:

```
CREATE FUNCTION myiter(myavg_state, integer)
RETURNING myavg_state
WITH (NOT VARIANT, PARALLELIZABLE)
EXTERNAL NAME ". . ."
LANGUAGE C;
```

The COMBINE function merges two state types into a new `state_type`. It has the following general declaration:

```
<state_type> = combine_function(<state_type>,
                                <state_type>);
```

The `mycombine()` function implementation is as follows:

```
myavg_state *mycombine(myavg_state *state1,
                       myavg_state *state2, MI_FPARAM *fp)
```

```
{
  myavg_state *retval;

  retval = (myavg_state *)mi_alloc(sizeof(myavg_state));
  retval->total = state1->total + state2->total;
  retval->count = state1->count + state2->count;

  return(retval);
}
```

The final step of the aggregation is to convert the last `myavg_state` variable into a type that is appropriate for the `return` value. This final function has the general syntax

```
<final_type> = final_function(<state_type>);
```

The `<final_type>` is any type that is considered appropriate for this specific aggregate function. The `myfinal()` function has the following implementation:

```
mi_double_precision *myfinal(myavg_state *state,
                             MI_FPARAM *fp)
{
  mi_double_precision *retval;

  retval = (mi_double_precision *)
           mi_alloc(sizeof(mi_double_precision));
  *retval = state->total / (state->count * 1.0);

  return(retval);
}
```

A DOUBLE PRECISION value is always returned as a pointer. For this reason, we must allocate memory for the return. The calculation of the average is done by dividing the `total` by the `count`. Since both values are integers, we convert one of the two values, count in this case, to a float so the result of the calculation is a floating point value instead of an integer. If we had kept the integer division, the result would have been an integer. The integer would then be converted to a DOUBLE PRECISION value without any possible fractional part. This means that the average of the set {1, 2} would be 1.0 instead of 1.5.

The `myfinal()` function has the following SQL declaration:

```
CREATE FUNCTION myfinal(myavg_state)
RETURNING double precision
WITH (NOT VARIANT, PARALLELIZABLE)
EXTERNAL NAME ". . ."
LANGUAGE C;
```

With this `final()` function created, we can use the new aggregate function on integer columns. Assuming that the `int_tab` table has an integer column named `col1`, the following statement would return the average of all the `col1` values:

```
SELECT myavg(col1) from int_tab;
```

This example shows how simple it is to implement the four support functions required for an aggregate function.

Processing `<STATE>` Arguments

The previous example creates a new state structure for each iteration. It then proceeds to copy new values into the new structure. It is also possible to reuse the state structure throughout the aggregation. We refer to this method as the in-place update.

The default memory duration within an aggregate function is `PER_ROUTINE`. This means that the memory is freed soon after the user-defined routine returns from its execution. We need to allocate the state structure with a duration of `PER_COMMAND` to preserve the memory until the end of the aggregation.

Top N Market Share Example

An aggregate function can accumulate values to process later in the aggregation. The following example assumes a table containing a revenue column. It calculates a running total and keeps the top N revenues. At the end, it adds up these values and calculates the percentage of the total revenue taken by the top N values.

This calculation can be looked at as the percentage of sales that go to the top *N* customers, the market share of the top *N* vendors in a market, and so on. If the values were divided by geography, it would be possible to calculate this value for each geographical area.

The aggregate implementation also uses the in-place update method to illustrate its use. We also make use of the initialization value to declare how many of the top *N* values are part of the calculation. To keep the example simple, we perform the operation on an integer column and limit the maximum number of values to ten.

This aggregate function requires the SQL declaration of a new DISTINCT TYPE, the four support functions, and the creation of the aggregate function itself:

```
CREATE DISTINCT TYPE myState_t AS pointer;

CREATE FUNCTION percentTot_init(integer, integer
    default 3)
RETURNING myState_t
WITH(HANDLESNULLS, NOT VARIANT)
EXTERNAL NAME '. . .'
LANGUAGE C;

CREATE FUNCTION percentTot_iter(myState_t, integer)
RETURNING myState_t
WITH(PARALLELIZABLE, NOT VARIANT)
EXTERNAL NAME '. . .'
LANGUAGE C;

CREATE FUNCTION percentTot_combine(myState_t,
    myState_t)
RETURNING myState_t
WITH(PARALLELIZABLE, NOT VARIANT)
EXTERNAL NAME '. . .'
LANGUAGE C;

CREATE FUNCTION percentTot_final(myState_t)
RETURNING float
WITH(PARALLELIZABLE, NOT VARIANT)
EXTERNAL NAME '. . .'
LANGUAGE C;
```

```
CREATE AGGREGATE percentTot
WITH (
  INIT = percentTot_init,
  ITER = percentTot_iter,
  COMBINE = percentTot_combine,
  FINAL = percentTot_final
);
```

The MyState_t distinct type is based on a built-in type called pointer. The database server then manipulates a four-byte value instead of the content of the internal structure, saving significant memory while copying. The aggregate support functions can still define their arguments as pointers to the appropriate structure and manipulate them as such.

Notwithstanding the DISTINCT TYPE, these SQL statements are similar to the ones shown in the previous example. The percentTot_init() function contains an additional declaration. The second parameter is given a default value of 3. This means that the following SQL statements are equivalent:

```
SELECT percentTot(col1) FROM int_tab;

SELECT percentTot(col1, 3) FROM int_tab;
```

Both statements will perform the calculation using the top three values of the col1 column. The second argument to the aggregate function in the first statement is provided by the default value instead of being explicitly put in the SQL statement. The arguments then match the percentTot_init() function signature.

We created a fixed-length opaque type as the state type for the aggregation. This type matches the following structure declaration:

```
typedef struct myState {
  mi_integer maxcount;
  mi_integer count;
  mi_real    running_total;
  mi_integer topN[10];
} myState_t;
```

This structure limits the number of top values to ten. We could easily use it to support a variable number of top values by using the same method as in Chap. 7. Since the `topN` array is at the end of the structure, we can allocate additional storage and assume a larger number of values.

The `percenttot_init()` function initializes a `myState_t` structure that is used throughout the aggregate processing:

```
myState_t *percenttot_init(mi_integer nil,
    mi_integer imax, MI_FPARAM *fp)
{
  myState_t *state;
  mi_integer i;

  state = (myState_t *)mi_dalloc(sizeof(myState_t),
                                 PER_COMMAND);
  state->maxcount = imax;
  state->count = 0;
  state->running_total = 0;

  return(state);
}
```

The allocation of the `myState_t` structure uses the `mi_dalloc()` API function with a memory duration of `PER_COMMAND`. This memory will not be reclaimed until the SQL statement terminates. This way the pointer that is manipulated throughout the aggregate statement will always refer to a valid memory buffer.

The `state` structure is initialized before being returned. The `maxcount` element represents the maximum number of values that must be saved. The `count` element represents the number of maximum values that are currently stored, and `running_total` stored the summation of all the values processed. Since we already know how many values we are holding, we don't need to initialize the `topN` array.

The `percenttot_iter()` function processes the column values and fills the `myState_t` structure:

```
myState_t *percenttot_iter(myState_t *state,
                           mi_integer value,
                           MI_FPARAM *fp)
{
  mi_integer i, j;
```

```
    state->running_total += value;

    for (i = 0; i < state->count; i++) {
      if (state->topN[i] < value)
        break;
    }
    if (i < state->maxcount) {
      state->count++;
      if (state->count > state->maxcount) {
        state->count-;
      }
      for (j = state->count - 1; j > i; j)
        state->topN[j] = state->topN[j - 1];
        state->topN[i] = value;

    }
    return(state);
}
```

The `percenttot_iter()` functions first updates the running total. Then it figures out if the value must be saved in the `topN` array. It finds the position where the value must be inserted and, if the position is within the bounds of `maxcount`, it moves down the values to make space for the new value and inserts it at that position. The `count` value limits the comparisons. If the `count` is zero, the `value` is inserted at position zero of the `topN` array.

The `percenttot_combine()` function merges two `myState_t` structures into one. Since we used the in-place method, it updates its first argument with the second one and returns the updated argument:

```
myState_t *percenttot_combine(myState_t *result1,
                       myState_t *result2, MI_FPARAM
   *fp)
{
  mi_integer i;

  for (i = 0; i < result2->count; i++)
    (void) percenttot_iter(result1, result2->topN[i], fp);
  result1->running_total += result2->running_total;

  mi_free((void *)result2);
```

```
          return(result1);
     }
```

We use `percenttot_iter()` to update the `result1` structure
with the `topN` values from the `result2` structure. Since `percent-
tot_iter()` returns a pointer to `result1`, we can ignore its
return value. We finish by updating the `running_total` element
before returning `result1`. The `result2` structure was allocated
with a PER_COMMAND memory duration. We could have left it to
the server to free it at the end of the processing but, by freeing it
ourselves explicitly, we make this memory available to the server
right away without delay.

The `percenttot_combine()` function is used only when the
aggregate is run in parallel. If a table has only one fragment,
only one copy of `percenttot_iter()` will execute, and its result
will be passed directly to `percenttot_final()`. This function is
as follows:

```
mi_double_precision *percenttot_final(myState_t *state,
                                      MI_FPARAM *fp)
{
   mi_integer i;
   mi_double_precision *retval;

   retval = (mi_double_precision *)
             mi_alloc(sizeof(mi_double_precision));
   for (i = 1; i < state->count; i++)
     state->topN[0] += state->topN[i];

   *retval = (100.0 * state->topN[0]) / state
   ->running_total;

   mi_free((void *)state);

   return(retval);
}
```

This function returns a DOUBLE PRECISION value. The return
value is allocated, the `topN` values are added together, and the
percentage is calculated using the `topN[0]` result and the `run-
ning_total` element. At this point, the `state` structure is not

needed anymore, so its memory can be returned to the server right away with the `mi_free()` API function.

Other Aggregation Usage

An aggregate function is expected to return one value. This value can be a base type or a user-defined type. The top N market share example above calculates the percentage of the total that a number of the largest values represent. It would also be possible to return a user-defined type containing information on the top N revenue producers and their percentage of the total. This user-defined type could be as simple as a character string containing the result or a more elaborate opaque type. Values could be extracted from the opaque type and used in other SQL statements to produce the planned business report.

An aggregate function could return a character string formatted as an XML document. We have to stop thinking that aggregate functions process only a numerical value and return only a single value. Since we can implement our own aggregate functions, we can take anything as argument and return whatever is required for the business processing.

Aggregate functions can group a data set into a new business type for more specific processing. The introduction of 64-bit implementations of IDS.2000 increases the potential available memory for processing. An aggregate function can take advantage of a larger memory model to create large business types from relational data.

The IDS.2000's user-defined aggregate feature is a powerful tool in business processing. Of course, even if a solution can be implemented using this feature, it does not mean that it is the best approach. Always be critical of your solution. Sometimes a solution is best implemented in a customized application. Evaluate your options carefully. However, if the best approach is to modify the database server to better fit your business environment, take advantage of it. It could give you a significant business advantage over your competitors.

Tracing and Debugging

Debugging is often the last thing on anybody's mind, so, it is also the last chapter of this book. The programming environment of user-defined routines is different from stand-alone application programs. We need to use the facilities provided in the DataBlade API to analyze what the functions are doing.

There is more to debugging than using a debugger or tracing the execution. This chapter gives some helpful suggestions on how to proceed in the development of user-defined routines. It does not intend to cover the subject in any depth but aims instead at giving some helpful hints and points out some simple problems that can make you waste hours.

We start by looking at the most common problems found during the testing of user-defined routines. We then provide some simple suggestions how to set up your development environment before proceeding with discussions of tracing, followed by debugging under UNIX and under Windows NT. Finally, we provide brief information how to look at a database server shared-memory dump.

Most Frequent Problems

There are some problems that can take a long time to figure out, even if they are simple. It does not help that the server generates messages in the database server log file that may appear, for example, as

```
06:41:57  (-1): ERROR: Loading Routine <. . .> procid=256
06:41:57  (35): ERROR: C Language Symbol <. . .> (procid
                256) not found in <. . .>


. . .


17:16:11  ERROR: Exception Segmentation Violation
                occurred
17:16:11  (5): ERROR: Routine execution trap --
                procname=<xxx> procid=300
```

This section covers some of the most common problems and their causes. Hopefully, the discussions in the subsections will help reduce time spent figuring out error messages and determining actual causes.

Old Library

Countless hours have been spent trying to figure out why changes made to a user-defined routine did not solve a specific problem. The timing in loading and unloading libraries may be the most frequent problem. Even when people are told to make sure the old library has been unloaded and the new one loaded, this problem still shows up from time to time.

IDS.2000 writes a message in its log file each time it loads and unloads a dynamic library. For example,

```
17:17:19  Loading Module <. . .>
17:17:23  C Language Module <. . .> loaded
17:17:23  Unloading Module <. . .>
17:17:27  C Language Module <. . .> unloaded
```

The ellipsis (. . .) represents the path to the dynamic shared library. We saw (see Chap. 2) how we can get a library to load or unload. Even if you follow these steps, though, something may prevent the old library from being unloaded. Sometimes, too, it appears that the only way to make sure a new library has been loaded is to bring the database server down and back up.

Even if you delete a library from the system and create a new one, the server may still be using the deleted library. Under UNIX, a file is removed only when no process has it open. Since the database server has the dynamic library opened, the deleted library still exists even though nobody else can see it. Creating a new library with the same pathname simply refers to a separate file.

Under Windows NT, the creation of a new dynamic library will fail if the database server has opened the dynamic library already. The message returned by the linker is

```
LINK : fatal error LNK1104: cannot open file ". . ."
```

This indicates that another process has already opened the file. You should then take steps to get the database server to unload the dynamic library. We will see later a way to ensure that your testing can replace a dynamic library at will.

Symbol Not Found

When IDS.2000 executes an SQL statement, it may not find the user-defined routine, or the routine execution may fail. Both cases are a variation on symbols that are not found.

The database server uses the function signature to find the desired routine. If a function with the proper signature is not found, the database server returns a message, such as

```
674: Routine (riskf) can not be resolved.
```

The database server log file does not include any additional message in this situation. In this case, verify the type of argument passed to the function. This problem can occur when processing a table hierarchy, even if no rows of that type are included.

The second case of symbol not found is when either a function is not found in a dynamic library or a symbol used by that function is not found. The following error is returned to the client attempting execution of such a function:

```
9794: User Defined Routine (bucket) load failed.
```

The database server log file contains a message similar to the following:

```
08:04:54   ERROR: C Language Symbol <Bucket> (procid
           311) not found in <. . .>
08:04:54   (-1): ERROR: Loading Routine <bucket>
                  procid=311
```

In the UNIX environment, the database server log may identify a symbol used by the user-defined routine as the symbol that cannot be resolved.

Under Windows NT, the error is reported at link time. The library will not be created unless the /FORCE:UNRESOLVED link option is used. Even then, a warning message will be generated that identifies the problem symbols.

There is one more situation that occurs under Windows NT. The dynamic library may be created without any problem, but execution may still fail because the function name is not found. The Windows NT environment has a concept of explicitly exporting symbols for use by other programs. This can be done in multiple ways, including Microsoft-specific keywords in the source code, link options, export file (.EXP), and module definition file (.DEF). The *Informix DataBlade Development Kit (DBDK)* favors the use of a module definition file, so we will use this method here. This file must be included in the LINK command to export the symbols that will be used by the database server. The module definition file supports several statements. In our case, we care about the EXPORTS statement. A simple data definition file for our purpose looks like this:

```
; Chapter 12 code
;
EXPORTS
  trace_level
```

```
trace_file
set_tracing
```

The lines starting with a semicolon (;) are comments. This file contains one keyword, EXPORTS, and a list of symbols that are exported for use in the server. The file is used in the LINK command with the /DEF option as follows:

```
/DEF:code12.def
```

When the database server reports that the user-defined routine cannot be found in the dynamic library, make sure that the name is properly spelled in the module definition file, the source file, and the CREATE FUNCTION SQL statement.

Value or Reference

A user-defined routine receives and returns values either as values or as pointers. These two methods are often referred to, respectively, as passing a parameter by value and passing a parameter by reference.

It is easy to see that a value could be mistaken for a pointer and vice versa. This could generate either an erroneous value or an exception in the execution of the user-defined routine. Chapter 4 was written especially to document the proper way to handle these two different data types.

Returning a pointer to a result can create several problems. Consider the following code fragment:

```
mi_double_precision retval;

retval = 3.1415926;
return(&retval);
```

This code returns a pointer to a DOUBLE PRECISION value as prescribed in Chap. 4. The problem is that it uses the address of a variable that was allocated on the stack. Once the function returns, the pointer is not valid any more and an error occurs. Each time a pointer is returned, the user-defined routine should allocate memory via the DataBlade API and return a pointer to that memory. The code fragment should have been

```
mi_double_precision *retval;

retval = (mi_double_precision *)
         mi_alloc(sizeof(mi_double_precision));
*retval = 3.1415926;
return(retval);
```

This way the pointer returned refers to a valid memory location.

Using Buffers

Throughout this book, we have seen code similar to

```
mi_char buffer[256];
. . .
/* use the buffer */
. . .
return(mi_string_to_lvarchar(buffer));
```

This is a proper use of automatic variables. It performs better than if we had to allocate the memory for a temporary buffer and release it before returning. However, since we are using a fixed-size buffer, we run the risk of writing past the end of the buffer by mistake, which would generate an exception. This comment is in no way meant to discourage use of these buffers. However, if the user-defined routine is modified, you should make sure that the buffer size will still be appropriate.

Using `mi_lvarchar` and `mi_bitvarying`

Both `mi_lvarchar` and `mi_bitvarying` are opaque structures that must be accessed using a set of DataBlade API functions. These structures are widely used to handle character strings and variable-length opaque types, among other things. Since these structures are equivalent, henceforth this discussion refers to both as `mi_lvarchar`.

When manipulating the content of a `mi_lvarchar` structure, it is common to extract a pointer to the data buffer by using `mi_get_vardata()`. The first problem comes from the fact that the data buffer is not NULL terminated. Any character manipulation function assuming a NULL-terminated string will continue past the end of the buffer and possibly try to write outside its boundary. This will most likely cause an exception.

A mi_lvarchar variable is always manipulated as a pointer to a structure. This variable must be allocated before it is used. This problem is similar to the one listed above in the mi_double_precision example.

When a mi_lvarchar structure is allocated, it receives either an explicit or an implicit length for its buffer. Consider the following statements:

```
lvar1 = mi_new_var(30);
lvar2 = mi_string_to_lvarchar(buffer);
```

The first statement allocates a mi_lvarchar structure that has a buffer area size of 30. The second statement allocates a structure with a buffer area large enough to store the content of the NULL-terminated character string passed as argument and initialize the content with the string.

Since the buffer area of a mi_lvarchar structure has a specific size, we need to make sure that we don't write past the end of the buffer. Otherwise, we may have a problem that can cause a database server exception.

Use of SPL

There are some situations where you need to test some ideas about how the processing is done or how the polymorphic calls operate. Don't hesitate to use SPL to test these ideas. For example, a quarter() function taking a date as argument and returning the quarter as a string can be written in SPL as follows:

```
CREATE FUNCTION quarter(dt date)
RETURNS varchar(10);

DEFINE yr    int;
DEFINE mon   int;
DEFINE qt    int;
```

```
LET yr = YEAR(dt);
LET mon = MONTH(dt);
LET qt = (mon - 1) / 3;

RETURN yr || 'Q' || qt;

END FUNCTION;
```

SPL is particularly useful when you want to execute SQL statements in your user-defined routine. It can also easily implement an iterator function, as illustrated below:

```
. . .
FOREACH SELECT id, items INTO aid, adoc FROM foo
   FOREACH EXECUTE FUNCTION do_iter1(adoc) INTO aitem
      RETURN aid, aitem WITH RESUME;
   END FOREACH;
END FOREACH;
. . .
```

We saw this code in Chap. 8. It illustrates the fact that we can execute SQL statements and user-defined routines. The iterator functionality is provided by the WITH RESUME clause in the RETURN statement.

In addition to being simple to code, SPL is advantageous for testing because it does not require a compilation step and the creation of a dynamic library. An SPL function can also be added and removed quickly. However, SPL has limited processing capabilities and does not support parallel execution.

Consider using SPL for your early functions development with the idea of rewriting the routines in C later.

Scripting Your Tests

The unloading of old dynamic libraries is probably the most common problem encountered during development. To avoid this problem, make sure to script the creation and removal of user-defined types and user defined routines. Sometimes, this can be done in one SQL script file, as in the case of testing a quarter() function:

```
CREATE FUNCTION quarter(date)
RETURNING varchar(10)
WITH (not variant)
EXTERNAL NAME
"$INFORMIXDIR/extend/udrbook/bin/chap12(quarter)"
LANGUAGE C;

CREATE TABLE tab_date (
  COL1 date
);

INSERT INTO tab_date VALUES('04/16/1999');
SELECT quarter(col1) FROM tab_date;
DROP FUNCTION quarter(date);
```

This way we ensure that the library is loaded when the script starts its execution and unloaded at the end because of the DROP FUNCTION at the end of the script. The script can be executed with the statement

```
dbaccess -e testdb quarter >errlog 2>&1
```

The -e option tells dbaccess to echo the commands that are entered. This way we see the SQL command and the result of the execution in the output. The output of the execution is redirected to the errlog file. The last part of the command indicates that the error messages should be redirected to the output file, errlog in this case. The syntax shown here works under both UNIX and Windows NT.

In many situations, it is not practical or possible to put every-thing in one script file. In this case, we can separate the script into three parts. The first script creates the types and functions, the second script executes the test, and the third removes all types and functions:

```
dbaccess -e testdb percent >errlog 2>&1
dbaccess -e testdb do_percent >>errlog 2>&1
dbaccess -e testdb percent_d >>errlog 2>&1
```

This example actually shows the execution of test scripts used in Chap. 11. We use a slightly different syntax here in the second and third command so that the output is appended to the existing `errlog` file. Once again, this syntax is valid on both UNIX and Windows NT.

The three commands above could be put in a command file without the output redirection. The redirection can be applied to the command file itself:

```
do_test >errlog 2>&1
```

This way, you decide where the output goes instead of having to modify the command file to change it.

Tracing

Since a user-defined routine executes in the server, it is not possible simply to print tracing statements to the standard output. The DataBlade API provides several functions and macros that facilitate tracing. They are listed in Table 12–1.

Before we can issue trace statements, we must define a tracing class and insert it into the SYSTRACESCLASSES table. In the following examples, we will use `myclass` as the tracing class, so we need to execute the following statement:

```
INSERT INTO systraceclasses(name)
        VALUES("myclass");
```

With this in place, we need to identify the level of tracing we want to use and where to put the result. Both of these values are set for the life of the user connection.

The trace level works as follow. Any trace statement that uses a level below or equal to the current trace level is printed to the trace file.

Table 12–1. Tracing API functions and macros.		
mi_tracefile_set()	mi_tracelevel_set()	DPRINTF()
tf()	tprintf()	

The trace file is set by default to the connection number followed by a ".trc" extension. The "/tmp" directory is the default directory for that trace file.

IDS.2000 does not provide a command to set the trace level and the trace file. The API calls can be put in the function we want to trace, but it make more sense to create a separate function that sets these values. We could create separate functions for trace level and trace file, but instead we write one that does both. The function has the following SQL declaration:

```
CREATE FUNCTION set_tracing(lvarchar, int, lvarchar)
RETURNING integer
WITH (NOT VARIANT, HANDLESNULLS)
EXTERNAL NAME
"$INFORMIXDIR/extend/udrbook/bin/code12.bld(set_tracing)"
LANGUAGE C;
```

We declare the function as taking three arguments. The first argument is the trace class name, the second argument is the class level, and the third argument is the pathname of the trace file. The function returns an integer that indicates whether it terminated normally.

The function handles NULL values, which allows us to set the trace level or the trace file independently of each other. The function is called as follows:

```
EXECUTE FUNCTION
set_tracing("myclass", 50, "/tmp/mytrace.trc");
```

The function sets the trace level at 50 and the trace file to /tmp/trace.trc. Both these values apply to the trace class myclass. The function implementation is

```
mi_integer set_tracing(mi_lvarchar *class, mi_integer lvl,
                       mi_lvarchar *tfile, MI_FPARAM
                          *fparam)
{
  mi_integer   ret;
  mi_string *str, buffer[80];

  /* if there is a trace file provided */
  if (mi_fp_argisnull(fparam, 2) != MI_TRUE) {
```

```
    str = mi_lvarchar_to_string(tfile);
    ret = mi_tracefile_set(str);
}
/* if both the class and level are not NULL */
if (mi_fp_argisnull(fparam, 0) != MI_TRUE &&
    (mi_fp_argisnull(fparam, 1)) != MI_TRUE) {
    str = mi_lvarchar_to_string(class);
    sprintf(buffer, "%s %d ", str, lvl);
    ret = mi_tracelevel_set(buffer);
}
return ret;
}
```

The function first tests whether the third argument is NULL. If not, it extracts the pathname from the tfile argument before calling the mi_tracefile_set() DataBlade API function. Then, if both the first and second arguments are not NULL, it sets the trace level for the specified class name.

A standard testing sequence could go as follows:

```
. . .
EXECUTE FUNCTION
    set_trace("my_class", 50, "/tmp/mytrace.trc");
SELECT quarter(col1) FROM tab_date;
. . .
```

If the quarter() function includes any tracing statements that use a trace level lower or equal to 50, they are written to the /tmp/mytrace.trc trace file.

The simplest tracing statement merely prints a message to the trace file. For example,

```
DPRINTF("myclass", 40, ("Entering quarter()"));
```

It is also possible to use the DPRINTF() macro to print the value of variables in the function being traced. The syntax is similar to the printf() function where the message string includes argument descriptions. For example, we can print an integer variable from the quarter() function:

```
DPRINTF("myclass", 40, ("Quarter value: %d", qt));
```

The parentheses are needed around the message string and the arguments in order for the DPRINTF() macro to consider them as one argument and process them properly.

If special processing is required for tracing, we can add conditional code that gets executed only if its trace level is below or equal to the current trace level set for the specified class. For example,

```
if (tf("myclass", 50)) {
   . . .
   tprintf("Quarter function, qt value: %d\n", qt);
}
```

The tf() function evaluates whether the class name and level are appropriate to execute the conditional code. It works the same way as the DPRINTF() macro. If the trace level passed as argument to tf() is lower than or equal to the current trace level set for the class name passed as argument one, the conditional code is executed.

Debugging

It is possible to use a source code debugger to go over your user-defined routine while it executes in the IDS.2000 server. Since the routine comes from a dynamic shared library, the compilation and the debugging setup itself is different from stand-alone programs. This section covers the requirements for debugging in the UNIX and Windows NT environment.

Debugging Under UNIX

The root user is the only user that can connect a debugger to a database server process. It is possible to create a private installation of the server so that another user can debug it. This is done by using the installserver script with the -c option. The -l option can also be used to create links to the original installation instead of copying the entire product directory structure. The following command shows how it can be done:

```
installserver -c -l /usr/home/jroy/myserver
```

The last parameter represents the target directory where you are installing your private database server. For more information on private installation, consult the *INFORMIX-Universal Server Installation Guide,* starting on page 19.

IDS.2000 implements its multithreaded architecture via several processes. For this reason, we must identify the virtual processor that runs the user-defined routine. Since the user-defined routine can run on any available CPU virtual processor, we must either use only one CPU VP or have the function run on an extended virtual processor. The processor is defined in the database configuration file with the statement

```
VPCLASS        UDR,num=1
```

This statement creates one instance of a new type of virtual processor of type UDR. With this virtual processor in place, we can declare a user-defined routine as running on this type of virtual processor. For example,

```
CREATE FUNCTION quarter(date)
RETURNING varchar(10)
WITH (CLASS='UDR')
. . .
```

The user-defined routine must be compiled with the appropriate debugging option. This is usually done by adding the "-g" option to the compilation. Other options may be required, depending on the platform and the environment setup. Under SOLARIS, if the object files (".o" files) are not available, you must use the "-xs" option to make sure the debugger will find symbols.

Our example shows that the quarter() user-defined routine must run on a UDR virtual processor. You can find the process number of the UDR virtual processor by executing either

```
onstat -g glo
```

or

```
onstat -g sch
```

Before you connect to the appropriate process using a debugger, make sure that the dynamic library is loaded. This can be done either by executing a function from the library or by executing a statement that loads the library without executing the function, as in the case of a SQL statement that does not return any rows. Once the library is loaded, you can use a debugger to attach to the UDR virtual processor process. With dbx you can connect to process 12345 with the following statements:

```
dbx - 12345
```

or

```
dbx
> debug -p 12345
```

In dbx, you can identify the source directory using the USE command. Then, you simply need to set a breakpoint in the user-defined routine before you execute the routine in another program like dbaccess. The debugger will stop the execution when it encounters the user-defined routine. You can then step through the routine in the source code and find out exactly what is happening with your function.

Debugging Under Windows NT

The Microsoft Windows NT provides a different environment. The Database server implementation of virtual processors is done through NT threads instead of processes, as in the UNIX implementation. Since all virtual processors run in the same process, we don't need to limit our function to a specific virtual processor as is needed in the UNIX environment.

Before a user-defined routine can be debugged, it must be compiled with the right option so that the debugger can find debugging information. IDS.2000 only supports Visual C++ under NT, so the debugger of choice is, of course, the Developer Studio's integrated debugger. The following options can be added to your makefile to create a dynamic library that can be debugged:

```
COPTS=/nologo /MTd /W3  /GX /Z7 /Od \
    /D "_DEBUG" /D "_WINDOWS" /YX /c

LOPTS=kernel32.lib user32.lib gdi32.lib winspool.lib\
    comdlg32.lib advapi32.lib shell32.lib ole32.lib\
    oleaut32.lib uuid.lib odbc32.lib odbccp32.lib\
    msvcrt.lib /subsystem:windows /pdb:none\
    /map:"$(PRODDIR)/$(PROJECT_TITLE).map" /debug\
    /machine:I386 /nodefaultlib:"libcmt.lib"\
    /nodefaultlib /implib:"$(PRODDIR)/$(PROJECT_
        TITLE).lib"
```

The COPTS entry represents the compiler options, and the
LOPTS entry represents the linking options. These entries reflect
the addition of debugging information for the makefiles used
for the examples throughout this book. All the examples can be
found on the accompanying CD. Some modifications are likely
required for your environment, specifically to represent the right
filenames in the link options.

Both COPTS and LOPTS may not represent the only possible set
of compiling and linking options that generate a debuggable
dynamic library. You can use them as a starting point, though,
and modify the options for your specific needs.

Once the library is created and the functions are registered,
you can use the debugger to connect to the database server
process to start debugging. The following discussion uses Visual
C++ version 5.0.

You connect to the database server using the Build -> Start
Debug -> Attach to Process sequence of menu items. Visual
Studio then displays a list of processes running on your system.
You need to select the oninit process.

At this point you need to select Project -> Settings to
identify the Dynamic Link Library (DLL) containing your user-
defined routine. Then go to the Debug tab and select the
Additional DLLs category to identify the dynamic library containing your function.

To set a breakpoint in your user-defined routine, you can first
open the source file using "File -> Open" and then position the
cursor on the line where you want to stop. Then, you need to use
"Edit -> Breakpoints" to set the breakpoint. There is a trick to

this: Instead of typing in a breakpoint location, you can use the right arrow following the "break at" field and select the line number of the cursor position. Then you need to reselect the right arrow and choose advanced to proceed. In the dialog box that is displayed, you need to fill in the executable file box. Its content is the pathname of the dynamic library containing the user-defined routine. You then press "Ok" to exit this dialog, and "Ok" to terminate the definition of the breakpoint.

You can then execute your user-defined routine through dbaccess or a client application. The debugger will stop execution at the breakpoint location. You can then step through the source code to debug your code.

When you exit the Visual Studio debugger or choose the Stop Debugging menu option, the debugger will terminate the oninit process, bringing your database server down.

Shared-Memory Dump

In some cases, a user-defined routine execution can generate errors that are unrecoverable. This does not imply that the database server will always be brought down; often, the error is isolated to a specific execution thread. The database server generates a shared-memory dump and a message file that are usually located in the /tmp directory. The shared-memory dump file name starts with "shmem" and "af." starts the message file name.

Both files can be used to look at the stack trace. The information on how to extract a stack trace from a shared-memory dump is available on the Informix Developer Network website (www.informix.com/idn). A stack trace can at least be used to identify which user-defined routine caused the problem. You can extract thread information and a thread stack trace from a shared-memory dump file with the following commands:

```
onstat -g ath <shmem file>
onstat -g stk <thread number> <shmem file>
```

Functions Reference

This appendix provides a summary description of the dataBlade API functions available and of the ESQL/C functions that can be used in a server-side function.

Functions Categories

Byte Operations (ESQL/C)

bycmpr()   bycopy()   byfill()   byleng()

Callbacks

mi_default_callback()   mi_err_desc_next()

mi_disable_callback()   mi_register_callback()

mi_enable_callback()   mi_retrieve_callback()

mi_err_desc_finish()   mi_unregister_callback()

Character Processing (ESQL/C)

ldchar()	rstol()	stcmpr()
rdownshift()	rupshift()	stcopy()
rstod()	stcat()	stleng()
rstoi()	stchar()	

Collections

mi_collection_close()	mi_collection_delete()	mi_collection_insert()
mi_collection_copy()	mi_collection_fetch()	mi_collection_open()
mi_collection_create()	mi_collection_free()	mi_collection_update()

Connecting and Disconnecting

mi_close()	mi_login()	mi_server_connect()
mi_init_library()	mi_open()	mi_server_reconnect()

Converting and Copying

mi_fix_integer()	mi_get_string()
mi_fix_smallint()	mi_put_bytes()
mi_get_bytes()	mi_put_date()
mi_get_date()	mi_put_datetime()
mi_get_datetime()	mi_put_decimal()
mi_get_decimal()	mi_put_double_precision()
mi_get_double_precision()	mi_put_int8()
mi_get_int8()	mi_put_integer()
mi_get_integer()	mi_put_interval()
mi_get_interval()	mi_put_money()
mi_get_money()	mi_put_real()
mi_get_real()	mi_put_smallint()
mi_get_smallint()	mi_put_string()

Conversion

mi_binary_to_date()	mi_decimal_to_string()
mi_binary_to_datetime()	mi_interval_to_string()
mi_binary_to_decimal()	mi_money_to_binary()
mi_binary_to_money()	mi_money_to_string()
mi_date_to_binary()	mi_string_to_date()
mi_date_to_string()	mi_string_to_datetime()
mi_datetime_to_binary()	mi_string_to_decimal()
mi_datetime_to_string()	mi_string_to_interval()
mi_decimal_to_binary()	mi_string_to_money()

Codeset Conversion

mi_convert_from_codeset()   mi_convert_to_codeset()

DATE Conversion (ESQL/C)

rdatestr()	rjulmdy()	rstrdate()
rdayofweek()	rleapyear()	rtoday()
rdefmtdate()	rmdyjul()	

DATETIME & INTERVAL (ESQL/C)

dtaddinv()	incvasc()	TU_DTENCODE	TU_FRAC
dtcurrent()	incvfmtasc()	TU_ENCODE	TU_HOUR
dtcvasc()	intoasc()	TU_END	TU_IENCODE
dtcvfmtasc()	intofmtasc()	TU_F1	TU_LEN
dtextend()	invdivdbl()	TU_F2	TU_MINUTE
dtsub()	invdivinv()	TU_F3	TU_MONTH
dtsubinv()	invextend()	TU_F4	TU_SECOND
dttoasc()	invmuldbl()	TU_F5	TU_START
dttofmtasc()	TU_DAY	TU_FLEN	TU_YEAR

DECIMAL Operations (ESQL/C)

decadd()	deccvint()	decmul()	dectoint()
deccmp()	deccvlong()	decround()	dectolong()
deccopy()	decdiv()	decsub()	dectrunc()
deccvasc()	dececvt()	dectoasc()	ifx_dececvt()
deccvdbl()	decfcvt()	dectodbl()	ifx_decfcvt()

Exception Handling

mi_db_error_raise()   mi_error_desc_is_copy()

mi_errmsg()   mi_error_level()

mi_error_desc_copy()   mi_error_sql_state()

mi_error_desc_destroy()   mi_error_sqlcode()

Function Execution

mi_cast_get()   mi_fp_setarglen()

mi_fp_argisnull()   mi_fp_setargprec()

mi_fp_arglen()   mi_fp_setargscale()

mi_fp_argprec()   mi_fp_setargtype()

mi_fp_argscale()   mi_fp_setfuncid()

mi_fp_argtype()   mi_fp_setfuncstate()

mi_fp_func_state()   mi_fp_setisdone()

mi_fp_getcolid()   mi_fp_setnargs()

mi_fp_getrow()   mi_fp_setnrets()

mi_fp_nargs()   mi_fp_setretlen()

mi_fp_nrets()   mi_fp_setretprec()

mi_fp_request()   mi_fp_setretscale()

mi_fp_retlen()   mi_fp_setrettype()

mi_fp_retprec()   mi_fp_setreturnisnull()

mi_fp_retscale()   mi_fp_usr_fparam()

mi_fp_rettype()   mi_fparam_allocate()

mi_fp_returnisnull()   mi_fparam_copy()

mi_fp_setargisnull()   mi_fparam_free()

```
mi_fparam_get()                    mi_routine_get()
mi_routine_end()                   mi_routine_get_by_typeid()
mi_routine_exec()                  mi_routine_id_get()
```

General Information About Results

```
mi_get_result()          mi_result_command_name()
mi_result_row_count()
```

General Information About Statements

```
mi_current_command_name()        mi_statement_command_name()
```

Handling NULL

```
mi_func_handlesnulls()
```

Information About the Current Statement

```
mi_binary_query()        mi_command_is_finished()
```

INT8 Access (ESQL/C)

```
ifx_getserial8()         ifx_int8cvdec()          ifx_int8toasc()
ifx_int8add()            ifx_int8cvint()          ifx_int8todbl()
ifx_int8cmp()            ifx_int8cvlong()         ifx_int8todec()
ifx_int8copy()           ifx_int8div()            ifx_int8toint()
ifx_int8cvasc()          ifx_int8mul()            ifx_int8tolong()
ifx_int8cvdbl()          ifx_int8sub()
```

LVARCHAR Manipulation

```
mi_get_vardata()         mi_set_vardata()         mi_var_copy()
mi_get_vardata_align()   mi_set_vardata_align()   mi_var_free()
mi_get_varlen()          mi_set_varlen()          mi_var_to_buffer()
mi_lvarchar_to_string()  mi_set_varptr()
mi_new_var()             mi_string_to_lvarchar()
```

Memory Management

```
mi_alloc()              mi_free()
mi_call()               mi_switch_memory_duration()
mi_dalloc()             mi_zalloc()
```

Multirepresentation ADT Support

```
mi_issmall_data()       mi_lo_expand()        mi_set_large()
```

Operating System File Interface

```
mi_file_allocate()   mi_file_read()     mi_file_unlink()
mi_file_close()      mi_file_seek()     mi_file_write()
mi_file_errno()      mi_file_sync()
mi_file_open()       mi_file_tell()
```

Parameters and Environment

```
mi_get_connection_info()           mi_set_connection_user_data()
mi_get_connection_user_data()      mi_set_default_connection_info()
mi_get_default_connection_info()   mi_set_default_database_info()
mi_get_default_database_info()     mi_set_parameter_info()
mi_get_id()                        mi_sysname()
mi_get_parameter_info()
```

Parameterized Queries and Cursors

```
mi_close_statement()            mi_parameter_nullable()
mi_drop_prepared_statement()    mi_parameter_precision()
mi_exec_prepared_statement()    mi_parameter_scale()
mi_fetch_statement()            mi_parameter_type_id()
mi_get_statement_row_desc()     mi_parameter_type_name()
mi_open_prepared_statement()    mi_prepare()
mi_parameter_count()
```

Retrieving Row and Row Data

mi_column_count()

mi_column_id()

mi_column_name()

mi_column_nullable()

mi_column_precision()

mi_column_scale()

mi_column_type_id()

mi_column_typedesc()

mi_get_row_desc()

mi_get_row_desc_from_type_desc()

mi_get_row_desc_without_row()

mi_get_type_source_type()

mi_next_row()

mi_row_create()

mi_row_desc_create()

mi_row_desc_free()

mi_row_free()

mi_type_align()

mi_type_byvalue()

mi_type_element_typedesc()

mi_type_full_name()

mi_type_length()

mi_type_maxlength()

mi_type_owner()

mi_type_precision()

mi_type_scale()

mi_type_typedesc()

mi_type_typename()

mi_typedesc_typeid()

mi_typeid_equals()

mi_typeid_is_collection()

mi_typeid_is_complex()

mi_typeid_is_distinct()

mi_typeid_is_list()

mi_typeid_is_multiset()

mi_typeid_is_row()

mi_typeid_is_set()

mi_typename_to_id()

mi_typename_to_typedesc()

mi_typestring_to_id()

mi_typestring_to_typedesc()

mi_value()

mi_value_by_name()

Save Sets

mi_save_set_count()

mi_save_set_create()

mi_save_set_delete()

mi_save_set_destroy()

mi_save_set_get_first()

mi_save_set_get_last()

mi_save_set_get_next()

mi_save_set_get_previous()

mi_save_set_insert()

mi_save_set_member()

Sending SQL Statements

```
mi_exec()        mi_query_finish()        mi_query_interupt()
```

Smart Large Object Creation

```
mi_lo_copy()        mi_lo_expand()
mi_lo_create()      mi_lo_from_file()
```

Smart Large Object I/O

```
mi_lo_close()              mi_lo_stat()
mi_lo_open()               mi_lo_tell()
mi_lo_read()               mi_lo_truncate()
mi_lo_readwithseek()       mi_lo_write()
mi_lo_seek()               mi_lo_writewithseek()
```

(Moving) Smart Large Objects to and from OS Files

```
mi_file_to_file()          mi_lo_from_file_by_lofd()
mi_lo_from_file()          mi_lo_to_file()
```

(Manipulating) Smart Large Object Handles

```
mi_lo_alter()          mi_lo_from_string()      mi_lo_lolist_create()
mi_lo_decrefcount()    mi_lo_increfcount()      mi_lo_to_string()
mi_lo_filename()       mi_lo_invalidate()       mi_lo_validate()
```

(Handling) Smart Large Object Specifications

```
mi_lo_colinfo_by_ids()     mi_lo_spec_free()
mi_lo_colinfo_by_name()    mi_lo_spec_init()
```

```
mi_lo_specget_estbytes()        mi_lo_specset_estbytes()
mi_lo_specget_extsz()           mi_lo_specset_extsz()
mi_lo_specget_flags()           mi_lo_specset_flags()
mi_lo_specget_maxbytes()        mi_lo_specset_maxbytes()
mi_lo_specget_sbspace()         mi_lo_specset_sbspace()
```

(Handling) Smart Large Object Statistics

```
mi_lo_stat()                    mi_lo_stat_mtime_sec()
mi_lo_stat_atime()              mi_lo_stat_mtime_usec()
mi_lo_stat_cspec()              mi_lo_stat_refcnt()
mi_lo_stat_ctime()              mi_lo_stat_size()
mi_lo_stat_free()               mi_lo_stat_uid()
```

Thread Management

```
mi_interupt_check()             mi_yield()
```

Transaction and Server Processing State Change

```
mi_transition_type()    mi_xact_state()
mi_xact_levels()
```

Tracing

```
DPRINTF()               tf()
mi_tracefile_set()      tprintf()
mi_tracelevel_set()
```

Type Conversion (ESQL/C)

rfmtdate()   rfmtdouble()

rfmtdec()   rfmtlong()

VARCHARs Manipulation (ESQL/C)

MAXVCLEN   VCMIN

VCLENGTH   VCSIZ

VCMAX

FUNCTIONS REFERENCE

bycmpr()

Syntax:	`int bycmpr(char *byte1, char *byte2, int len);`
Description:	Compares two groups of contiguous bytes
Return value:	Less than (-1), equal (0), greater than (1)

bycopy()

Syntax:	`void bycopy(char *from, char *to, int len);`
Description:	Copies byte from one location to another
Return value:	No return

byfill()

Syntax:	`void byfill(char *to, int length, char ch);`
Description:	Fills an area with a specific character
Return value:	No return

byleng()

Syntax:	`int byleng(char *from, int count);`
Description:	Counts number of characters, not considering trailing blanks
Return value:	Number of characters

decadd()

Syntax: `int decadd(dec_t *n1, dec_t *n2, dec_t *sum);`
Description: Adds two decimal type values
Return value: Success (0), overflow (-1200), underflow (-1201)

deccmp()

Syntax: `int deccmp(dec_t *n1, dec_t *n2);`
Description: Compares two decimal type values
Return value: Less than (-1), equal (0), greater than (1)

deccopy()

Syntax: `void deccopy(dec_t *source,`
                `            dec_t *target);`
Description: Copies one decimal structure to another
Return value: No return

deccvasc()

Syntax: `int deccvasc(char *strng_val, int len,`
                `             dec_t *dec_val);`
Description: Converts an ASCII string to a decimal type number
Return value: Success (0), Overflow (-1200), Underflow (-1201),
                nonnumeric string (-1213), bad exponent (-1216)

deccvdbl()

Syntax: `int deccvdbl(double double_val,`
                `             dec_t *dec_val);`
Description: Converts a double value to a decimal value
Return value: Success (0), failure (<0)

deccvint()

Syntax: `int deccvint(int int_val, dec_t *dec_val);`
Description: Converts from an integer to a decimal type
Return value: Success (0), failure (<0)

deccvlong()

Syntax:	`int deccvlong(long long_val,` `                 dec_t *dec_val);`
Description:	Converts from a long to a decimal type
Return value:	Success (0), failure (<0)

decdiv()

Syntax:	`int decdiv(dec_t *dividend,` `dec_t *divisor, dec_t *result);`
Description:	Divides two decimal type values
Return value:	Success (0), Overflow (-1200), Underflow (-1201), divide by 0 (-1202)

dececvt()

Syntax:	`char *dececvt(dec_t *dec_val, int` `ndigits, int *decpt, int *sign);`
Description:	Converts a decimal to a character string. **Not thread safe.**
Return value:	Resulting string pointer

decfcvt()

Syntax:	`char *decfcvt(dec_t *dec_val, int` `ndigits, int *decpt, int *sign);`
Description:	Converts a decimal to a character string. **Not thread safe.**
Return value:	Resulting string pointer

decmul()

Syntax:	`int decmul(dec_t *n1, dec_t *n2,` `                 dec_t *result);`
Description:	Multiplies two decimal values
Return value:	Success (0), Overflow (-1200), Underflow (-1201)

decround()

Syntax:	`void decround(dec_t *d, int s);`
Description:	Rounds a decimal number to a number of fractional digits
Return value:	No return

Syntax: int decsub(dec_t *n1, dec_t *n2,
                                dec_t *difference);

Description: Subtracts n2 from n1

Return value: Success (0), Overflow (-1200), Underflow (-1201)

Syntax: int dectoasc(dec_t *dec_val, char
                *string_val, int len, int right);

Description: Converts a decimal value to a character string

Return value: Success (0), failure (<0)

Syntax: int dectodbl(dec_t *dec_val,
                                double *double_val);

Description: Converts a decimal type to a double type

Return value: Success (0), failure (<0)

Syntax: int dectoint(dec_t *dec_val, int *int_val);

Description: Converts a decimal type to an integer type

Return value: Success (0), failure (<0), decimal value greater than
                32767 (-1200)

Syntax: int dectolong(dec_t *dec_val,
                                long *long_val);

Description: Converts a decimal type to a long type

Return value: Success (0), decimal value greater than
                2,147,483,647 (–1200)

Syntax: void dectrunc(dec_t dec_val, int s);

Description: Truncates a decimal value to s fractional digits

Return value: No return value

DPRINTF()

Syntax:
```
void DPRINTF(mi_string *trace_class,
             mi_integer threshold,
             (format [, arg]...));
```

Description: Macro used to print tracing information conditional to being under the current threshold of the trace_class specified

Return value: None

dtaddinv()

Syntax:
```
int dtaddinv(dtime_t *dt, intrvl_t *inv,
             dtime_t *res);
```

Description: Adds an interval to a datetime

Return value: Success (0), Error in addition (<0)

dtcurrent()

Syntax:
```
void dtcurrent(dtime_t *dt);
```

Description: Assigns the current date and time to a datetime variable

Return value: No return value

dtcvasc()

Syntax:
```
int dtcvasc(char *inbuf,
            dtime_t *dtvalue);
```

Description: Converts a properly formatted string to a datetime value

Return value: Success (0), conversion impossible (-1260), Too many digits in first field (-1261), Nonnumeric character (-1262), Out of range or incorrect (-1263), Extra trailing character (-1264), Overflow occurred (-1265), incompatible operation (-1266), Out of range computation (-1267), invalid qualifier (-1268)

dtcvfmtasc()

Syntax:
```
int dtcvfmtasc(char *inbuf,
char *fmtstring, dtime_t *dtvalue);
```

Description:	Converts a string to a datetime value using a formatting mask
Return value:	Success (0), failure (<0)

Syntax:	`int dtextend(dtime_t *in_dt,` `            dtime_t *out_dt);`
Description:	Changes the precision of a datetime field to match the output field precision
Return value:	Success (0), invalid datetime qualifier (-1268)

dtsub()

Syntax:	`int dtsub(dtime_t *n1, dtime_t *n2,` `          intrvl_t *result);`
Description:	Subtracts n2 from n2 giving an interval between dates
Return value:	Success (0), failure (<0)

dtsubinv()

Syntax:	`int dtsubinv(dtime_t *dt, intrvl_t *inv,` `             dtime_t *res);`
Description:	Subtracts an interval from a datetime
Return value:	Success (0), failure (<0)

dttoasc()

Syntax:	`int dttoasc(dtime_t *dtvalue,` `            char *outbuf);`
Description:	Converts a datetime field to an ASCII string
Return value:	Success (0), failure (<0)

dttofmtasc()

Syntax:	`int dttofmtasc(dtime_t *dtvalue, char` `*outbuf, int buflen, char *fmtstring);`
Description:	Converts a datetime field to a character string using a formatting mask
Return value:	Success (0), failure (<0)

ifx_dececvt()

Syntax:
```
int ifx_dececvt(register dec_t *np,
    register int ndigit, int *decpt,
    int *sign, char *decstr,
    int decstrlen);
```

Description: Thread-safe version of dececvt()

Return value: Success (0), Failure (<0), buffer NULL or too small (-1273)

ifx_decfcvt()

Syntax:
```
int ifx_decfcvt(register dec_t *np,
    register int ndigit, int *decpt,
    int *sign, char *decstr,
    int decstrlen);
```

Description: Thread-safe version of decfcvt()

Return value: Success (0), Failure (<0), buffer NULL or too small (-1273)

ifx_getserial8()

Syntax:
```
void ifx_getserial8(
    ifx_int8_t
    *serial8_val);
```

Description: Returns the serial8 value of the last inserted row

Return value: No return value

ifx_int8add()

Syntax:
```
int ifx_int8add(ifx_int8_t *n1,
    ifx_int8_t *n2, ifx_int8_t *sum);
```

Description: Adds two int8 values

Return value: Success (0), Overflow or underflow (-1284)

ifx_int8cmp()

Syntax:
```
int ifx_int8cmp(ifx_int8_t *n1,
                ifx_int8_t *n2);
```

Description: Compares two int8 values

Return value: n1 < n2 (-1), n1 == n2 (0), n1 > n2 (1)

Syntax:
```
void ifx_int8copy(ifx_int8_t *source,
                  ifx_int8_t *target);
```

Description: Copies an int8 structure to another

Return value: No return value

Syntax:
```
int ifx_int8cvasc(char *string_val,
int len, ifx_int8_t *int8_val);
```

Description: Converts a character string to an int8 value

Return value: Success (0), String has nonnumeric characters (-1213), Overflow or underflow (-1284)

Syntax:
```
int ifx_int8cvdbl(double double_val,
    ifx_int8_t *int8_val);
```

Description: Converts a double value to an int8 value

Return value: Success (0), Failure (<0)

Syntax:
```
int ifx_int8cvdec(dec_t *dec_val,
    ifx_int8_t *int8_val);
```

Description: Converts a decimal value to an int8 value

Return value: Success (0), Failure (<0)

Syntax:
```
int ifx_int8cvflt(float *flt_val,
    ifx_int8_t *int8_val);
```

Description: Converts a float value to an int8 value

Return value: Success (0), Failure (<0)

Syntax:
```
int ifx_int8cvint(int int_val,
    ifx_int8_t *int8_val);
```

Description: Converts an int value to an int8 value

Return value: Success (0), Failure (<0)

ifx_int8cvlong()

Syntax:	int ifx_int8cvlong(long long_val, ifx_int8_t *int8_val);
Description:	Converts a long value to an int8 value
Return value:	Success (0), Failure (<0)

ifx_int8div()

Syntax:	int ifx_int8div(ifx_int8_t *n1, ifx_int8_t *n2, ifx_int8_t *result);
Description:	Divides n1 by n2
Return value:	Success (0), divide by 0 (-1202)

ifx_int8mul()

Syntax:	int ifx_int8mul(ifx_int8_t *n1, ifx_int8_t *n2, ifx_int8_t *result);
Description:	Multiplies two int8 values
Return value:	Success (0), Overflow or underflow (-1284)

ifx_int8sub()

Syntax:	int ifx_int8sub(ifx_int8_t *n1, ifx_int8_t *n2, ifx_int8_t *diff);
Description:	Subtracts n2 from n1
Return value:	Success (0), Overflow or underflow (-1284)

ifx_int8toasc()

Syntax:	int ifx_int8toasc(ifx_int8_t *int8_val, char *string_val, int len);
Description:	Converts an int8 value to a character string
Return value:	Success (0), string too small (-1207)

ifx_int8todbl()

Syntax:	int ifx_int8todbl(ifx_int8_t *int8_val, double *double_val);
Description:	Converts an int8 value to a double value
Return value:	Success (0), Failure (<0)

Syntax: `int ifx_int8todec(ifx_int8_t *int8_val,`
`dec_t *dec_val);`

Description: Converts an int8 value to a decimal value

Return value: Success (0), Failure (<0)

Syntax: `int ifx_int8toflt(ifx_int8_t *int8_val,`
`float *float_val);`

Description: Converts an int8 value to a float value

Return value: Success (0), Failure (<0)

Syntax: `int ifx_int8toint(ifx_int8_t *int8_val,`
`int *int_val);`

Description: Converts an int8 value to an int value

Return value: Success (0), Failure (<0)

Syntax: `int ifx_int8tolong(ifx_int8_t *int8_val,`
`long *long_val);`

Description: Converts an int8 value to a long value

Return value: Success (0), int8 value greater than 2,147,483,647
(-1200)

Syntax: `int incvasc(char *inbuf,`
`intrvl_t *invvalue);`

Description: Converts a formatted string to an interval

Return value: Success (0), conversion impossible (-1260), Too
many digits in first field (-1261), Nonnumeric
character (-1262), Out of range or incorrect (-1263),
Extra trailing character (-1264), Overflow occurred
(-1265), incompatible operation (-1266), Out of
range computation (-1267), invalid qualifier (-1268)

incvfmtasc()

Syntax:	`int incvfmtasc(char *inbuf,` `        char *fmtstring, intrvl_t *invvalue);`
Description:	Converts a string to an interval using a formatting mask
Return value:	Success (0), failure (<0)

intoasc()

Syntax:	`int intoasc(intrvl_t *invalue, char *outbuf);`
Description:	Converts an interval value to an character string
Return value:	Success (0), failure (<0)

intofmtasc()

Syntax:	`int intofmtasc(intrvl_t *invalue, char` `*outbuf, int buflen, char *fmtstring);`
Description:	Converts an interval value to a character string using a formatting mask
Return value:	Success (0), failure (<0)

invdivdbl()

Syntax:	`int invdivdbl(intrvl_t *iv, double num,` `        intrvl_t *ov);`
Description:	Divides an interval value by a double value
Return value:	Success (0), failure (<0), magnitude too large (-1200), magnitude too small (-1201), divide by 0 (-1202), Overflow (-1265), Interval incompatible with operation (-1266), Invalid interval qualifier (-1268)

invdivinv()

Syntax:	`int invdivinv(intrvl_t *i1,` `        intrvl_t *i2, double *num);`
Description:	Divides an interval value (i1) by another interval value (i2)
Return value:	Success (0), failure (<0), magnitude too large (-1200), magnitude too small (-1201), Interval incompatible with operation (-1266), Invalid interval qualifier (-1268)

Syntax:
```
int invextend(intrvl_t *in_inv,
              intrvl_t *out_inv);
```

Description: Copies an interval value to another one with a different precision

Return value: Success (0), failure (<0), Interval incompatible with operation (-1266), Invalid interval qualifier (-1268)

Syntax:
```
int invmuldbl(intrvl_t *iv, double num,
              intrvl_t *ov);
```

Description: Multiplies an interval value by a double value

Return value: Success (0), failure (<0), magnitude too large (-1200), magnitude too small (-1201), Interval incompatible with operation (-1266), Invalid interval qualifier (-1268)

Syntax:
```
void ldchar(char *from, int count, char *to);
```

Description: Copies a fixed-length string into a NULL-terminated string and removes any trailing blanks

Return value: No return

Syntax:
```
MAXVCLEN
```

Description: Macro returning the maximum number of characters that can be stored in a VARCHAR column

Return value: The current value is 255

Syntax:
```
void *mi_alloc(mi_integer size);
```

Description: The mi_alloc() function allocates a bloc of memory of a given size

Return value: Pointer to the allocated memory block or NULL

mi_binary_query()

Syntax:
```
mi_integer mi_binary_query(
        MI_CONNECTION *conn);
```

Description: Reports whether the current statement on a particular connection returns a binary value

Return value: Binary value (1), ascii value (0), error (MI_ERROR)

mi_binary_to_date()

Syntax:
```
mi_lvarchar *mi_binary_to_date(
        mi_date date);
```

Description: Creates a date string from the internal representation

This function will be deprecated sometime after the 9.14 release

Return value: A pointer to the buffer that contains the resulting date string

mi_binary_to_datetime()

Syntax:
```
mi_lvarchar *mi_binary_to_datetime(
        mi_datetime *dt_data);
```

Description: Creates a datetime string from the internal representation

This function will be deprecated sometime after the 9.14 release

Return value: A pointer to the buffer that contains the resulting datetime string

mi_binary_to_decimal()

Syntax:
```
mi_lvarchar *mi_binary_to_decimal(
        mi_decimal *dec_data);
```

Description: Creates a decimal string from the internal representation

This function will be deprecated sometime after the 9.14 release

Return value: A pointer to the buffer that contains the resulting decimal string

Syntax: `mi_lvarchar *mi_binary_to_money(`
                              `mi_money *money_data);`

Description: Creates a money string from the internal
               representation

               This function will be deprecated sometime after the
               9.14 release

Return value: A pointer to the buffer that contains the resulting
               money string

Syntax: `mi_integer mi_call(mi_integer *retval,`
                              `mi_integer (fn)(),`
                              `mi_integer nargs, ...);`

Description: Allocates a new thread stack for the execution of
               the function

Return value: Memory allocation error (`MI_NOMEM`), more than 10
               arguments (`MI_TOOMANY`), stack large enough
               (`MI_CONTINUE`), call done and return value in retval
               (`MI_DONE`)

Syntax: `MI_FUNC_DESC * mi_cast_get(`
                              `MI_CONNECTION *conn,`
                              `MI_TYPEID *from_type,`
                              `MI_TYPEID *to_type,`
                              `mi_char *cast_status);`

Description: Looks up a registered cast function and returns its
               function descriptor

Return value: Function descriptor pointer or `NULL`. The error status
               is in cast_status. The available values are: get failed
               (`MI_ERROR_CAST`), no cast available but cast
               needed (`MI_NO_CAST`), no cast needed and no
               function required for the cast (`MI_NOP_CAST`),
               casting is between built-in types (`MI_SYSTEM_CAST`),
               user-defined routine provided (`MI_UDR_CAST`),
               explicit cast (`MI_EXPLICIT_CAST`), implicit cast
               (`MI_IMPLICIT_CAST`)

mi_client()

      Syntax: `mi_integer mi_client();`

      Description: Indicates whether the function is running in the client or the server

      Return value: 1 if it is in a client, 0 if it is in the server

mi_client_locale()

      Syntax: `mi_char1 *mi_client_locale();`

      Description: Returns the name of the client locale

      Return value: The name of the client locale

mi_close()

      Syntax: `mi_integer mi_close(MI_CONNECTION *conn);`

      Description: Closes a connection

      Return value: Success (`MI_OK`), failure (`MI_ERROR`)

mi_close_statement()

      Syntax: `mi_integer mi_close_statement(`
                                     `MI_STATEMENT *stmtptr);`

      Description: Closes a previously opened statement

      Return value: Success (`MI_OK`), cannot close the statement (`MI_ERROR`)

mi_collection_close()

      Syntax: `mi_integer mi_collection_close(`
                                       `MI_CONNECTION *conn,`
                                       `MI_COLL_DESC *colldesc);`

      Description: Closes a collection

      Return value: Success (`MI_OK`), failure (`MI_ERROR`)

mi_collection_copy()

      Syntax: `MI_COLLECTION *mi_collection_copy(`
                                       `MI_CONNECTION *conn,`
                                       `MI_COLL_DESC *colldesc);`

Description:	Makes a copy of a collection to a newly allocated collection
Return value:	`MI_COLLECTION` pointer on success, `NULL` on error

mi_collection_create()

Syntax:	`MI_COLLECTION *mi_collection_create(`
	`        MI_CONNECTION *conn,`
	`        MI_TYPEID *typeid);`

Description:	Creates a collection.
Return value:	Collection pointer or `NULL` if an error occured

mi_collection_delete()

Syntax:	`mi_integer mi_collection_delete(`
	`        MI_CONNECTION *conn,`
	`        MI_COLL_DESC *colldesc,`
	`        MI_CURSOR_ACTION action,`
	`        mi_integer jump);`

Description:	Deletes a single element of a collection
	`action:`
	`MI_CURSOR_NEXT`: deletes the next element after the current cursor position
	`MI_CURSOR_PRIOR`: deletes the previous element from the current cursor position
	`MI_CURSOR_FIRST`: deletes the first element
	`MI_CURSOR_LAST`: deletes the last element
	`MI_CURSOR_ABSOLUTE`: deletes the element at jump position
	`MI_CURSOR_RELATIVE`: moves jump elements from the current position then delete the current element
	`MI_CURSOR_CURRENT`: deletes the current element
	`jump`: offset for deletion (lists only) or 0
Return value:	Success (`MI_OK`), bad jump value (`MI_NULL_VALUE`), failure (`MI_ERROR`)

mi_collection_fetch()

Syntax:	`mi_integer mi_collection_fetch(MI_CONNECTION *conn, MI_COLL_DESC *colldesc, MI_CURSOR_ACTION action, mi_integer jump, MI_DATUM *retdatum, mi_integer *retlen);`
Description:	Fetches an element of a collection

`action`:

`MI_CURSOR_NEXT`: fetches the next element after the current cursor position

`MI_CURSOR_PRIOR`: fetches the previous element from the current cursor position

`MI_CURSOR_FIRST`: fetches the first element

`MI_CURSOR_LAST`: fetches the last element

`MI_CURSOR_ABSOLUTE`: fetches the element at jump position

`MI_CURSOR_RELATIVE`: moves jump elements from the current position, then fetches the current element

`MI_CURSOR_CURRENT`: fetches the current element

`jump`: offset for fetch (lists only) or 0. The first element has a jump value of 1

Return value: NULL data (`MI_NULL_VALUE`), no more values (`MI_END_OF_DATA`), invalid connection (`MI_ERROR`), value is a row (`MI_ROW_VALUE`), value is a collection (`MI_COLLECTION_VALUE`), success (`MI_NORMAL_VALUE`)

mi_collection_free()

Syntax:	`mi_integer mi_collection_free(MI_CONNECTION *conn, MI_COLLECTION *coll);`
Description:	Frees a collection
Return value:	Success (`MI_OK`), failure (`MI_ERROR`)

mi_collection_insert()

Syntax:	`mi_integer mi_collection_insert(MI_CONNECTION *conn, MI_COLL_DESC *colldesc, MI_DATUM datum, MI_CURSOR_ACTION action, mi_integer jump);`

Description:	Inserts an element into a collection
	`action:`
	`MI_CURSOR_NEXT`: inserts the next element after the current cursor position
	`MI_CURSOR_PRIOR`: inserts the previous element from the current cursor position
	`MI_CURSOR_FIRST`: inserts the first element
	`MI_CURSOR_LAST`: inserts the last element
	`MI_CURSOR_ABSOLUTE`: inserts the element at jump position
	`MI_CURSOR_RELATIVE`: moves jump elements from the current position, then inserts the current element
	`MI_CURSOR_CURRENT`: deletes the current element
	`jump`: offset for insertion (lists only) or 0
Return value:	Success (`MI_OK`), bad jump value (`MI_NULL_VALUE`), failure (`MI_ERROR`)

mi_collection_open()

Syntax:	`MI_COLL_DESC * mi_collection_open(MI_CONNECTION *conn, MI_COLLECTION *coll);`
Description:	Opens a collection
Return value:	Collection pointer or `NULL` on error

[9.20] mi_collection_open_with_options()

Syntax:	`MI_COLL_DESC * mi_collection_open_with_options(MI_CONNECTION *conn,MI_COLLECTION *coll, mi_integer open_flags);`
Description:	Opens a collection. Opens_flags bit mask: `MI_COLL_READONLY, MI_COLL_NOSCROLL`
Return value:	Collection pointer or `NULL` on error

mi_collection_update()

Syntax:	`mi_integer mi_collection_update(MI_CONNECTION *conn, MI_COLL_DESC *colldesc, MI_DATUM datum, MI_CURSOR_ACTION action, mi_integer jump);`

Description:	Updates a collection
	`action:`
	`MI_CURSOR_NEXT:` updates the next element after the current cursor position
	`MI_CURSOR_PRIOR:` updates the previous element from the current cursor position
	`MI_CURSOR_FIRST:` updates the first element
	`MI_CURSOR_LAST:` updates the last element
	`MI_CURSOR_ABSOLUTE:` updates the element at jump position
	`MI_CURSOR_RELATIVE:` Moves jump elements from the current position, then updates the current element
	`MI_CURSOR_CURRENT:` updates the current element
	`jump:` offset for update (lists only)
Return value:	Success (`MI_OK`), bad jump value (`MI_NULL_VALUE`), failure (`MI_ERROR`)

mi_column_count()

Syntax:	`mi_integer mi_column_count(` `        MI_ROW_DESC *rdesc);`
Description:	Returns the number of columns in the row descriptor
Return value:	Number of columns or `MI_ERROR`

mi_column_id()

Syntax:	`mi_integer mi_column_id(`
	`        MI_ROW_DESC *rdesc,`
	`        mi_string *colname);`

Description:	Returns the position of a column in a row
Return value:	Column position or `MI_ERROR`

mi_column_name()

Syntax:	`mi_string *mi_column_name(`
	`        MI_ROW_DESC *rdesc, mi_integer`
	`        column_no);`

Description:	Returns a pointer to a NULL-terminated string containing the column name
Return value:	Column name or NULL on failure

Syntax:	`mi_integer mi_column_nullable(`
	`        MI_ROW_DESC *rdesc,`
	`        mi_integer column_no);`

Description:	Indicates whether a column can contain a NULL value
Return value:	Accepts NULL (1), no NULL allowed (0), failure (MI_ERROR)

Syntax:	`mi_integer mi_column_precision(`
	`MI_ROW_DESC *rdesc, mi_integer`
	`column_no);`

Description:	Returns the precision of the specified column
Return value:	Column precision, 0 if there is no precision, MI_ERROR on failure

Syntax:	`mi_integer mi_column_scale (`
	`MI_ROW_DESC *rdesc, mi_integer`
	`column_no);`

Description:	Returns the scale of the specified column (for money and decimal types)
Return value:	Scale of the column, 0 if not applicable, MI_ERROR on failure

Syntax:	`MI_TYPEID *mi_column_type_id (`
	`MI_ROW_DESC *rdesc,`
	`mi_integer column_no);`

Description:	Returns the type ID of the specified column
Return value:	Pointer to a NULL-terminated type ID, or NULL on failure

mi_column_typedesc()

Syntax:	```MI_TYPE_DESC * mi_column_typedesc(```
	```MI_ROW_DESC *rdesc,```
	```mi_integer column_no);```

Description:	Gets the type descriptor of the specified column
Return value:	Type descriptor or NULL on failure

mi_command_is_finished()

Syntax:	```mi_integer mi_command_is_finished(``` ``` MI_CONNECTION *conn);```
Description:	Reports whether the current statement or command is finished executing
Return value:	Statement active(1), statement completed(0), error (MI_ERROR)

mi_convert_from_codeset()

Syntax:	```mi_integer mi_convert_from_codeset(```
	``` char *string,```
	``` char *locale_name);```

Description:	Converts data from a specified code set
Return value:	Pointer to the resulting data

mi_convert_to_codeset()

Syntax:	```mi_integer mi_convert_to_codeset(```
	``` char *string,```
	``` char *locale_name);```

Description:	Converts data to a specified code set
Return value:	Pointer to the resulting data

mi_current_command_name()

Syntax:	```mi_string *mi_current_command_name(``` ``` MI_CONNECTION *conn);```
Description:	Retrieves the name of the last statement or command sent on this connection
Return value:	Command name on success, NULL on failure

Syntax: `void * mi_dalloc(mi_integer size,`
                `     MI_MEMORY_DURATION duration);`

Description: Allocates a specified amount of memory with the specified memory duration

                Memory duration: `PER_FUNCTION`/`PER_ROUTINE`, `PER_COMMAND`

                Undocumented: `PER_STATEMENT`, `PER_TRANSACTION`, `PER_SESSION`, `PER_SYSTEM`

Return value: Pointer to memory or `NULL`

Syntax: `mi_date mi_date_to_binary(`
                `     mi_lvarchar *date_string);`

Description: Converts a string representation of a date to its binary presentation

                This function will be deprecated sometime after the 9.14 release

Return value: Date value

Syntax: `mi_string *mi_date_to_string(`
                `     mi_date date);`

Description: Creates a string representation of a date value

Return value: Pointer to a string

Syntax: `mi_datetime *mi_datetime_to_binary(`
                `mi_lvarchar *datetime_string);`

Description: Converts a string representation of a datetime to its binary representation

                This function will be deprecated sometime after the 9.14 release

Return value: Pointer to a datetime

mi_datetime_to_string()

Syntax: `mi_string *mi_datetime_to_string(`
`mi_datetime *dtvalue);`

Description: Converts a datetime to its character representation

Return value: Pointer to a string

mi_db_error_raise()

Syntax: `mi_integer`

`mi_db_error_raise(MI_CONNECTION *conn,`
`mi_integer msg_type, mi_char *msg, ...);`

Description: Raises an error or warning

The `MI_CONNECTION` pointer can be `NULL`

Return value: Success (`MI_OK`), error (`MI_ERROR`), may not return

mi_decimal_to_binary()

Syntax: `mi_decimal`
`*mi_decimal_to_binary(`
` mi_lvarchar *decimal_string);`

Description: Converts a string to a decimal value

This function will be deprecated sometime after the 9.14 release

Return value: Pointer to a decimal value

mi_decimal_to_string()

Syntax: `mi_string *mi_decimal_to_string(`
`mi_decimal *decimal);`

Description: Converts a decimal value to a string

Return value: Pointer to a string

mi_disable_callback()

Syntax: `mi_integer mi_disable_callback(`
`MI_CONNECTION *conn, MI_EVENT_TYPE`
`event_type, MI_CALLBACK_HANDLE *handle);`

Description: Disables a callback for a single event or for all events

The MI_CONNECTION pointer must be NULL in a
server-side function

Return value: Success (MI_OK), failure (MI_ERROR)

mi_drop_prepared_statement()

Syntax:
```
mi_integer mi_drop_prepared_statement(
        MI_STATEMENT *stmtPtr);
```

Description: Drops a previously prepared statement

Return value: Success (MI_OK), failure (MI_ERROR)

mi_enable_callback()

Syntax:
```
mi_integer mi_enable_callback(
MI_CONNECTION *conn, MI_EVENT_TYPE
event_type, MI_CALLBACK_HANDLE *handle);
```

Description: Enables a callback for a single event or for all event
types

The MI_CONNECTION pointer can be NULL

Return value: Success (MI_OK), failure (MI_ERROR)

mi_err_desc_finish()

Syntax:
```
mi_integer mi_err_desc_finish(
MI_ERROR_DESC *error_desc);
```

Description: Completes processing of the current exception list

Return value: Success (MI_OK), failure (MI_ERROR)

mi_err_desc_next()

Syntax:
```
MI_ERROR_DESC *mi_err_desc_next(
MI_ERROR_DESC *desc);
```

Description: Gets the next error descriptor from the list of current
exceptions

Return value: Error exception, or NULL if no more error exceptions
or failure

mi_errmsg()

Syntax:
```
void mi_errmsg(MI_ERROR_DESC *desc,
        char *buf, mi_integer buflen);
```

Description:	Copies an error or warning message from the message descriptor into the specified buffer
Return value:	No return

mi_error_desc_copy()

Syntax:	`MI_ERROR_DESC *mi_error_desc_copy(` `                MI_ERROR_DESC *source);`
Description:	Returns a copy of a given `MI_ERROR_DESC` structure
Return value:	Newly allocated copy, or `NULL` on error

mi_error_desc_destroy()

Syntax:	`mi_integer mi_error_desc_destroy(` `                MI_ERROR_DESC *desc);`
Description:	Frees the `MI_ERROR_DESC` structure
Return value:	Success (`MI_OK`), failure (`MI_ERROR`)

mi_error_desc_is_copy()

Syntax:	`mi_integer mi_error_desc_is_copy(` `                MI_ERROR_DESC *desc);`
Description:	Finds out if the structure is a user copy
Return value:	`MI_TRUE` is a copy, `MI_FALSE` not a copy, `MI_ERROR` on failure

mi_error_level()

Syntax:	`mi_integer mi_error_level(` `                MI_ERROR_DESC *desc);`
Description:	Returns the exception level associated with the server exception
Return value:	Success: exception level: `MI_MESSAGE`, `MI_EXCEPTION`, failure: (`MI_ERROR`)

mi_error_ sqlcode()

Syntax:	`mi_integer mi_error_sqlcode(`
	`                MI_ERROR_DESC *desc,`
	`                mi_integer *sqlcodep);`

Description:	Retrieves the value of `SQLCODE`
Return value:	Success (`MI_OK`), failure (`MI_ERROR`)

Syntax:
```
mi_integer mi_error_ sql_state(
MI_ERROR_DESC *desc, char *buf,
mi_integer buflen);
```

Description: Gets the SQLSTATE value

Return value: Success (MI_OK), failure (MI_ERROR)

Syntax:
```
mi_integer
mi_exec(MI_CONNECTION *conn, const
        mi_string *cmd, mi_integer
        control);
```

Description: Sends a SQL statement for execution

```
control: MI_QUERY_NORMAL, MI_QUERY_BINARY
```

Return value: Success (MI_OK), failure (MI_ERROR)

Syntax:
```
mi_integer mi_exec_prepared_statement(
MI_STATEMENT *stmt, mi_integer control,
mi_integer are_binary, mi_integer
nparams, MI_DATUM values[], mi_integer
lengths[], mi_integer nulls[], mi_string
*types[], mi_integer retlen, mi_string
*rettypes[]);
```

Description: Executes a prepared statement (For SELECT it opens a cursor)

Return value: Success (MI_OK), failure (MI_ERROR)

Syntax:
```
mi_integer mi_fetch_statement(
MI_STATEMENT *stmt, MI_CURSOR_ACTION
orient, mi_integer jump, mi_integer
count);
```

Description: Sets up the fetch cursor for the statement

```
orient: MI_CURSOR_<NEXT|PRIOR|FIRST|LAST|
ABSOLUTE|RELATIVE>
```

Return value: Success (MI_OK), failure (MI_ERROR)

mi_file_allocate()

Syntax:	`mi_integer mi_file_allocate(mi_integer n);`
Description:	Ensures that a specified number of file descriptors are available to open files
Return value:	Number of file descriptors allocated on success, `MI_ERROR` on failure

mi_file_close()

Syntax:	`void mi_file_close(mi_integer fd);`
Description:	Closes a file that was previously opened with `mi_file_open()`
Return value:	No return value

mi_file_errno()

Syntax:	`mi_integer mi_file_errno();`
Description:	Retrieves the errno value for the last file operation
Return value:	Errno value

mi_file_open()

Syntax:	`mi_integer mi_file_open(const char *name,` `mi_integer flags,` `mi_integer mode);`
Description:	Opens a file. This function is tailored after the `open()` system call
Return value:	File descriptor on success, `MI_ERROR` on failure

mi_file_read()

Syntax:	`mi_integer mi_file_read(mi_integer fd,` `char *buf, mi_integer count);`
Description:	Reads from an open file into a buffer. This is tailored after the `read()` system call.
Return value:	Number of bytes read on success, `MI_ERROR` on failure

Syntax: `mi_integer mi_file_seek(mi_integer fd, mi_integer offset, mi_integer whence);`

Description: Changes the current position within a file. Similar to the `lseek()` system call.

Return value: Position in bytes from the beginning of the file on success, `MI_ERROR` on failure

Syntax: `mi_integer mi_file_sync(mi_integer fd);`

Description: Flushes all pages belonging to this file to disk

Return value: Success `MI_OK`, failure `MI_ERROR`

Syntax: `mi_integer mi_file_tell(mi_integer fd);`

Description: Provides the current position in the file as the number of bytes from the beginning of the file

Return value: Current position on success, `MI_ERROR` on failure

Syntax: `char *mi_file_to_file(MI_CONNECTION *conn, const char *fromfile, mi_integer fromflags, const char *tofile, mi_integer toflags);`

Description: Copies files between the database server and a client

Flags: `MI_O_<EXCL|TRUNC|APPEND|RDWR|RDONLY|TEXT|SERVER_FILE|CLIENT_FILE>`

Return value: Destination path on success, `NULL` on failure

Syntax: `mi_integer mi_file_unlink(mi_integer fd);`

Description: Removes a file previously opened

Return value: `MI_OK` on success, `MI_EROR` on failure

mi_file_write()

Syntax:	`mi_integer mi_file_write(mi_integer fd, const char *buf, mi_integer count);`
Description:	Writes a number of bytes to a file. Similar to the `write()` system call.
Return value:	Actual number of bytes written on success, `MI_ERROR` on failure

mi_fix_integer()

Syntax:	`mi_unsigned_integer mi_fix_integer( mi_unsigned_integer val);`
Description:	Converts the specified value to or from the client byte ordering
Return value:	The value in the desired byte ordering

mi_fix_smallint()

Syntax:	`mi_unsigned_integer mi_fix_smallint( mi_unsigned_integer val);`
Description:	Converts the specified value to or from the client byte ordering
Return value:	The value in the desired byte ordering

mi_fp_argisnull()

Syntax:	`mi_unsigned_char1 mi_fp_argisnull( MI_FPARAM *fparam, mi_integer argno);`
Description:	Returns if argument number argno is `NULL`. The first argument is argument number 0.
Return value:	`MI_TRUE` if the argument is `NULL`, `MI_FALSE` if not

mi_fp_arglen()

Syntax:	`mi_integer mi_fp_arglen( MI_FPARAM *fparam, mi_integer argno);`
Description:	Returns the length of argument number argno. The first argument is argument number 0.
Return value:	Argument length

Syntax: `mi_integer mi_fp_argprec(`
                 `MI_FPARAM *fparam, mi_integer argno);`

Description: Gets the precision of argument number argno. The
                 first argument is argument number 0.

Return value: Argument precision

Syntax: `mi_integer mi_fp_argscale(`
                 `MI_FPARAM *fparam, mi_integer argno);`

Description: Gets the scale of argument number argno. The first
                 argument is argument number 0.

Return value: Scale of the argument

Syntax: `MI_TYPEID *mi_fp_argtype(`
                 `MI_FPARAM *fparam, mi_integer argno);`

Description: Gets the typeid of argument number argno. The first
                 argument is argument number 0.

Return value: Argument typeid

Syntax: `void *mi_fp_funcstate(`
                 `        MI_FPARAM *fparam);`

Description: Returns a pointer to a user-defined memory buffer
                 that was saved in a previous invocation of the UDR

Return value: Pointer to a user-defined memory area

Syntax: `mi_integer mi_fp_getcolid(`
                 `        MI_FPARAM *fparam);`

Description: The colum number of the associated row context.
                 This is valid in limited contexts and in `assign()`,
                 `destroy()`, and `import()`.

Return value: Row number or `MI_ERROR`

mi_fp_getrow()

Syntax: `MI_ROW *mi_fp_getrow(MI_FPARAM *fparam);`

Description: Retrieves the row context of the function. This is valid only in `assign()`, `destroy()`, and `import()`. It is valid in other functions depending on how they are used.

Return value: `MI_ROW` pointer, or `NULL`

mi_fp_nargs()

Syntax: `mi_integer mi_fp_nargs(MI_FPARAM *fparam);`

Description: Gets the number of arguments required by the routine

Return value: Number of arguments

mi_fp_nrets()

Syntax: `mi_integer mi_fp_nrets(`
`MI_FPARAM *fparam);`

Description: Gets the number of return values for this function

Return value: Always 1 for C functions

mi_fp_request()

Syntax: `MI_SETREQUEST mi_fp_request(`
`MI_FPARAM *fparam);`

Description: Gets the type of operation being performed Essential for iterator functions

Return value: `SET_INIT, SET_RETONE, SET_END,`
`SET_INVALID`

mi_fp_retlen()

Syntax: `mi_integer mi_fp_retlen(`
`MI_FPARAM *fparam, mi_integer argno);`

Description: Gets the length of the argno return value. The only valid argno for C functions is 0.

Return value: Return value length

Syntax: `mi_integer mi_fp_retprec(`
`MI_FPARAM *fparam, mi_integer argno);`

Description: Gets the precision of the argno return value. The
only valid argno for C functions is 0.

Return value: Return value precision

Syntax: `mi_integer mi_fp_retscale(`
`MI_FPARAM *fparam, mi_integer argno);`

Description: Gets the scale of the argno return value. The only
valid argno for C functions is 0.

Return value: Return value scale

Syntax: `MI_TYPEID *mi_fp_rettype(`
`MI_FPARAM *fparam, mi_integer argno);`

Description: Gets the type of the argno return value. The only
valid argno for C functions is 0.

Return value: Return value `typeid`

Syntax: `mi_boolean mi_fp_returnisnull(`
`MI_FPARAM *fparam, mi_integer argno);`

Description: Returns if the return value is identified as `NULL`

Return value: `MI_TRUE` or `MI_FALSE`

Syntax: `void mi_fp_setargisnull(`
`MI_FPARAM *fparam, mi_integer argno,`
`mi_integer value);`

Description: Sets argument number argno to `NULL`. The first
argument is argument number 0.

Return value: No return value

mi_fp_setarglen()

Syntax:	`void mi_fp_setarglen(MI_FPARAM *fparam,` `    mi_integer argno, mi_integer len);`
Description:	Sets the length of the argno argument. The first argument is argument number 0.
Return value:	No return value

mi_fp_setargprec()

Syntax:	`void mi_fp_setargprec(MI_FPARAM *fparam,` `    mi_integer argno, mi_integer prec);`
Description:	Sets the precision of the argno argument. The first argument is argument number 0.
Return value:	No return value

mi_fp_setargscale()

Syntax:	`void mi_fp_setargscale(MI_FPARAM *fparam,` `    mi_integer argno, mi_integer scale);`
Description:	Sets the scale of the argno argument. The first argument is argument number 0.
Return value:	No return value

mi_fp_setargtype()

Syntax:	`void mi_fp_setargtype(MI_FPARAM *fparam,`
	`    mi_integer argno, MI_TYPEID`
	`    *typeid);`

Description:	Sets the typeid of the argno argument. The first argument is argument number 0.
Return value:	No return value

mi_fp_setfuncid()

Syntax:	`void mi_fp_setfuncid(MI_FPARAM *fparam,` `    mi_funcid func);`
Description:	Sets the function identifier of the MI_FPARAM argument
Return value:	No return value

Syntax: void mi_fp_setfuncstate(
                    MI_FPARAM *fparam, void *value);

Description: Sets the function state of the MI_FPARAM structure

Return value: No return value

Syntax: void mi_fp_setisdone(
                    MI_FPARAM *fparam,
                    mi_integer value);

Description: Indicates that the set functions execution is
                complete

Return value: No return value

Syntax: void mi_fp_setnargs(
                    MI_FPARAM *fparam,
                    mi_integer value);

Description: Sets the number of arguments

Return value: No return value

Syntax: void mi_fp_setnrets(
                    MI_FPARAM *fparam,
                    mi_integer value);

Description: Sets the number of return values. Always 1 for C
                functions.

Return value: No return value

Syntax: void mi_fp_setretlen(MI_FPARAM *fparam,
                    mi_integer argno, mi_integer len);

Description: Sets the length of the argno return value. For C
                functions, the only valid value for argno is 0.

Return value: No return value

mi_fp_setretprec()

Syntax:
```
void mi_fp_setretprec(MI_FPARAM *fparam,
mi_integer argno, mi_integer len);
```

Description: Sets the precision of the argno return value. For C functions, the only valid value for argno is 0.

Return value: No return value

mi_fp_setretscale()

Syntax:
```
void mi_fp_setretscale(MI_FPARAM *fparam,
mi_integer argno, mi_integer len);
```

Description: Sets the scale of the argno return value. For C functions, the only valid value for argno is 0.

Return value: No return value

mi_fp_setrettype()

Syntax:
```
void mi_fp_setrettype(MI_FPARAM *fparam,
mi_integer argno, MI_TYPEID *typeid);
```

Description: Sets the typeid of the argno return value. For C functions, the only valid value for argno is 0.

Return value: No return value

mi_fp_setreturnisnull()

Syntax:
```
void
mi_fp_setreturnisnull(MI_FPARAM *fparam,
mi_integer argno, mi_integer truefalse);
```

Description: Indicates that the argno return value is NULL or not. For C functions, the only valid value for argno is 0.

Return value: No return value

mi_fp_usr_fparam()

Syntax:
```
mi_boolean mi_fp_usr_fparam(
          MI_FPARAM *fparam);
```

Description: Returns if the MI_FPARAM was allocated on behalf of the UDR or by the database server

Return value: True if it was allocated on behalf of the user-defined routine

mi_fparam_allocate()

Syntax:
```
MI_FPARAM *mi_fparam_allocate(
        mi_integer nargs);
```

Description: Allocates an `MI_FPARAM` structure on behalf of the function

Return value: Pointer to a `MI_FPARAM` structure, or `NULL` on failure

mi_fparam_copy()

Syntax:
```
MI_FPARAM *mi_fparam_copy(
        MI_FPARAM *fparam);
```

Description: Copies an `MI_FPARAM` structure into a newly allocated one

Return value: Pointer to a `MI_FPARAM` structure, or `NULL` on failure

mi_fparam_free()

Syntax:
```
mi_integer mi_fparam_free(
        MI_FPARAM *fparam);
```

Description: Frees the memory that was allocated to an `MI_FPARAM` structure

Return value: `MI_OK` on success, `MI_ERROR` on failure

mi_fparam_get()

Syntax:
```
MI_FPARAM *mi_fparam_get(
        MI_CONNECTION *conn,
        MI_FUNC_DESC *fdesc);
```

Description: Retrieves the `MI_FPARAM` structure associated with the function descriptor

Return value: A pointer to a `MI_FPARAM` structure or `NULL` on failure

mi_free()

Syntax:	`void mi_free(void *ptr);`
Description:	Frees previously allocated memory through the API memory allocation functions
Return value:	No return value

[9.20] mi_func_desc_by_typeid()

Syntax:	`MI_FUNC_DESC`
	`*mi_func_desc_by_typeid(`
	`MI_CONNECTION *conn,`
	`mi_funcid *funcid);`

Description:	Returns a function descriptor
Return value:	Function descriptor pointer, or NULL on error

mi_func_handlesnulls()

Syntax:	`mi_integer mi_func_handlesnulls(` `                MI_FUNC_DESC *funcdesc);`
Description:	Reports whether the function associated with the function descriptor can handle NULL values
Return value:	1 if it handles NULLs, 2 if not, MI_ERROR on failure

[9.20] mi_func_is_variant()

Syntax:	`mi_integer`
	`mi_func_is_variant(`
	`MI_FUNC_DESC *funcdesc);`

Description:	Indicates if the function is a variant
Return value:	1 if variant, 2 if not variant, MI_ERROR on error

[9.20] mi_func_negator()

Syntax:	`mi_integer`
	`mi_func_negator(`
	`MI_FUNC_DESC *funcdesc);`

Description:	Indicates if the function has a negator function
Return value:	1 if it has a negator, 2 if not, MI_ERROR on error

[9.20] **mi_funcarg_get_argtype()**

Syntax:
```
MI_FUNC_ARG_TYPE

mi_funcarg_get_argtype(
MI_FUNC_ARG *funcarg);
```

Description: Returns the argument type

Return value: MI_FUNCARG_COLUMN, MI_FUNCARG_CONSTANT, MI_FUNCARG_PARAM, MI_ERROR

[9.20] **mi_funcarg_get_colno()**

Syntax:
```
mi_integer

mi_funcarg_get_colno(
MI_FUNC_ARG *funcarg);
```

Description: Returns the argument column number

Return value: Column number

[9.20] **mi_funcarg_get_datalen()**

Syntax:
```
mi_integer

mi_funcarg_get_datalen(
MI_FUNC_ARG *funcarg);
```

Description: Returns the argument length

Return value: length

[9.20] **mi_funcarg_get_datatype()**

Syntax:
```
MI_TYPEID *

mi_funcarg_get_datatype(
MI_FUNC_ARG *funcarg);
```

Description: Returns the argument type identifier

Return value: Type identifier

[9.20] **mi_funcarg_get_distrib()**

Syntax:
```
mi_bitvarying *

mi_funcarg_get_distrib(
MI_FUNC_ARG *funcarg);
```

Description: Returns the argument distribution

Return value: Distribution result

[9.20] mi_funcarg_get_routine_id()

Syntax:	`mi_integer`
	`mi_funcarg_get_routine_id(` `MI_FUNC_ARG *funcarg);`
Description:	Returns the argument routine identifier
Return value:	Routine identifier

[9.20] mi_funcarg_get_routine_name()

Syntax:	`mi_string *`
	`mi_funcarg_get_routine_name(` `MI_FUNC_ARG *funcarg);`
Description:	Returns the argument routine name
Return value:	Routine name

[9.20] mi_funcarg_get_tabid()

Syntax:	`mi_integer`
	`mi_funcarg_get_tabid(` `MI_FUNC_ARG *funcarg);`
Description:	Returns the argument table identifier
Return value:	Table identifier

[9.20] mi_funcarg_isnull()

Syntax:	`mi_boolean`
	`mi_funcarg_isnull (MI_FUNC_ARG *funcarg);`
Description:	Determines if the argument contains an SQL NULL value
Return value:	`MI_TRUE` if it contains a `NULL`, `MI_FALSE` otherwise

mi_get_bytes()

Syntax:	`mi_unsigned_char1 *`
	`mi_get_bytes(mi_unsigned_char1 *from,` `mi_char1 *to, mi_integer nbytes);`
Description:	Copies bytes from one buffer to another
Return value:	The address in the "from" buffer

Syntax:
```
mi_integer
mi_get_connection_info(MI_CONNECTION
*conn, MI_CONNECTION_INFO *conninfo);
```

Description: Populates a user-provided structure with information about an open connection

Return value: MI_OK on success, MI_ERROR on failure

[9.20] mi_get_connection_option()

Syntax:
```
mi_integer
mi_get_connection_option(MI_CONNECTION
*conn, mi_integer options, mi_integer
*result);
```

Description: Finds out if a specific option is in use

options: MI_IS_ANSI_DB, MI_IS_LOGGED_DB, MI_IS_EXCLUSIVE_DB

result: MI_TRUE or MI_FALSE

Return value: MI_OK on success, MI_ERROR on failure

mi_get_connection_user_data()

Syntax:
```
mi_integer mi_get_connection_user_data(
MI_CONNECTION *conn, void **user_date);
```

Description: Gets the user value associated with a connection

Return value: MI_OK on success, MI_ERROR on failure

[9.20] mi_get_cursor_table()

Syntax:
```
mi_lvarchar *mi_get_cursor_table(
             mi_lvarchar *cursor_name);
```

Description: Gets the name of the table associated with this cursor name

Return value: Table name or NULL

[9.20] mi_get_database_info()

Syntax:
```
mi_integer mi_get_database_info(
             MI_CONNECTION *conn,
             MI_DATABASE_INFO *db_info);
```

Description:	Populates the dbinfo argument; retrieves the same information as mi_get_default_database_info()
Return value:	MI_OK, or MI_ERROR

mi_get_date()

Syntax:	`mi_unsigned_char1 *mi_get_date(` `mi_unsigned_char1 *from, mi_date *to);`
Description:	Copies a date value from a buffer regardless of alignment
Return value:	An address in the "from" buffer

mi_get_datetime()

Syntax:	`mi_unsigned_char1 *mi_get_datetime(`
	`mi_unsigned_char1 *from, mi_datetime`
	`*to);`

Description:	Copies a datetime value from a buffer regardless of alignment
Return value:	An address in the "from" buffer

mi_get_decimal()

Syntax:	`mi_unsigned_char1 *mi_get_decimal(` `mi_unsigned_char1 *from, mi_decimal *to);`
Description:	Copies a decimal value from a buffer regardless of alignment
Return value:	A new "from"address

mi_get_default_connection_info()

Syntax:	`mi_integer`
	`mi_get_default_connection_info(`
	`MI_CONNECTION_INFO *info);`

Description:	Populates the MI_CONNECTION_INFO structure
Return value:	MI_OK on success, MI_ERROR on failure

mi_get_default_database_info()

Syntax:	`mi_integer mi_get_default_database_info(` `MI_DATABASE_INFO *info);`

Description:	Populates the MI_DATABASE_INFO structure with the appropriate system defaults
Return value:	MI_OK on success, MI_ERROR on failure

mi_get_double_precision()

| Syntax: | ```
mi_unsigned_char1
*mi_get_double_precision(
mi_unsigned_char1 *from,
mi_double_precision *to);
``` |
|---|---|
| Description: | Copies a double precision value from a buffer regardless of alignment |
| Return value: | Address of the "from" buffer |

mi_get_id()

| Syntax: | ```
mi_integer mi_get_ id(
            MI_CONNECTION *conn,
            mi_integer type);
``` |
|---|---|
| Description: | Obtains a statement or a session identifier based on the type: MI_STATEMENT_ID, MI_SESSION_ID |
| Return value: | 0, no identifier available, >0, identifier |

mi_get_int8()

| Syntax: | ```
mi_unsigned_char1
*mi_get_int8(mi_unsigned_char1
*from, mi_int8 *to);
``` |
|---|---|
| Description: | Copies an int8 value from a buffer regardless of alignment |
| Return value: | Address of the "from" buffer |

mi_get_integer()

| Syntax: | ```
mi_unsigned_char1 *mi_get_integer(
mi_unsigned_char1 *from, mi_integer *to);
``` |
|---|---|
| Description: | Copies an integer value from a buffer regardless of alignment |
| Return value: | Address of the "from" buffer |

mi_get_interval()

Syntax:
```
mi_unsigned_char1 *mi_get_interval(
mi_unsigned_char1 *from,
mi_interval *to);
```

Description: Copies an interval value from a buffer regardless of alignment

Return value: Address of the "from" buffer

[9.20] mi_get_lo_handle()

Syntax:
```
mi_unsigned_char1 *mi_get_lo_handle(
mi_unsigned_char1 *from,
MI_LO_HANDLE *to);
```

Description: Copies a LO_HANDLE, considering the changes in alignment and byte ordering between client and server computers

Return value: "from" data buffer, or NULL

mi_get_money()

Syntax:
```
mi_unsigned_char1 *mi_get_money(
mi_unsigned_char1 *from, mi_money *to);
```

Description: Copies a money value from a buffer regardless of alignment

Return value: Address of the "from" buffer

mi_get_parameter_info()

Syntax:
```
mi_integer mi_get_parameter_info(
        MI_PARAMETER_INFO *paraminfo);
```

Description: Populates the MI_PARAMETER_INFO structure from the system parameter file or environment

Return value: MI_OK on success, MI_ERROR on failure

mi_get_real()

Syntax:
```
mi_unsigned_char1 *mi_get_real(
mi_unsigned_char1 *from, mi_real *to);
```

Description: Copies a real value from a buffer regardless of alignment

Return value: Address of the "from" buffer

Syntax: mi_integer mi_get_result(
                    MI_CONNECTION *conn);

Description: Reports on how a statement sent to the database
               has completed

Return value: MI_ERROR, MI_NO_MORE_RESULTS, MI_ROWS,
               MI_DML, MI_DDL

mi_get_row_desc()

Syntax: MI_ROW_DESC *mi_get_row_desc(
                    MI_ROW *row);

Description: Gets a pointer to the row descriptor

Return value: Pointer to a MI_ROW_DESC on success, NULL on
               failure

mi_get_row_desc_from_type_desc()

Syntax: MI_ROW_DESC
               *mi_get_row_desc_from_type_desc(
               MI_TYPE_DESC *typedesc);

Description: Gets the row descriptor associated with the type
               descriptor

Return value: Pointer to a MI_ROW_DESC on success, NULL on
               failure

mi_get_row_desc_without_row()

Syntax: MI_ROW_DESC *mi_get_row_desc_without_row(
                    MI_CONNECTION *conn);

Description: Gets a pointer to the row descriptor for the last
               statement that returned a row

Return value: Pointer to a MI_ROW_DESC on success, NULL on
               failure

[9.20] mi_get_serverenv()

Syntax: mi_integer mi_get_serverenv(
                    char1 *name, char **value);

Description: Obtains the value for an environment variable or
               an onconfig parameter

Return value: MI_OK, or MI_ERROR

mi_get_smallint()

Syntax:	`mi_unsigned_char1 *mi_get_smallint(`
	`mi_unsigned_char1 *from,`
	`mi_smallint *to);`

Description:	Copies a smallint value from a buffer regardless of alignment
Return value:	Address of the "`from`" buffer

mi_get_statement_row_desc()

Syntax:	`MI_ROW_DESC *mi_get_statement_row_desc(` `MI_STATEMENT *stmt);`
Description:	Gets a row descriptor from a prepared statement
Return value:	Pointer to a `MI_ROW_DESC` on success, `NULL` on failure

mi_get_string()

Syntax:	`mi_unsigned_char1 *mi_get_string(`
	`mi_unsigned_char1 *from, mi_string`
	`**to, mi_integer len);`

Description:	Copies a string value from a buffer, performing code-set conversion from client to server if necessary
Return value:	Address of the "`from`" buffer

mi_get_type_source_type()

Syntax:	`MI_TYPE_DESC *mi_get_type_source_type(` `MI_TYPE_DESC *ref);`
Description:	Gets the source of a distinct type
Return value:	`MI_TYPE_DESC` structure of the source type

mi_get_vardata()

Syntax:	`char *mi_get_vardata(mi_lvarchar *var);`
Description:	Returns a pointer to the data contained in an `mi_lvarchar` or `mi_bitvarying` structure
Return value:	Pointer to the data

mi_get_vardata_align()

Syntax: `char *mi_get_vardata_align(mi_lvarchar *var, mi_integer align);`

Description: Returns a pointer to the data contained in an `mi_lvarchar` or `mi_bitvarying` structure and adjusts for any initial padding requirement to align the data

Return value: Pointer to the data

mi_get_varlen()

Syntax: `mi_integer mi_get_varlen(mi_lvarchar *var);`

Description: Gets the length of the data in an `mi_lvarchar` or `mi_bitbarying` structure

Return value: Length of the variable-length structure

mi_init_library()

Syntax: `mi_integer mi_init_library( mi_integer flags);`

Description: Initializes the DataBlade API library. The argument flags should be 0.

Return value: `MI_OK` on success, `MI_ERROR` on failure

mi_interupt_check()

Syntax: `mi_integer mi_interupt_check(void);`

Description: Checks for a user interupt

Return value: Zero if the client interupted the operation, nonzero otherwise

mi_interval_to_string()

Syntax: `mi_string *mi_interval_to_string( mi_interval *interval);`

Description: Converts an interval value to a string

Return value: Pointer to a string

mi_issmall_data()

Syntax:
```
mi_boolean mi_issmall_data(
            mi_integer size);
```

Description: Finds out if a multirepresentational data type is set to `MI_MULTIREP_LARGE`

Return value: `MI_TRUE` if it is not set to `MI_MULTIREP_LARGE`, `MI_FALSE` if it is set

[9.20] mi_last_serial()

Syntax:
```
mi_integer mi_last_serial(
            MI_CONNECTION *conn,
            mi_integer *val);
```

Description: Gets the last generated serial value that was inserted

Return value: `MI_OK` or `MI_ERROR`

[9.20] mi_last_serial8()

Syntax:
```
mi_integer mi_last_serial8(
MI_CONNECTION *conn, mi_int8 *val);
```

Description: Gets the last generated serial8 value that was inserted

Return value: `MI_OK` or `MI_ERROR`

mi_library_version()

Syntax:
```
mi_integer mi_library_version(
            mi_char *buf, mi_integer len);
```

Description: Returns a version string in the provided buffer. The string is similar to:
`"INFORMIX-Universal Server Version 9.xx.xxx"`

Return value: `MI_OK`, or `MI_ERROR`

mi_lo_alter()

Syntax:
```
mi_integer mi_lo_alter(MI_CONNECTION *conn,
MI_LO_HANDLE *loptr, MI_LO_SPEC *lospec);
```

Description: Alters the attibutes of a smart large object

Return value: `MI_OK` on success, `MI_ERROR` on failure

Syntax:	`mi_integer mi_lo_close(` `MI_CONNECTION *conn, MI_LO_FD lofd);`
Description:	Closes a smart large object
Return value:	`MI_OK` on success, `MI_ERROR` on failure

Syntax:	`mi_integer mi_lo_colinfo_by_ids(` `MI_CONNECTION *conn, MI_ROW *row,` `mi_integer colno, MI_LO_SPEC *lospec);`
Description:	Sets the fields of a `MI_LO_SPEC` structure, given the row and column IDs
Return value:	`MI_OK` on success, `MI_ERROR` on failure

Syntax:	`mi_integer mi_lo_colinfo_by_name(` `MI_CONNECTION *conn, const char` `*colspec, MI_LO_SPEC *lospec);`
Description:	Sets the fields of a `MI_LO_SPEC` structure, given the column name
Return value:	`MI_OK` on success, `MI_ERROR` on failure

Syntax:	`MI_LO_FD mi_lo_copy(MI_CONNECTION *conn,` `MI_LO_HANDLE *srclo, MI_LO_SPEC *spec,` `mi_integer flags, MI_LO_HANDLE **dstlo);`
Description:	Makes a copy of a smart large object and opens the copy
	`flags: MI_LO_RDONLY, MI_LO_WRONLY,` `MI_LO_RDWR, MI_LO_DIRTY_READ`
Return value:	`MI_LO_FD` on success, `MI_ERROR` on failure

Syntax:	`MI_LO_FD mi_lo_create(MI_CONNECTION` `*conn, MI_LO_SPEC *spec, mi_integer` `flags, MI_LO_HANDLE **lohandle);`

Description:	Creates and opens a smart large object, returns a `MI_LO_FD` and its unique named pointer as an output parameter
Return value:	`MI_LO_FD` on success, `MI_ERROR` on failure

mi_lo_decrefcount()

Syntax:	`mi_integer mi_lo_decrefcount( MI_CONNECTION *conn, MI_LO_HANDLE *loptr);`
Description:	Decrements the reference count of a smart large object
Return value:	New reference count on success, `MI_ERROR` on failure

mi_lo_expand()

Syntax:	`MI_LO_FD mi_lo_expand(MI_CONNECTION *conn, MI_LO_HANDLE **hbuf, MI_MULTIREP_DATA *mrptr, mi_integer len, mi_integer flags, MI_LO_SPEC *lospec);`
Description:	Converts a multirepresentational data into a smart large object
Return value:	Pointer to a smart large object on success, `MI_ERROR` on failure

mi_lo_filename()

Syntax:	`const char *mi_lo_filename(MI_CONNECTION *conn, MI_LO_HANDLE *loptr, const char *fnamespec);`
Description:	Constructs an ASCII representation of a `MI_LO_HANDLE` value.
	The caller is responsible for freeing the return value.
Return value:	A pointer to the resulting name

[9.20] mi_lo_from_buffer()

Syntax:	`mi_integer mi_lo_from_buffer(MI_CONNECTION *conn, MI_LO_HANDLE *lohandle, mi_integer size, mi_char * buffer);`

Description:	Copies a number of bytes from a buffer to a large object
Return value:	`>=0`: number of bytes copied, or `MI_ERROR`

mi_lo_from_file()

Syntax:	`MI_LO_FD mi_lo_from_file(MI_CONNECTION *conn, MI_LO_HANDLE **lohandle, const char *fspec, mi_integer flags, mi_integer offset, mi_integer amount, MI_LO_SPEC *lospec);`
Description:	Copies an operating system file to a large object
	Flags: `MI_O_<EXCL|TRUNC|APPEND|RDWR|RDONLY|TEXT|SERVER_FILE|CLIENT_FILE>`
Return value:	An open `MI_LO_FD` on success, `MI_ERROR` on failure

mi_lo_from_file_by_lofd()

Syntax:	`mi_integer mi_lo_from_file_by_lofd (MI_CONNECTION *conn, MI_LO_FD lofd, const char *fspec, mi_integer flags, mi_integer offset, mi_integer amount);`
Description:	Copies a smart large object from a file using an open smart large object descriptor
	`flags: MI_O_<EXCL|TRUNC|APPEND|RDWR|RDONLY|TEXT|SERVER_FILE|CLIENT_FILE>`
Return value:	`MI_OK` on success, `MI_ERROR` on failure

mi_lo_from_string()

Syntax:	`MI_LO_HANDLE *mi_lo_from_string( char *str);`
Description:	Converts an ASCII representation of a smart large object handle to its binary form
Return value:	Handle on success, `NULL` on failure

mi_lo_increfcount()

Syntax:	`mi_integer mi_lo_increfcount( MI_CONNECTION *conn, MI_LO_HANDLE *loptr);`

Description:	Increments the reference count of a smart large object
Return value:	New reference count on success, MI_ERROR on failure

mi_lo_invalidate()

Syntax:	mi_integer mi_lo_invalidate(MI_CONNECTION *conn, MI_LO_HANDLE *lohandle);
Description:	Marks the smart large object handle as invalid
Return value:	MI_OK on success, -1 if the connection is invalid or the handle illegal

mi_lo_lolist_create()

Syntax:	mi_integer mi_lo_lolist_create(MI_CONNECTION *conn, mi_integer locount, MI_LO_HANDLE **lohandles, MI_LO_LIST **lolist);
Description:	Converts an array of large object handles into a MI_LO_LIST structure
Return value:	Size in byte of the MI_LO_LIST structure on success, 0 on failure

[9.20] mi_lo_lock()

Syntax:	mi_integer mi_lo_lock(MI_CONNECTION *conn, MI_LO_FD fd, mi_int8 *offset, mi_integer whence, mi_int8 *nbytes, mi_integer lmode);
Description:	Obtains a byte-range lock
	whence: MI_LO_SEEK_<SET|CUR|END>
	lmode: MI_LO_SHARED_MODE, MI_LO_EXCLUSIVE_ MODE
Return value:	MI_OK, or MI_ERROR

mi_lo_open()

Syntax:	MI_LO_FD mi_lo_open(MI_CONNECTION *conn, MI_LO_HANDLE *loptr, mi_integer flags);

Description:	Opens an existing smart large object
	flags: MI_LO_<RDONLY	WRONLY	RDWR	TRUNC	APPEND	RANDOM	SEQUENTIAL	BUFFER	NOBUFFER>
Return value:	Opened LO descriptor on success, MI_ERROR on failure

mi_lo_ptr_cmp()

Syntax:	mi_integer mi_lo_ptr_cmp(MI_CONNECTION *conn, MI_LO_HANDLE *loptr1, MI_LO_HANDLE *loptr2);
Description:	Compares two LO-pointer handles to determine if they reference the same object
Return value:	0 if they are the same, 1 if not, MI_ERROR on failure

mi_lo_read()

Syntax:	mi_integer mi_lo_read(MI_CONNECTION *conn, MI_LO_FD lofd, char *buf, mi_integer nbytes);
Description:	Reads data from an open smart large object
Return value:	Number of bytes read on success, MI_ERROR on failure

mi_lo_readwithseek()

Syntax:	mi_integer mi_lo_readwithseek(MI_CONNECTION *conn, MI_LO_FD lofd, char *buf, mi_integer nbytes, mi_int8 off, mi_integer whence);
Description:	Reads a smart large object starting at the given position
	whence: MI_LO_SEEK_<SET	CUR	END>
Return value:	Number of bytes read on success, MI_ERROR on failure

[9.20] mi_lo_release()

Syntax:	mi_integer mi_lo_release(MI_CONNECTION *conn, MI_LO_HANDLE *handle);

Description:	Tells the database server that the resources associated with the handle can be released
Return value:	MI_OK or MI_ERROR

mi_lo_seek()

Syntax:	mi_integer mi_lo_seek(MI_CONNECTION *conn, MI_LO_FD lofd, mi_int8 off, mi_integer whence, mi_int8 *seekpos);
Description:	Changes the current position in a smart large object for the next read or write and returns the new position in seekpos
	whence: MI_LO_SEEK_<SET|CUR|END>
Return value:	MI_OK on success, MI_ERROR on failure

mi_lo_spec_free()

Syntax:	mi_integer mi_lo_spec_free(MI_CONNECTION *conn, MI_LO_SPEC *lospec);
Description:	Deallocates the MI_LO_SPEC structure
Return value:	MI_OK on success, MI_ERROR on failure

mi_lo_spec_init()

Syntax:	mi_integer mi_lo_spec_init(MI_CONNECTION *conn, MI_LO_SPEC **lospec);
Description:	Allocates and initializes a MI_LO_SPEC structure
Return value:	MI_OK on success, MI_ERROR on failure

[9.20] mi_lo_specget_def_open()

Syntax:	mi_integer mi_lo_specget_def_open(MI_LO_SPEC *lospec);
Description:	Gets the default open flags for a large object
Return value:	MI_OK on success, MI_ERROR on failure

mi_lo_specget_estbytes()

Syntax:	mi_integer mi_lo_specget_estbytes(MI_LO_SPEC *spec, mi_int8 *count);

Description:	Get the estimated size of a smart large object returning the result in count
Return value:	MI_OK on success, MI_ERROR on failure

mi_lo_specget_extsz()

Syntax:	`mi_integer mi_lo_specget_extsz(` `        MI_LO_SPEC *spec);`
Description:	Gets the extent size of a smart large object
Return value:	Extent size in kilobytes

mi_lo_specget_flags()

Syntax:	`mi_integer mi_lo_specget_flags(` `        MI_LO_SPEC *spec);`
Description:	Returns the create flags of the smart large object
Return value:	Create flags

mi_lo_specget_maxbytes()

Syntax:	`mi_integer mi_lo_specget_maxbytes(` `MI_LO_SPEC *spec, mi_int8 *maxcount);`
Description:	Gets the maximum number of bytes allowed in a smart large object, returning the result in maxcount
Return value:	MI_OK on success, MI_ERROR on failure

mi_lo_specget_sbspace()

Syntax:	`mi_integer mi_lo_specget_sbspace(`
	`MI_LO_SPEC *spec, char *outbuf,`
	`mi_integer size);`

Description:	Gets the sbspace name where the smart large object is located
Return value:	MI_OK on success, MI_ERROR on failure

[9.20] mi_lo_specset_def_open()

Syntax:	`mi_integer mi_lo_specset_def_open(` `MI_LO_SPEC *spec, mi_integer open_flags);`
Description:	Sets the default open flags for a smart large object
Return value:	MI_OK on success, MI_ERROR on failure

mi_lo_specset_estbytes()

Syntax: mi_integer mi_lo_specset_estbytes(
                 MI_LO_SPEC *spec, mi_int8 *size);

Description: Sets the estimated size in bytes of a smart large object

Return value: MI_OK on success, MI_ERROR on failure

mi_lo_specset_extsz()

Syntax: mi_integer mi_lo_specset_extsz(
                 MI_LO_SPEC *spec, mi_integer size);

Description: Sets the extent size

Return value: MI_OK on success, MI_ERROR on failure

mi_lo_specset_flags()

Syntax: mi_integer mi_lo_specset_flags(
                 MI_LO_SPEC *spec, mi_integer flags);

Description: Sets the create flags

Return value: MI_OK on success, MI_ERROR on failure

mi_lo_specset_maxbytes()

Syntax: mi_integer mi_lo_specset_maxbytes(
                 MI_LO_SPEC *spec, mi_int8 *size);

Description: Sets the maximum number of bytes allowed in the
                 specified large object

Return value: MI_OK on success, MI_ERROR on failure

mi_lo_specset_sbspace()

Syntax: mi_integer mi_lo_specset_sbspace(
                 MI_LO_SPEC *spec, const char *val);

Description: Sets the sbspace name of a smart large object

Return value: MI_OK on success, MI_ERROR on failure

mi_lo_stat()

Syntax: mi_integer mi_lo_stat(
                 MI_CONNECTION *conn, MI_LO_FD lofd,
                 MI_LO_STAT **lostat);

Description:	Gets statistics information about the smart large object
Return value:	`MI_OK` on success, `MI_ERROR` on failure

mi_lo_stat_atime()

Syntax:	`mi_integer mi_lo_stat_atime(` `        MI_LO_STAT *stat);`
Description:	Gets the access time statistics
Return value:	Access time in seconds on success, `MI_ERROR` on failure

mi_lo_stat_cspec()

Syntax:	`MI_LO_SPEC *mi_lo_stat_cspec(` `        MI_LO_STAT *stat);`
Description:	Gets the specification structure
Return value:	Structure on success, `NULL` on failure

mi_lo_stat_ctime()

Syntax:	`mi_integer mi_lo_stat_ctime(` `        MI_LO_STAT *stat);`
Description:	Gets the creation time
Return value:	Creation time in seconds on success, `MI_ERROR` on failure

mi_lo_stat_free()

Syntax:	`mi_integer mi_lo_stat_free(` `MI_CONNECTION *conn, MI_LO_STAT *stat);`
Description:	Deallocates the `MI_LO_STAT` structure
Return value:	`MI_OK` on success, `MI_ERROR` on failure

mi_lo_stat_mtime_sec()

Syntax:	`mi_integer mi_lo_stat_mtime_sec(` `        MI_LO_STAT *stat);`
Description:	Gets the modification time in seconds
Return value:	Modification time on success, `MI_ERROR` on failure

mi_lo_stat_mtime_usec()

Syntax:	`mi_integer mi_lo_stat_mtime_usec(` `MI_LO_STAT *stat);`
Description:	Gets the modification time, microseconds part
Return value:	Modification time on success, `MI_ERROR` on failure

mi_lo_stat_refcnt()

Syntax:	`mi_integer mi_lo_stat_refcnt(` `MI_LO_STAT *stat);`
Description:	Gets the reference count
Return value:	Reference count on success, `MI_ERROR` on failure

mi_lo_stat_size()

Syntax:	`mi_integer mi_lo_stat_size(` `MI_LO_STAT *stat, mi_int8 *size);`
Description:	Gets the size of the large object into the size argument
Return value:	`MI_OK` on success, `MI_ERROR` on failure

mi_lo_stat_uid()

Syntax:	`mi_integer mi_lo_stat_uid(MI_LO_STAT *stat);`
Description:	Gets the user ID of the owner
Return value:	User ID on success, `MI_ERROR` on failure

mi_lo_tell()

Syntax:	`mi_integer mi_lo_tell(`
	`MI_CONNECTION *conn, MI_LO_FD lofd,`
	`mi_int8 *seekpos);`

Description:	Gets the current position in the large object into seekpos
Return value:	`MI_OK` on success, `MI_ERROR` on failure

[9.20] mi_lo_to_buffer()

Syntax:	`mi_integer mi_lo_to_buffer(`
	`MI_CONNECTION *conn, MI_LOHANDLE *loptr,`
	`mi_integer size, mi_char **buffer);`

Description:	Copies a number of bytes from a smart large object to a buffer
Return value:	Number of bytes transferred, or MI_ERROR

mi_lo_to_file()

Syntax:	```Const char *mi_lo_to_file(
MI_CONNECTION *conn, MI_LOHANDLE *loptr,
const char *fnamespec, mi_integer flags,
mi_integer *size);```
Description:	Copies a smart large object to a file returning its size in the size argument
	flags: MI_O_<EXCL|TRUNC|APPEND|RDWR| WRONLY|BINARY|TEXT|SERVER_FILE|CLIENT_FILE>
Return value:	File name on success, NULL on failure

mi_lo_to_string()

Syntax:	```char *mi_lo_to_string(MI_LO_HANDLE *lo);```
Description:	Converts a handle to its ASCII representation with current memory duration
Return value:	Pointer to ASCII representation on success, NULL on failure

mi_lo_truncate()

Syntax:	```mi_integer mi_lo_truncate(
MI_CONNECTION *conn, MI_LO_FD lofd,
mi_int8 *offset);```
Description:	Truncates a smart large object at a specified offset
Return value:	MI_OK on success, MI_ERROR on failure

[9.20] mi_lo_unlock()

Syntax:	```mi_integer mi_lo_unlock(MI_CONNECTION
*conn, MI_LO_FD fd, mi_int8 *offset,
mi_integer whence, mi_int8 *nbytes);```
Description:	Releases a byte range lock on a smart large object
	whence: MI_LO_SEEK<SET|CUR|END>
Return value:	MI_OK, or MI_ERROR

mi_lo_validate()

Syntax: `mi_integer mi_lo_validate(MI_CONNECTION *conn, MI_LO_HANDLE *lohandle);`

Description: Check the validity of a handle

Return value: 0 if valid, 1 if invalid, -1 if the connection is invalid

mi_lo_write()

Syntax: `mi_integer mi_lo_write(MI_CONNECTION *conn, MI_LO_FD lofd, const char *buf, mi_integer size);`

Description: Writes a buffer at the current position of a smart large object

Return value: Number of bytes written on success, `MI_ERROR` on failure

mi_lo_writewithseek()

Syntax: `mi_integer mi_lo_writewithseek( MI_CONNECTION *conn, MI_LO_FD lofd, const char *buf, mi_integer size, mi_int8 *offset, mi_integewr whence);`

Description: Writes a buffer at a specified offset into a smart large object

      whence: `MI_LO_SEEK_<SET|CUR|END>`

Return value: Number of bytes written on success, `MI_ERROR` on failure

mi_login()

Syntax: `mi_integer mi_login(MI_CONNECTION *conn, const MI_DATABASE_INFO *dbinfo);`

Description: Opens a database on the current connection

Return value: `MI_OK` on success, `MI_ERROR` on failure

mi_lvarchar_to_string()

Syntax: `mi_string *mi_lvarchar_to_string( mi_lvarchar *lv);`

Description:	Converts the `mi_lvarchar` to a newly allocated string
Return value:	Pointer on success, `NULL` on failure

mi_money_to_binary()

Syntax:	`mi_money *mi_money_to_binary(` `        mi_lvarchar *moneystring);`
Description:	Converts a string representation of a money type to its binary representation
	This function will be deprecated sometime after the 9.14 release.
Return value:	Pointer to a money type

mi_money_to_string()

Syntax:	`mi_string *mi_money_to_string(mi_money` `*money);`
Description:	Converts a money value to a string
Return value:	Pointer to a string

mi_new_var()

Syntax:	`mi_lvarchar *mi_new_var(mi_integer len);`
Description:	Creates a new lvarchar of a given length
Return value:	Pointer to an `mi_lvarchar`

mi_next_row()

Syntax:	`MI_ROW *mi_next_row(MI_CONNECTION *conn,` `        mi_integer *error);`
Description:	Fetches the next row from the given connection with an error status in error
Return value:	Pointer to a row type on success, `NULL` on failure or no more row

mi_open()

Syntax:	`MI_CONNECTION *mi_open(char *dbname,` `char *username, char *password);`

Description:	Connects to a database server
Return value:	Connection on success, `NULL` on failure

mi_open_prepared_statement()

Syntax:	`mi_integer mi_open_prepared_statement(`
	`MI_STATEMENT *stmt, mi_integer control,`
	`mi_integer arebinary, mi_integer nparams,`
	`MI_DATUM values[], mi_integer lengths[],`
	`mi_integer nulls[], mi_string *types[],`
	`mi_string *name, mi_integer retlen,`
	`mi_string *rettypes[]);`

Description:	Opens a cursor on a prepared statement
	`control:` `MI_BINARY`, `MI_SEND_SENSITIVE`, `MI_SEND_READ`, `MI_SEND_SCROLL`
Return value:	`MI_OK` on success, `MI_ERROR` on failure

mi_parameter_count()

Syntax:	`mi_integer mi_parameter_count(` `        MI_STATEMENT *stmt);`
Description:	Returns the number of parameters in the prepared statement
Return value:	Number of parameters on success, `MI_ERROR` on failure

mi_parameter_nullable()

Syntax:	`mi_integer mi_parameter_nullable(` `MI_STATEMENT *stmt, mi_integer paramno);`
Description:	Indicates whether an input parameter is nullable. For `INSERT` statements only
Return value:	1 if nullable, 0 if not, `MI_ERROR` on failure

mi_parameter_precision()

Syntax:	`mi_integer mi_parameter_precision(` `MI_STATEMENT *stmt, mi_integer paramno);`
Description:	Returns the precision of a parameter
Return value:	Precision of the parameter (length of character parameters) on success, `MI_ERROR` on failure

Syntax:

```
mi_integer mi_parameter_scale(
            MI_STATEMENT *stmt,
            mi_integer paramno);
```

Description: Returns the scale of a parameter

Return value: Scale for decimal or money type, 0 otherwise on success, MI_ERROR on failure

mi_parameter_type_id()

Syntax:

```
MI_TYPEID *mi_parameter_type_id(
MI_STATEMENT *stmt, mi_integer paramno);
```

Description: Returns the type_id of a parameter

Return value: Type id

mi_parameter_type_name()

Syntax: ·

```
mi_string *mi_parameter_type_name(
            MI_STATEMENT *stmt,
            mi_integer paramno);
```

Description: Returns the type_name of a parameter

Return value: Type name

mi_prepare()

Syntax:

```
MI_STATEMENT * mi_prepare(
MI_CONNECTION *conn, mi_string *query,
mi_string *name);
```

Description: Prepares an SQL statement

Return value: Statement handle on success, NULL on failure

mi_put_bytes()

Syntax:

```
mi_unsigned_char1 *mi_put_bytes(
mi_unsigned_char1 *to, mi_char1 *from,
mi_integer nbytes);
```

Description: Copies a given number of bytes to a buffer regardless of alignment

Return value: Return a new "to" address

mi_put_date()

Syntax:	`mi_unsigned_char1 *mi_put_date(` `mi_unsigned_char1 *to, mi_date *from);`
Description:	Copies a date value to a buffer regardless of alignment
Return value:	An address in the "`to`" buffer

mi_put_datetime()

Syntax:	`mi_unsigned_char1 *mi_put_datetime(`
	`mi_unsigned_char1 *to,`
	`mi_datetime *from);`

Description:	Copies a datetime value to a buffer regardless of alignment
Return value:	An address in the "`to`" buffer

mi_put_decimal()

Syntax:	`mi_unsigned_char1 *mi_put_decimal(` `mi_unsigned_char1 *to, mi_decimal *from);`
Description:	Copies a decimal value to a buffer regardless of alignment
Return value:	An address in the "`to`" buffer

mi_put_double_precision()

Syntax:	`mi_unsigned_char1`
	`*mi_put_double_precision(`
	`mi_unsigned_char1 *to,`
	`mi_double_precision *from);`

Description:	Copies a double-precision value to a buffer regardless of alignment
Return value:	An address in the "`to`" buffer

mi_put_int8()

Syntax:	`mi_unsigned_char1 *mi_put_int8(` `mi_unsigned_char1 *to, mi_int8 *from);`
Description:	Copies an int8 value to a buffer regardless of alignment
Return value:	Returns a new "`to`" address

mi_put_integer()

Syntax:	`mi_unsigned_char1 *mi_put_integer(` `mi_unsigned_char1 *to, mi_integer from);`
Description:	Copies an integer value to a buffer regardless of alignment
Return value:	Returns a new "`to`" address

mi_put_interval()

Syntax:	`mi_unsigned_char1`
	`*mi_put_interval(mi_unsigned_char1 *to,`
	`                 mi_interval *from);`

Description:	Copies an interval value to a buffer regardless of alignment
Return value:	An address in the "`to`" buffer

mi_put_money()

Syntax:	`mi_unsigned_char1 *mi_put_money(` `mi_unsigned_char1 *to, mi_money *from);`
Description:	Copies a money value to a buffer regardless of alignment
Return value:	An address in the "`to`" buffer

mi_put_real()

Syntax:	`mi_unsigned_char1 *mi_put_real(` `mi_unsigned_char1 *to, mi_real *from);`
Description:	Copies a real value to a buffer regardless of alignment
Return value:	An address in the "`to`" buffer

mi_put_smallint()

Syntax:	`mi_unsigned_char1 *mi_put_smallint(` `mi_unsigned_char1 *to, mi_integer from);`
Description:	Copies a smallint value to a buffer regardless of alignment
Return value:	An address in the "`to`" buffer advanced by the size of a `mi_integer`

mi_put_string()

Syntax:	`mi_unsigned_char1 *mi_put_string(`
	`mi_unsigned_char1 *to, mi_string *from,`
	`mi_integer len);`

Description:	Copies a string value to a buffer regardless of alignment
Return value:	An address in the "`to`" buffer

mi_query_finish()

Syntax:	`mi_integer mi_query_finish(` `          MI_CONNECTION *conn);`
Description:	Terminates an active query
Return value:	`MI_OK` on success, `MI_ERROR` on failure

mi_query_interupt()

Syntax:	`mi_integer mi_query_interupt(` `MI_CONNECTION *conn, mi_integer block);`
Description:	Interupts the current statement; "block" is currently ignored
Return value:	`MI_OK` on success, `MI_ERROR` if an exception was encountered

mi_register_callback()

Syntax:	`MI_CALLBACK_HANDLE *mi_register_callback(`
	`MI_CONNECTION *conn, MI_EVENT_TYPE event,`
	`MI_CALLBACK_FUNC func, void *userdata,`
	`MI_CALLBACK_HANDLE *parent);`

Description:	Registers a user callback for one or all event types; "`parent`" must be `NULL`
Return value:	Handle to the newly registered callback

mi_result_command_name()

Syntax:	`mi_char *mi_result_command_name(` `          MI_CONNECTION *conn);`
Description:	Returns the last statement submitted on this connection
Return value:	String on success, `NULL` on failure

mi_result_row_count()

Syntax:
```
mi_integer mi_result_row_count(
        MI_CONNECTION *conn);
```

Description: Returns the number of rows affected by the current statement

Return value: Number of rows on success, MI_ERROR on failure

mi_retrieve_callback()

Syntax:
```
mi_integer mi_retrieve_callback(
MI_CONNECTION *conn, MI_EVENT_TYPE event,
MI_CALLBACK_HANDLE *handle,
MI_CALLBACK_FUNC *func, void **userdata);
```

Description: Retrieves the details of a registered callback

Return value: MI_OK on success, MI_ERROR on failure

mi_routine_end()

Syntax:
```
mi_integer mi_routine_end(
        MI_CONNECTION *conn,
        MI_FUNC_DESC *fdesc);
```

Description: Frees the MI_FUNC_TYPE structure

Return value: MI_OK on success, MI_ERROR on failure

mi_routine_exec()

Syntax:
```
MI_DATUM mi_routine_exec(MI_CONNECTION
*conn, MI_FUNC_DESC *fdesc, mi_integer
*error, argument_list);
```

Description: Executes the function associated with the function descriptor with status in "error."

Return value: Return value of the executed function

mi_routine_get()

Syntax:
```
MI_FUNC_DESC *mi_routine_get(
MI_CONNECTION *conn,
mi_integer flags, char *sig);
```

Description: Looks up a function by signature. The "flags" must be 0.

Return value: Function descriptor on success, NULL on failure

mi_routine_get_by_typeid()

Syntax: MI_FUNC_DESC *mi_routine_get_by_typeid(
MI_CONNECTION *conn, mi_integer udrtype,
char *udrname, char *owner,
MI_UDR_TYPE argcount, MI_TYPE_ID
*argtypes);

Description: Looks up a function by its list of arguments

Return value: Function descriptor on success, NULL on failure

mi_routine_id_get()

Syntax: mi_integer mi_routine_id_get(
MI_CONNECTION *conn,
MI_FUNC_DESC *fdesc);

Description: Returns a unique identifier for the given UDR

Return value: Unique identifier on success, NULL on failure

mi_row_create()

Syntax: MI_ROW *mi_row_create(
MI_CONNECTION *conn,
MI_ROW_DESC *rowdesc,
MI_DATUM coldata[],
mi_boolean colisnull[]);

Description: Gets a row by transforming a row descriptor into a row

Return value: Row on success, NULL on failure

mi_row_desc_create()

Syntax: MI_ROW_DESC *mi_row_desc_create(
MI_TYPEID *typeid);

Description: Creates a row descriptor

Return value: Row descriptor

mi_row_desc_free()

Syntax: void mi_row_desc_free(
MI_ROW_DESC *rowdesc);

Description: Frees a row descriptor

Return value: No return

mi_row_free()

Syntax: `mi_integer mi_row_free(MI_ROW *row);`

Description: Frees a row

Return value: MI_OK on success, MI_ERROR on failure

mi_save_set_count()

Syntax: `mi_integer mi_save_set_count(`
                `        MI_SAVE_SET *saveset);`

Description: Returns the number of rows in the save set

Return value: Number of rows on success, MI_ERROR on failure

mi_save_set_create()

Syntax: `MI_SAVE_SET *mi_save_set_create(`
                `        MI_CONNECTION *conn);`

Description: Creates a save set on the current connection

Return value: Save set pointer on success, NULL on failure

mi_save_set_delete()

Syntax: `mi_integer mi_save_set_delete(`
                `        MI_ROW *row);`

Description: Removes the specified row from the save set

Return value: MI_OK on success, MI_ERROR on failure

mi_save_set_destroy()

Syntax: `mi_integer mi_save_set_destroy(`
                `        MI_SAVE_SET *saveset);`

Description: Destroys a save set and frees its resources

Return value: MI_OK on success, MI_ERROR on failure

mi_save_set_get_first()

Syntax: `MI_ROW *mi_save_set_get_first(`
                `        MI_SAVE_SET *saveset,`
                `        mi_integer *error);`

Description: Retrieves the first row from a save set

Return value: Row on success, NULL and "error" set to 0 if empty,
                NULL and "error" set to MI_ERROR on failure

mi_save_set_get_last()

Syntax:	`MI_ROW *mi_save_set_get_last(` `MI_SAVE_SET *saveset, mi_integer *error);`
Description:	Retrieves the last row from a save set
Return value:	Row on success, `NULL` and "`error`" set to 0 if empty, `NULL` and "`error`" set to `MI_ERROR` on failure

mi_save_set_get_next()

Syntax:	`MI_ROW *mi_save_set_get_next(` `MI_SAVE_SET *saveset, mi_integer *error);`
Description:	Retrieves the next row from a save set
Return value:	Row on success, `NULL` and "`error`" set to 0 if empty, `NULL` and "`error`" set to `MI_ERROR` on failure

mi_save_set_get_previous()

Syntax:	`MI_ROW *mi_save_set_get_previous(` `MI_SAVE_SET *saveset, mi_integer *error);`
Description:	Retrieves the previous row from a save set
Return value:	Row on success, `NULL` and "`error`" set to 0 if empty, `NULL` and "`error`" set to `MI_ERROR` on failure

mi_save_set_insert()

Syntax:	`MI_ROW *mi_save_set_insert(` `MI_SAVE_SET *saveset, MI_ROW *row);`
Description:	Appends a copy of a row at the end of a save set
Return value:	Pointer to the row on success, `NULL` on failure

mi_save_set_member()

Syntax:	`mi_integer mi_save_set_member(` `        MI_ROW *row);`
Description:	Reports if a row is part of any save set
Return value:	1 if it is a member, 0 if not, `MI_ERROR` on failure

mi_server_connect()

Syntax:	`MI_CONNECTION *mi_server_connect(` `        MI_CONNECTION_INFO *info);`

Description:	Establishes a connection to a server
Return value:	Connection pointer

mi_server_reconnect()

Syntax:	`mi_integer mi_server_reconnect(` `        MI_CONNECTION *conn);`
Description:	Reestablishes a dropped connection
Return value:	`MI_OK` on success, `MI_ERROR` on failure

mi_set_connection_user_data()

Syntax:	`mi_integer mi_set_connection_user_data(`
	`        MI_CONNECTION *conn,`
	`        void *userdata);`

Description:	Associates a user value with a connection
Return value:	`MI_OK` on success, `MI_ERROR` on failure

mi_set_default_connection_info()

Syntax:	`mi_integer`
	`mi_set_default_connection_info(`
	`MI_CONNECTION_INFO *info);`

Description:	Sets the default connection parameters
Return value:	`MI_OK` on success, `MI_ERROR` on failure

mi_set_default_database_info()

Syntax:	`mi_integer mi_set_default_database_info(` `        MI_DATABASE_INFO *info);`
Description:	Sets the fields of the database info structure to the default values
Return value:	`MI_OK` on success, `MI_ERROR` on failure

mi_set_large()

Syntax:	`mi_integer mi_set_large(mi_integer size);`
Description:	Sets its argument to a `MI_MULTIREP_LARGE` value. A `mi_lo_expand()` should be called next.
Return value:	`MI_OK` on success, `MI_ERROR` on failure

mi_set_parameter_info()

Syntax:	`mi_integer mi_set_parameter_info(` `const MI_PARAMETER_INFO *info);`
Description:	Sets the fields in the user-provided structure
Return value:	`MI_OK` on success, `MI_ERROR` on failure

mi_set_vardata()

Syntax:	`void mi_set_vardata(mi_lvarchar *var,` `char *data);`
Description:	Sets the data in the lvarchar structure
Return value:	No return value

mi_set_vardata_align()

Syntax:	`void mi_set_vardata_ align(`
	`mi_lvarchar *var, char *data,`
	`mi_integer align);`

Description:	Sets the data in the lvarchar structure with initial padding for alignment
Return value:	No return value

mi_set_varlen()

Syntax:	`void mi_set_varlen(` `mi_lvarchar *var, mi_integer len);`
Description:	Sets the length of an `lvarchar`
Return value:	No return value

mi_set_varptr()

Syntax:	`void mi_set_varptr(` `mi_lvarchar *var, char *data);`
Description:	Sets the data pointer in the `lvarchar` structure
Return value:	No return value

mi_statement_command_name()

Syntax:	`mi_string *mi_statement_command_name(` `MI_STATEMENT *stmt);`

Description:	Returns a NULL-terminated string representing the verb of the command
Return value:	String on success, NULL on failure

mi_string_to_date()

Syntax:	`mi_date mi_string_to_date(` `        mi_string *string);`
Description:	Converts a date string to a date
Return value:	mi_date on success, NULL on error

mi_string_to_datetime()

Syntax:	`mi_datetime *mi_string_to_datetime(`
	`        mi_string *dt,`
	`        mi_string *range);`

Description:	Converts a datetime string to a datetime
Return value:	mi_datetime pointer on success, NULL on failure

mi_string_to_decimal()

Syntax:	`mi_decimal *mi_string_to_decimal(` `        mi_string *string);`
Description:	Converts a decimal string to a decimal value
Return value:	mi_decimal pointer on success, NULL on failure

mi_string_to_interval()

Syntax:	`mi_interval *mi_string_to_interval(`
	`        mi_string *intrval,`
	`        mi_string *range);`

Description:	Converts an interval string to an interval
Return value:	mi_interval pointer on success, NULL on failure

mi_string_to_lvarchar()

Syntax:	`mi_lvarchar *mi_string_to_lvarchar(` `        mi_string *string);`
Description:	Create a new lvarchar structure based on the given NULL-terminated string
Return value:	lvarchar pointer on success, NULL on failure

mi_string_to_money()

Syntax:
```
mi_money *mi_string_to_money(
            mi_string *string);
```

Description: Converts a money string to a money value

Return value: `mi_money` pointer on success, `NULL` on failure

mi_switch_memory_duration()

Syntax:
```
MI_MEMORY_DURATION
mi_switch_memory_duration(
MI_MEMORY_DURATION md);
```

Description: Changes the default memory duration
(`PER_ROUTINE`, `PER_COMMAND`)

Return value: Previous memory duration

mi_sysname()

Syntax:
```
char *mi_sysname(char *sysname);
```

Description: Attempts to set the value of the current system

Return value: Current system name on success, `NULL` on failure

mi_td_cast_get()

Syntax:
```
MI_FUNC_DESC *mi_td_cast_get(
MI_CONNECTION *conn, MI_TYPE_DESC *from,
MI_TYPE_DESC *to, mi_char *caststatus);
```

Description: Looks up a registered cast function

Caststatus output: `MI_ERROR_CAST`, `MI_NO_CAST`,
`MI_NOP_CAST`, `MI_SYSTEM_CAST`, `MI_UDR_CAST`,
`MI_EXPLICIT_CAST`, `MI_IMPLICIT_CAST`

Return value: Function descriptor on success, NULL on failure

mi_tracefile_set()

Syntax:
```
mi_integer mi_tracefile_set(
            const mi_string *filename);
```

Description: Sets the file where trace messages go to

Return value: `MI_OK` on success, `MI_ERROR` on failure

mi_tracelevel_set()

Syntax:
```
mi_integer mi_tracelevel_set(
            const mi_string *cmds);
```

Description: Sets the tracing level for the specified trace classes

Return value: `MI_OK` on success, `MI_ERROR` on failure

mi_transition_type()

Syntax:
```
MI_TRANSITION_TYPE mi_transition_type(
MI_TRANSITION_DESC *desc);
```

Description: Finds the type of state transition that occurred for the callback

Return value: `MI_BEGIN, MI_NORMAL_END, MI_ABORT_END`

mi_type_align()

Syntax:
```
mi_integer mi_type_align(
            MI_TYPE_DESC *td);
```

Description: Gets the alignment for a given type

Return value: Alignment in bytes

mi_type_byvalue()

Syntax:
```
mi_boolean mi_type_byvalue(
            MI_TYPE_DESC *td);
```

Description: Finds out if a type is passed by value or by reference

Return value: 1 if passed by value, 0 if passed by reference

mi_type_element_typedesc()

Syntax:
```
MI_TYPE_DESC *mi_type_element_typedesc(
            MI_TYPE_DESC *td);
```

Description: Returns the type of the elements in a collection type

Return value: Pointer to a type descriptor

mi_type_full_name()

Syntax:
```
mi_string *mi_type_full_name(
            MI_TYPE_DESC *td);
```

Description:	Gets the full name (owner.typename) of a type
Return value:	Pointer to a string containing the full name

mi_type_length()

Syntax:	`mi_integer mi_type_length(` `        MI_TYPE_DESC *td);`
Description:	Returns the length of a type
Return value:	Length of the type or -1 for character types

mi_type_maxlength()

Syntax:	`mi_integer mi_type_maxlength(` `        MI_TYPE_DESC *td);`
Description:	Returns the maximum length of a type
Return value:	Maximum length of the given type

mi_type_owner()

Syntax:	`mi_string *mi_type_owner(` `        MI_TYPE_DESC *td);`
Description:	Returns the owner of a type
Return value:	String pointer to the owner of the given type

mi_type_precision()

Syntax:	`mi_integer mi_type_precision(` `        MI_TYPE_DESC *td);`
Description:	Returns the precision of a type if applicable
Return value:	Precision of the given type

[9.20] mi_type_qualifier()

Syntax:	`mi_integer mi_type_qualifier(` `        MI_TYPE_DESC *td);`
Description:	Returns the qualifier of a data type if applicable
Return value:	If >=0 qualifier, otherwise `MI_ERROR`

Syntax: `mi_integer mi_type_scale(MI_TYPE_DESC *td);`

Description: Returns the scale of a type if applicable

Return value: Scale of the given type

Syntax:
```
MI_TYPE_DESC *
mi_type_typedesc(MI_CONNECTION *conn,
                 MI_TYPEID *tid);
```

Description: Returns the type descriptor of the specified type ID

Return value: Type descriptor

Syntax:
```
mi_string *mi_type_typename(
          MI_TYPE_DESC *td);
```

Description: Returns the name of the type

Return value: Pointer to the type name

Syntax:
```
MI_TYPEID *mi_typedesc_typeid(
          MI_TYPE_DESC *td);
```

Description: Return the type ID of the type

Return value: Type ID

Syntax:
```
mi_boolean mi_typeid_equals(
MI_TYPEID *tid1, MI_TYPEID *tid2);
```

Description: Finds out if two type IDs are the same

Return value: `MI_TRUE` if equal, `MI_FALSE` if not

[9.20] mi_typeid_is_builtin()

Syntax:
```
mi_boolean mi_typeid_is_builtin(
          MI_TYPEID *tid);
```

Description: Finds out if it is a builtin type

Return value: MI_TRUE if it is, MI_FALSE if not

mi_typeid_is_collection()

Syntax:
```
mi_boolean mi_typeid_is_collection(
          MI_TYPEID *tid);
```

Description: Finds out if it is a collection type

Return value: MI_TRUE if it is, MI_FALSE if not

mi_typeid_is_complex()

Syntax:
```
mi_boolean mi_typeid_is_complex(
          MI_TYPEID *tid);
```

Description: Finds out if it is a complex type

Return value: MI_TRUE if it is, MI_FALSE if not

mi_typeid_is_distinct()

Syntax:
```
mi_boolean mi_typeid_is_distinct(
          MI_TYPEID *tid);
```

Description: Finds out if it is a distinct type

Return value: MI_TRUE if it is, MI_FALSE if not

mi_typeid_is_list()

Syntax:
```
mi_boolean mi_typeid_is_list(
          MI_TYPEID *tid);
```

Description: Finds out if it is a list type

Return value: MI_TRUE if it is, MI_FALSE if not

mi_typeid_is_multiset()

Syntax:
```
mi_boolean mi_typeid_is_multiset(
          MI_TYPEID *tid);
```

Description: Finds out if it is a multiset type

Return value: MI_TRUE if it is, MI_FALSE if not

Syntax:
```
mi_boolean mi_typeid_is_row(
        MI_TYPEID *tid);
```

Description: Finds out if it is a row type

Return value: MI_TRUE if it is, MI_FALSE if not

Syntax:
```
mi_boolean mi_typeid_is_set(
        MI_TYPEID *tid);
```

Description: Finds out if it is a set type

Return value: MI_TRUE if it is, MI_FALSE if not

Syntax:
```
MI_TYPEID *mi_typename_to_id(
MI_CONNECTION *conn, mi_lvarchar *name);
```

Description: Finds the type ID given the type name

Return value: Type ID if found, NULL if not

Syntax:
```
MI_TYPE_DESC
*mi_typename_to_typedesc(MI_CONNECTION
*conn, mi_lvarchar *name);
```

Description: Creates a type descriptor, given the type name

Return value: Type descriptor if found, NULL if not

Syntax:
```
MI_TYPEID * mi_typestring_to_id(
        MI_CONNECTION *conn, char *name);
```

Description: Finds the type ID given the type name

Return value: Type ID if found, NULL if not

Syntax:
```
MI_TYPE_DESC *mi_typestring_to_typedesc(
MI_CONNECTION *conn, mi_string *name);
```

Description:	Creates a type descriptor, given the type name
Return value:	Type descriptor if found, NULL if not

mi_unregister_callback()

Syntax:	`mi_integer mi_unregister_callback(`
	`MI_CONNECTION *conn, MI_EVENT_TYPE type,`
	`MI_CALLBACK_HANDLE *handle);`

Description:	Deletes a callback for one or all event types
Return value:	MI_OK on success, MI_ERROR on failure

mi_value()

Syntax:	`mi_integer mi_value(MI_ROW *row,`
	`mi_integer colno, MI_DATUM *retbuf,`
	`mi_integer *retlen);`

Description:	Retrieves a value (column) from a row. The "colno" starts at 0.
Return value:	MI_NORMAL_VALUE, MI_COLLECTION_VALUE, MI_ROW_VALUE, MI_NULL_VALUE, MI_ERROR

mi_value_by_name()

Syntax:	`mi_integer mi_value_by_name(`
	`MI_ROW *row, char *colname,`
	`MI_DATUM *retbuf, mi_integer *retlen);`

Description:	Retrieves a value (column) from a row
Return value:	MI_NORMAL_VALUE, MI_COLLECTION_VALUE, MI_ROW_VALUE, MI_NULL_VALUE, MI_ERROR

mi_var_copy()

Syntax:	`mi_lvarchar *mi_var_copy(` `mi_lvarchar *lv);`
Description:	Creates and allocates a new lvarchar based on the given one
Return value:	mi_lvarchar pointer

mi_var_free()

Syntax:	`mi_integer mi_var_free(mi_lvarchar *lv);`

| Description: | Frees the lvarchar structure |
| Return value: | MI_OK on success, MI_ERROR on failure |

mi_var_to_buffer()

| Syntax: | ```void mi_var_to_buffer(mi_lvarchar *lv,
                            char *buffer);``` |
| Description: | Copies the lvarchar to the buffer |
| Return value: | No return value |

mi_xact_levels()

| Syntax: | ```void mi_xact_levels(void *data,
       mi_integer *oldlevel,
       mi_integer newlevel);``` |
| Description: | Gets the transaction level before and after the transaction |
| Return value: | No return value |

mi_xact_state()

| Syntax: | ```mi_integer mi_xact_state(
          void *clientdata);``` |
| Description: | Finds out what kind of transaction has occurred |
| Return value: | MI_XACT_BEGIN, MI_XACT_END, MI_XACT_ABORT |

mi_yield()

Syntax:	void mi_yield();
Description:	Yields processing to other server threads
Return value:	No return value

mi_zalloc()

Syntax:	void *mi_zalloc(mi_integer size);
Description:	Allocates sero-filled memory
Return value:	Pointer to memory on success, NULL on failure

rdatestr()

Syntax:	`int rdatestr(long jdate, char *outbuf);`
Description:	Converts a date to a character string
Return value:	Success (0), Failure (<0), conversion not possible (-1210), DBDATE invalid (-1212)

rdayofweek()

Syntax:	`int rdayofweek(long jdate);`
Description:	Returns a day of the week starting with 0 for Sunday
Return value:	Zero if Sunday, One if monday, . . . 6 if Saturday

rdefmtdate()

Syntax:	`int rdefmtdate(long *jdate,` `        char *fmtstring, char *inbuf);`
Description:	Converts a character string to a date using a formatting mask
Return value:	Success (0), invalid year (-1204), invalid month (-1205), invalid day (-1206), input format problem (-1209), invalid formatting string (-1212)

rdownshift()

Syntax:	`void rdownshift(char *s)`
Description:	Changes all uppercase characters to lowercase in a NULL-terminated string
Return value:	No return value

rfmtdate()

Syntax:	`int rfmtdate(long jdate, char` `*fmtstring, char *outbuf);`
Description:	Converts a date into a character string using a formatting mask
Return value:	Success (0), cannot convert (-1210), out of memory (-1211)

Syntax:	`int rfmtdec(dec_t *dec_val,` `        char *fmtstring, char *outbuf);`
Description:	Converts a decimal value to a character string using a formatting string
Return value:	Success (0), memory allocation error (-1211), format string too large (-1217)

Syntax:	`int rfmtdouble(double double_val,` `        char *fmtstring, char *outbuf);`
Description:	Converts a double to a character string using a formatting mask
Return value:	Success (0), memory allocation error (-1211), format string too large (-1217)

Syntax:	`int rfmtlong(long long_val,` `        char *fmtstring, char *outbuf);`
Description:	Converts a long to a character string using a formatting mask
Return value:	Success (0), memory allocation error (-1211), format string too large (-1217)

Syntax:	`int rjulmdy(long jdate, short mdy[3]);`
Description:	Creates an array of 3 values representing the month, day, and year of the given date
Return value:	Success (0), Failure (<0), Conversion error (-1210)

Syntax:	`int rleapyear(int year);`
Description:	Returns true if the given year is a leap year
Return value:	True (1), False (0)

rmdyjul()

Syntax:	`int rmdyjul(short mdy[3], long *jdate);`
Description:	Creates a date from an array representing month, day, year
Return value:	Success (0), invalid year (-1204), invalid month (-1205), invalid day (-1206)

rstod()

Syntax:	`int rstod(char *string,` `double *double_val);`
Description:	Converts a NULL-terminated string into a double value
Return value:	Success (0), error(!= 0)

rstoi()

Syntax:	`int rstoi(char *string, int int_val);`
Description:	Converts a NULL-terminated string to a short integer
Return value:	Success (0), error(!= 0)

rstol()

Syntax:	`int rstol(char *string, long long_val);`
Description:	Converts a NULL-terminated string to a long integer
Return value:	Success (0), error(!= 0)z

rstrdate()

Syntax:	`int rstrdate(char *inbuf, long *jdate);`
Description:	Converts a character string to a date
Return value:	Success (0), failure (<0), inbuf invalid year (-1204), inbuf invalid month (-1205), inbuf invalid day (-1206), invalid DBDATE (-1212), invalid date in inbuf (-1218)

rtoday()

Syntax:	`void rtoday(long *today);`
Description:	Returns today's date
Return value:	No return value

Syntax:	`void rupshift(char *s);`
Description:	Converts all characters in a NULL-terminated string to uppercase
Return value:	No return

Syntax:	`void stcat(char *s, char *dest);`
Description:	Concatenates one NULL-terminated string at the end of another
Return value:	No return

Syntax:	`void stchar(char *from, char *to,` `              int count);`
Description:	Stores a NULL-terminated string into a fixed-length string, padding it with blanks if necessary
Return value:	No return

Syntax:	`int stcmpr(char *s1, char *s2);`
Description:	Compares two NULL-terminated strings
Return value:	Less than (-1), equal (0), greater than (1)

Syntax:	`void stcopy(char *from, char *to);`
Description:	Copies a NULL-terminated string from one location to another
Return value:	No return value

Syntax:	`int stleng(char *s);`
Description:	Gets the length of a NULL-terminated string
Return value:	Length of the string

tf()

Syntax:	`mi_boolean tf(mi_string *trace_class,` `                mi_integer threshold);`
Description:	Tests if the condition fits the threshold value for tracing in a specific class
Return value:	`MI_TRUE, or MI_FALSE`

tprintf()

Syntax:	`void tprintf(mi_string *format` `                [, arg] ...);`
Description:	Prints a message to the trace file. This function takes the same arguments as a printf() function.
Return value:	None

TU_DAY

Syntax:	`TU_DAY`
Description:	Macro used to identify the DAY precision in a qualifier field
Return value:	Field number for DAY

TU_DTENCODE

Syntax:	`TU_DTENCODE(begin, end)`
Description:	Creates a datetime qualifier with the given range Example: `TU_DTENCODE(TU_YEAR, TU_DAY)`
Return value:	qualifier

TU_ENCODE

Syntax:	`TU_ENCODE(precision, begin, end)`
Description:	Creates a qualifier ranging from begin to end. The precision represents the number of digits allocated to the begin field.
Return value:	qualifier

Syntax: `TU_END(qualifier)`

Description: Returns the trailing field number for the given qualifier

Return value: Field number

Syntax: `TU_F1`

Description: Name for datetime-ending field of FRACTION(1)

Return value: Field number

Syntax: `TU_F2`

Description: Name for datetime-ending field of FRACTION(2)

Return value: Field number

Syntax: `TU_F3`

Description: Name for datetime-ending field of FRACTION(3)

Return value: Field number

Syntax: `TU_F4`

Description: Name for datetime-ending field of FRACTION(4)

Return value: Field number

Syntax: `TU_F5`

Description: Name for datetime-ending field of FRACTION(5)

Return value: Field number

TU_FLEN

Syntax:	TU_FLEN(qualifier)
Description:	Length in digits of the first field of an interval qualifier
Return value:	Number of digits

TU_FRAC

Syntax:	TU_FRAC
Description:	Macro used to identify the FRACTION precision in a qualifier field
Return value:	Field number

TU_HOUR

Syntax:	TU_HOUR
Description:	Macro used to identify the HOUR precision in a qualifier field
Return value:	Time unit of the HOUR qualifier

TU_IENCODE

Syntax:	TU_IENCODE(precision, begin, end)
Description:	Creates an interval qualifier ranging from begin to end. Precision represents the number of digits allocated to the begin unit.
Return value:	Interval qualifier

TU_LEN

Syntax:	TU_LEN(qualifier)
Description:	Returns the length in digits of the qualifier
Return value:	Qualifier length

TU_MINUTE

Syntax:	TU_MINUTE

Description:	Macro used to identify the MINUTE precision in a qualifier field
Return value:	Field number

TU_MONTH

Syntax:	TU_MONTH
Description:	Macro used to identify the MONTH precision in a qualifier field
Return value:	Field number

TU_SECOND

Syntax:	TU_SECOND
Description:	Macro used to identify the SECOND precision in a qualifier field
Return value:	Field number

TU_START

Syntax:	TU_START (qualifier)
Description:	Returns the field number representing the precision of the leading field
Return value:	Field number

TU_YEAR

Syntax:	TU_YEAR
Description:	Macro used to identify the YEAR precision in a qualifier field
Return value:	Field number

VCLENGTH

Syntax:	VCLENGTH (s)
Description:	Allocation length required for a variable that will be used for a VARCHAR column of maximum size "s."
Return value:	integer

VCMAX

Syntax: `VCMAX(s)`

Description: Maximum number of characters you can store in the `VARCHAR` column. The "s" is obtained from: `select collength` from `syscolumns` ...

Return value: integer

VCMIN

Syntax: `VCMIN(s)`

Description: Minimum size that must be stored in a `VARCHAR` column. The "s" is obtained from: `select collength` from `syscolumns` ...

Return value: Integer, minimum size

VCSIZ

Syntax: `VCSIZ(min, max)`

Description: Encodes a size value for a `VARCHAR` column

Return value: integer

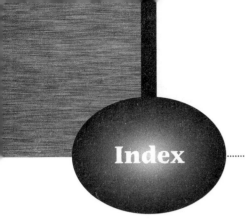

Index

Hardware components and
performance, 14–16

I

Ill-behaved functions, 43–44
Implicit cast, 60, 61
Importbinary function, 165–66
Import function, 161–62
Index access methods, 12
Index block, 18
Indexes, 8
  b+tree, 12
  b-tree, 170
  collection type, 142
  functional, 10, 129
  row type, 129
  r-tree, 11, 171
Informix DataBlade Development
  Kit (DBDK), 289
"$INFORMIXDIR/etc" directory, 216
$INFORMIXDIR variable, 66
Informix Dynamic Server.2000
  (IDS.2000), 20–22
  aggregate functions, 265–66
  benefit of, 3
  capabilities, 1
  features, 4–12
    access method, 11–12
    distinct type, 5–6
    functional index, 10
    list, 6
    multiset, 6
    opaque type, 6
    polymorphism, 8–9
    row type, 6
    r-tree index, 11
    set, 6
    smart blobs, 11
    table/row type inheritance, 7–8
    user-defined aggregate, 9–10
    user-defined routine, 6–7
  multithreading, 37–38
Informix Dynamic Server
  architecture, 5
Informix function, 208–9
Informix threading model, 38
info structure, 193
Inheritance, 27
  table, 125
  table/row type, 7–8
INIT function, 57, 273
INIT modifier, 58
I-node, 18
In-place update method, 280
input() function, 158–61, 250, 251
INSERT INTO statement, 128,
  141, 244
Institute of Electrical and Electronics
  Engineers (IEEE) Computer
  Society, 37

INT8 data type, 90
INT data type, 89–90, 97
Inter() function, 172
Interleaving, 14
INTERNAL function, 75
INTERNAL function, 66
Interprocess communication, 31
INTERVAL data type, 91
ioctl(), 41
IPX/SPX, 21
Item extraction function, 181–88
Iterator functions, 177–99
  countdown, 179–81
  DataBlade API elements, 177–78
  item extraction, 181–88
  joining with, 199
  limitations, 188–89
  limitations work-around, 190–99
Iterator limitations, 188–89
ITER function, 57, 273–74
ITER modifiers, 58

K

Kernel-level thread, 36
Keywords
  DISTINCT, 265
  EXPORTS, 290
  minus(), 170
  negate(), 170
  OPCLASS, 72
  OUT, 68
  UNIQUE, 265
  VARIABLE, 70

L

Large object API functions, 233–50
Large objects
  creating, 241–44
  and opaque types, 245–50
  processing, 234–36
  specifications, 239–41
  statistics, 237–39
  storage specifications, 262–63
  structures, 234
lessthan() function, 66, 167
lessthan() operator, 72, 170
lessthanorequal() function,
  167, 170
Library loading and unloading,
  48–49
Light-weight processes (LWPs), 36
like function, 174–75
LIKE operator, 46, 105
List, 6
LIST collection type, 141
List constructors, 128
LIST data type, 91–92
LoadLibrary(), 40
lohandles() function, 252–53
lospec() function, 240

LOTOCOPY, 232
LOTOFILE, 232
LVARCHAR data type, 49, 85, 92–93,
  105, 107

M

malloc(), 41
MATCHES, 46
matches function, 174–75
Math functions, 169–70
MAX() function, 266
Memory, 14
Memory allocation, 53–54, 116–17
Memory caches, 14
Memory management, 17
Messages, 31
mi_alloc() function, 117, 121, 161,
  187–88
mi_bitvarying, 291–92
mi_cast_get() function, 201–2,
  203–8, 206, 224–25
mi_collection_fetch() function,
  144, 145
mi_collection_open()
  function, 144
MI_COLLECTION_VALUE, 140
mi_column, 132
mi_column_count() API
  function, 132
mi_column_type_id() function, 135
MI_CONNECTION usage, 149
Microsoft NT environment, 20–21
Microsoft Windows NT threads, 37
MI_CURSOR_ABSOLUTE cursor
  action, 146
MI_CURSOR_RELATIVE, 146
mi_dalloc() function, 184
MI_DATUM variable, 82–83, 133
mi_db_error_raise() function,
  111, 112, 113, 206
MI_DDL statement, 138
MI_DML statement, 138
mi_double_precision type, 203
MI_ERROR, 140, 178
MI_ERROR_CAST, 202
MI_EXCEPTION, 112
mi_exec() function, 137, 138
MI_EXPLICIT_CAST, 202
MI_FPARAM argument, 52–53
mi_fparam_get() function, 222–23
MI_FPARAM pointer, 52, 110
MI_FPARAM structure, 171, 192
mi_fp_argisnull(), 109
mi_fp_argtype () function, 131
mi_fp_funcstate(), 53, 178
mi_fp_getcolid(), 250
mi_fp_getrow() function, 250
mi_fp_nargs() function, 224
mi_fp_request() function, 53,
  178, 180, 192

INFORMIX-ONLINE DYNAMIC SERVER HANDBOOK

CARLTON DOE

Hands-on information that will help Informix-OnLine Dynamic Server administrators get their job done as effectively as possible.

- Hands-on techniques and ideas for effective administration.
- Covers the entire process of starting up and running an Informix-OnLine Dynamic Server database environment
- CD-ROM contains a library of administration scripts saving you hundreds of hours.

1997, 496pp., paper, 0-13-605296-7

A BOOK/CD-ROM PACKAGE

PROGRAMMING INFORMIX SQL/4GL:
A Step-By-Step Approach, Second Edition
CATHY KIPP

The most thorough, up-to-date primer on INFORMIX SQL/4GL database design and programming.

- Revised and updated to cover new Informix product features, especially the INFORMIX-4GL Interactive Debugger.
- Includes an overview of relational database design, and step-by-step techniques for building and maintaining databases.
- New CD-ROM includes extensive SQL/4GL software tools.

1998, 512pp, Paper, 0-13-675919-X

A BOOK/CD-ROM PACKAGE

INFORMIX PERFORMANCE TUNING
Second Edition
ELIZABETH SUTO

1997, 192 pp, Cloth,
0-13-239237-2

INFORMIX STORED PROCEDURE PROGRAMMING
MICHAEL L. GONZALES

1996, 200 pp, Paper,
0-13-206723-4

EVOLUTION OF THE HIGH PERFORMANCE DATABASE
INFORMIX SOFTWARE

1997, 432 pp, Cloth,
0-13-594730-8

OPTIMIZING INFORMIX APPLICATIONS
ROBERT SCHNEIDER

1995, 300 pp, Paper,
0-13-149238-1

ADVANCED INFORMIX-4GL PROGRAMMING
ART TAYLOR

1995, 400pp, Paper,
0-13-301318-9

ALSO AVAILABLE...

SELECTED DOCUMENTATION FROM INFORMIX SOFTWARE, INC.

INFORMIX-4GL BY EXAMPLE
0-13-100355-0

INFORMIX GUIDE TO SQL:
Reference • 0-13-100363-1

INFORMIX GUIDE TO SQL:
Tutorial • 0-13-100371-2

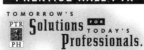

PRENTICE HALL PTR

TOMORROW'S
Solutions FOR TODAY'S
Professionals.

LICENSE AGREEMENT AND LIMITED WARRANTY

READ THE FOLLOWING TERMS AND CONDITIONS CAREFULLY BEFORE OPENING THIS CD PACKAGE. THIS LEGAL DOCUMENT IS AN AGREEMENT BETWEEN YOU AND PRENTICE-HALL, INC. (THE "COMPANY"). BY OPENING THIS SEALED CD PACKAGE, YOU ARE AGREEING TO BE BOUND BY THESE TERMS AND CONDITIONS. IF YOU DO NOT AGREE WITH THESE TERMS AND CONDITIONS, DO NOT OPEN THE CD PACKAGE. PROMPTLY RETURN THE UNOPENED CD PACKAGE AND ALL ACCOMPANYING ITEMS TO THE PLACE YOU OBTAINED THEM FOR A FULL REFUND OF ANY SUMS YOU HAVE PAID.

1.   **GRANT OF LICENSE:** In consideration of your purchase of this book, and your agreement to abide by the terms and conditions of this Agreement, the Company grants to you a nonexclusive right to use and display the copy of the enclosed software program (hereinafter the "SOFTWARE") on a single computer (i.e., with a single CPU) at a single location so long as you comply with the terms of this Agreement. The Company reserves all rights not expressly granted to you under this Agreement.

2.   **OWNERSHIP OF SOFTWARE:** You own only the magnetic or physical media (the enclosed CD) on which the SOFTWARE is recorded or fixed, but the Company and the software developers retain all the rights, title, and ownership to the SOFTWARE recorded on the original CD copy(ies) and all subsequent copies of the SOFTWARE, regardless of the form or media on which the original or other copies may exist. This license is not a sale of the original SOFTWARE or any copy to you.

3.   **COPY RESTRICTIONS:** This SOFTWARE and the accompanying printed materials and user manual (the "Documentation") are the subject of copyright. The individual programs on the CD are copyrighted by the authors of each program. Some of the programs on the CD include separate licensing agreements. If you intend to use one of these programs, you must read and follow its accompanying license agreement. You may not copy the Documentation or the SOFTWARE, except that you may make a single copy of the SOFTWARE for backup or archival purposes only. You may be held legally responsible for any copying or copyright infringement which is caused or encouraged by your failure to abide by the terms of this restriction.

4.   **USE RESTRICTIONS:** You may not network the SOFTWARE or otherwise use it on more than one computer or computer terminal at the same time. You may physically transfer the SOFTWARE from one computer to another provided that the SOFTWARE is used on only one computer at a time. You may not distribute copies of the SOFTWARE or Documentation to others. You may not reverse engineer, disassemble, decompile, modify, adapt, translate, or create derivative works based on the SOFTWARE or the Documentation without the prior written consent of the Company.

5.   **TRANSFER RESTRICTIONS:** The enclosed SOFTWARE is licensed only to you and may not be transferred to any one else without the prior written consent of the Company. Any unauthorized transfer of the SOFTWARE shall result in the immediate termination of this Agreement.

6.   **TERMINATION:** This license is effective until terminated. This license will terminate automatically without notice from the Company and become null and void if you fail to comply with any provisions or limitations of this license. Upon termination, you shall destroy the Documentation and all copies of the SOFTWARE. All provisions of this Agreement as to warranties, limitation of liability, remedies or damages, and our ownership rights shall survive termination.

7.   **MISCELLANEOUS:** This Agreement shall be construed in accordance with the laws of the United States of America and the State of New York and shall benefit the Company, its affiliates, and assignees.

8.   **LIMITED WARRANTY AND DISCLAIMER OF WARRANTY:** The Company warrants that the SOFTWARE, when properly used in accordance with the Documentation, will operate in substantial conformity with the description of the SOFTWARE set forth in the Documentation. The Company does not warrant that the SOFTWARE will meet your requirements or that the operation

of the SOFTWARE will be uninterrupted or error-free. The Company warrants that the media on which the SOFTWARE is delivered shall be free from defects in materials and workmanship under normal use for a period of thirty (30) days from the date of your purchase. Your only remedy and the Company's only obligation under these limited warranties is, at the Company's option, return of the warranted item for a refund of any amounts paid by you or replacement of the item. Any replacement of SOFTWARE or media under the warranties shall not extend the original warranty period. The limited warranty set forth above shall not apply to any SOFTWARE which the Company determines in good faith has been subject to misuse, neglect, improper installation, repair, alteration, or damage by you. EXCEPT FOR THE EXPRESSED WARRANTIES SET FORTH ABOVE, THE COMPANY DISCLAIMS ALL WARRANTIES, EXPRESS OR IMPLIED, INCLUDING WITHOUT LIMITATION, THE IMPLIED WARRANTIES OF MERCHANTABILITY AND FITNESS FOR A PARTICULAR PURPOSE. EXCEPT FOR THE EXPRESS WARRANTY SET FORTH ABOVE, THE COMPANY DOES NOT WARRANT, GUARANTEE, OR MAKE ANY REPRESENTATION REGARDING THE USE OR THE RESULTS OF THE USE OF THE SOFTWARE IN TERMS OF ITS CORRECTNESS, ACCURACY, RELIABILITY, CURRENTNESS, OR OTHERWISE.

IN NO EVENT, SHALL THE COMPANY OR ITS EMPLOYEES, AGENTS, SUPPLIERS, OR CONTRACTORS BE LIABLE FOR ANY INCIDENTAL, INDIRECT, SPECIAL, OR CONSEQUENTIAL DAMAGES ARISING OUT OF OR IN CONNECTION WITH THE LICENSE GRANTED UNDER THIS AGREEMENT, OR FOR LOSS OF USE, LOSS OF DATA, LOSS OF INCOME OR PROFIT, OR OTHER LOSSES, SUSTAINED AS A RESULT OF INJURY TO ANY PERSON, OR LOSS OF OR DAMAGE TO PROPERTY, OR CLAIMS OF THIRD PARTIES, EVEN IF THE COMPANY OR AN AUTHORIZED REPRESENTATIVE OF THE COMPANY HAS BEEN ADVISED OF THE POSSIBILITY OF SUCH DAMAGES. IN NO EVENT SHALL LIABILITY OF THE COMPANY FOR DAMAGES WITH RESPECT TO THE SOFTWARE EXCEED THE AMOUNTS ACTUALLY PAID BY YOU, IF ANY, FOR THE SOFTWARE.

SOME JURISDICTIONS DO NOT ALLOW THE LIMITATION OF IMPLIED WARRANTIES OR LIABILITY FOR INCIDENTAL, INDIRECT, SPECIAL, OR CONSEQUENTIAL DAMAGES, SO THE ABOVE LIMITATIONS MAY NOT ALWAYS APPLY. THE WARRANTIES IN THIS AGREEMENT GIVE YOU SPECIFIC LEGAL RIGHTS AND YOU MAY ALSO HAVE OTHER RIGHTS WHICH VARY IN ACCORDANCE WITH LOCAL LAW.

ACKNOWLEDGMENT

YOU ACKNOWLEDGE THAT YOU HAVE READ THIS AGREEMENT, UNDERSTAND IT, AND AGREE TO BE BOUND BY ITS TERMS AND CONDITIONS. YOU ALSO AGREE THAT THIS AGREEMENT IS THE COMPLETE AND EXCLUSIVE STATEMENT OF THE AGREEMENT BETWEEN YOU AND THE COMPANY AND SUPERSEDES ALL PROPOSALS OR PRIOR AGREEMENTS, ORAL, OR WRITTEN, AND ANY OTHER COMMUNICATIONS BETWEEN YOU AND THE COMPANY OR ANY REPRESENTATIVE OF THE COMPANY RELATING TO THE SUBJECT MATTER OF THIS AGREEMENT.

Should you have any questions concerning this Agreement or if you wish to contact the Company for any reason, please contact in writing at the address below.

Robin Short

Prentice Hall PTR

One Lake Street

Upper Saddle River, New Jersey 07458

ABOUT THE CD-ROM

Source Code

The CD-ROM contains C source code, makefiles, SQL scripts, and test scripts that implement examples of all the subjects covered in the book.

The CD-ROM organization follows the book chapters where each sub-directory name contains the chapter number it relates to. Each directory contains code implementing the examples covered in its related chapter and sometimes more. The CD-ROM also contains already compiled code for Microsoft Windows NT and Sun Solaris so examples can be executed without the need for a compiler and a linker.

Finally, a fully functional development version of Informix DBDK software and a link for acquiring Informix Client SDK have been included for your convenience.

DBDK

DBDK allows you to easily develop user-defined types and routines to extend the IDS.2000 environment. DBDK supports C and C++ development environments and automatic generation of ActiveX components. It provides a complete graphical development environment that allows developers to easily design and implement the extensions used by IDS.2000. DBDK's automatic generation of C and C++ code significantly speeds development of IDS.2000 extensions.

Before installing, you must register this copy of the Informix DBDK online at http://www.informix.com/dbdkreg and obtain your activation key. This key will give you a single-user development license. Once you have your key, run the installation program SETUP.EXE located in the Informix directory. Further information about the software can be found in the appropriate ReadMe file.

Client SDK

The Client SDK is a freely available product from Informix. Informix Client SDK is a package of several applications programming interfaces (APIs) needed to develop applications for Informix servers. These interfaces allow developers to write applications in the language they are familiar with—Java, C++, C, or ESQL. You can download it by following the Informix Client SDK link at http://www.intraware.com/informix/. If you wish to order the Client SDK on media, please call your Informix Sales office. The Informix Sales offices in the United States are listed at http://www.informix.com/informix/contact/offices/us.htm and those outside of the United States are listed at http://www.informix.com/informix/contact/offices/international.htm.

License Agreement

Use of the software accompanying *Informix Dynamic Server.2000: Server-Side Programming in C* is subject to the terms of the License Agreement and Limited Warranty, found on the previous page.

Technical Support

Prentice Hall does not offer technical support for any of the programs on the CD-ROM. However, if the CD-ROM is damaged, you may obtain a replacement copy by sending an email that describes the problem to: disc_exchange@prenhall.com.